THE AFRIC-AMERICAN PICTURE GALLERY

THE AFRIC-AMERICAN PICTURE GALLERY

William J. Wilson's Speculative Museum of Black Art

BRITT RUSERT

Duke University Press
Durham and London
2026

Printed in the United States of America on acid-free paper ∞
Project Editor: Livia Tenzer
Designed by A. Mattson Gallagher
Typeset in Minion Pro, Pelago, and Poetica Std
by Westchester Publishing Services

Library of Congress Cataloging-in-Publication Data
Names: Rusert, Britt author
Title: The Afric-American Picture Gallery : William J. Wilson's speculative museum of black art / Britt Rusert.
Other titles: William J. Wilson's speculative museum of black art
Description: Durham : Duke University Press, 2026. | Includes bibliographical references and index.
Identifiers: LCCN 2025053869 (print)
LCCN 2025053870 (ebook)
ISBN 9781478039075 paperback
ISBN 9781478034124 hardcover
ISBN 9781478062691 ebook
Subjects: LCSH: Wilson, William J. 1818–1878 | Wilson, William J. 1818–1878—Criticism and interpretation | American literature—African American authors—History and criticism | African Americans—New York (State)—New York—Intellectual life—History—19th century | Literature, Experimental—New York (State)—New York—History and criticism | Aesthetics, Black—United States—History—19th century | Art in literature | African American art—19th century | African Americans
Classification: LCC PS153.B53 R875 2026 (print) | LCC PS153.B53 (ebook) | DDC 810.9/896073—dc23/eng/20260520
LC record available at https://lccn.loc.gov/2025053869
LC ebook record available at https://lccn.loc.gov/2025053870

Cover art: Genevieve Gaignard, *Family Tree*, 2022. Mixed media, vintage wallpaper, 10 ft. × 9 ft. ½ in. × 54 in. (304.8 × 275.59 × 137.16 cm). Courtesy of the artist and Vielmetter Los Angeles. Photo: Jeff McLane.

Contents

Preface

This book is an extended study of William J. Wilson's "Afric-American Picture Gallery" (February–October 1859), an experimental periodical series from the late antebellum period that imagines the first museum of Black art in the United States. I first encountered this little-known text while finishing my first monograph, *Fugitive Science*. Hiding in plain sight in the pages of the *Anglo-African Magazine*, a Black intellectual magazine published monthly out of New York City right before the start of the Civil War, the series is a fascinating and, in some ways, singular publication from the early African American print sphere. Among other things, the Picture Gallery is a deeply visual text that reproduces no actual images.

I began teaching the "Afric-American Picture Gallery" regularly in 2013, and in 2015, with Leif Eckstrom, I edited a digital edition of the series for the American Antiquarian Society's *Just Teach One: Early African American Print* project. Even with a teachable version of the text out in the world, I felt there was still so much to learn about William J. Wilson, his social and artistic networks, and his voluminous contributions to antebellum and postbellum periodicals. A book-length study of the Picture Gallery also allows us—reading after the experience of the COVID-19 pandemic lockdown, in which our access to physical spaces of collective art viewership was drastically constricted—to return to the text with renewed attention to Wilson's own necessarily mediated relationship to visual art. Wilson did not have the luxury of regularly viewing art in private studios and art academies. He was routinely subjected to de facto regimes of segregation in antebellum New York, where white people could bar access to museums, galleries, and other spaces of display whenever they wanted to. Wilson could have been let in to an exhibition one day and then denied access the next. Black access to art in this period was, in this way, controlled by white whim. How do you write on art when you are denied access to it and when daily life is structured by the need to be hypervigilant about your survival? Where did one find the time to contemplate aesthetic questions amid the racial emergencies and daily cataclysms that marked the years leading up to the Civil War? Studio visits offered one crucial haven for Wilson, as did the homes of those few members in his community who had the means to purchase and display fine art in their homes.[1] The print sphere also enabled Wilson to view visual works from the protection of his parlor, a space that, as Jasmine Nichole Cobb has shown, played a crucial role in both the private and political lives of free African Americans in the antebellum period.[2]

The intensification of racial surveillance, scapegoating, and violence unleashed in the aftermath of the pandemic lockdown and the George Floyd rebellions in the summer of 2020 also brought into heightened relief the conditions of state violence, social emergency, and vigilante "justice" under which Wilson was producing his art in late antebellum New York, a notoriously racist city in a nation riven by anti-Black violence and mounting tensions over sectionalism and slavery. In some ways it feels incredible that anyone was writing anything in 1859—as the nation flew headlong toward social anarchy and war—let alone a text as rich, as experimental, and as wide-ranging as the "Afric-American Picture Gallery." Wilson, his wife, Mary, his child, Annie, and his students were subjected to routine harassment on the city streets, faced housing and employment discrimination, and navigated incessant threats of violence and even kidnapping. Jonathan Wells has described New York City as the largest proslavery bastion in the North. His account of "the Kidnapping Club"—a network of police, private investigators, judges, industrialists, and other thugs who captured African Americans in the city for profit in the years following the passage of the Fugitive Slave Act in 1850—offers a chilling picture of the manifold threats that surrounded Black New Yorkers at every turn.[3] Throughout the 1850s, African Americans were being stolen from the streets of New York, including adults and children who had never been enslaved. Writing within and against these conditions of political instability, anti-Black violence, and family separation, Wilson somehow found the physical and mental space to write.

In this way, I have come to understand the sheer existence of the "Afric-American Picture Gallery" to be nothing less than a miracle. I hope that the pages that follow capture and honor the miracle of Black art as works that find their way into the world in the face of white supremacy's stultifying repressions and violences. Through speculative prose and radical imagination Wilson wills another world into existence, but to do so, he must continually confront the machinations of this one.

Introduction

> All is tranquil in Gotham, and around the Heights, at least, within the *black world*.
>
> **Ethiop**, *Frederick Douglass' Paper*, March 25, 1853

In 2008, art historian Richard Powell coined the phrase "the new black portraiture" to name the proliferation of a particular kind of figural work in contemporary art and to describe the specificities of a diasporic practice. For Powell, Black portraiture, both past and present, depends on a special relationship between the artist and the subject rather than between the subject and the viewer; it is also rooted in the subject's power to upend dominant regimes of racial representation and stereotypes through self-representation, self-adornment, and self-composure. Highlighting ideas of "collaboration, agency, and introspection," since "black people are often active participants in spectatorship—either as knowing spectacles, willing actors, or self-scrutinizers," Black portraiture is a dynamic field that "invests black subjects with social capital."[1]

Portraiture has indeed become a vibrant site of practice and experimentation among diasporic artists working in diverse mediums and styles, as well as a popular topic for scholarly analysis and curatorial framing.[2] But the new Black portraiture also connects to a much longer debate about racial representation in fine art. In 1853, William J. Wilson was already meditating on the glaring absence of what he called "distinguished black" figures in museums and galleries. Writing to *Frederick Douglass' Paper*, he concluded, "we must begin to tell our own story, write our own lecture, paint our own picture, chisel our own bust."[3] In 1859, Wilson answered his own call with the serial publication of his "Afric-American Picture Gallery." Responding to the absence of fine art representing Black subjects as well as the mass circulation of anti-Black imagery in popular culture, Wilson's gallery turned to the resources of an expanding transatlantic print sphere to provide an alternative visual archive of Blackness, one wrought, somewhat paradoxically, completely in textual form.

The "Afric-American Picture Gallery" imagines the first museum of Black art before any such institution existed in the United States. Published in seven installments in the *Anglo-African Magazine*, the text is a fascinating experiment in both form and authorship. The *Anglo-African Magazine*, itself an experiment, was a short-lived yet intellectually rich and historically significant magazine edited by the African American bookseller and printer Thomas Hamilton. Hamilton's shop on Beekman Street was a block away from Printing House Square, the hub of New York's vibrant publishing industry.[4] It was also adjacent to the historic Black neighborhood in Lower Manhattan that has been chronicled in loving detail by Carla Peterson, a literary scholar and descendant of that very community.[5] Hamilton's shop, the city's printing center, and Manhattan's free Black community were also all proximate to Wilson's beloved Brooklyn.

Wilson wrote under the pen name Ethiop in Black periodicals during the period and was a frequent contributor to those publications. Beginning in 1851, he served as the Brooklyn correspondent for *Frederick Douglass' Paper*. For his Picture Gallery series, he transformed Ethiop into a fully developed literary character: a docent, curator, art critic, sketch artist, and flaneur who gives a virtual tour of an imaginary museum of art and later embarks on a mysterious journey to the Black Forest. The text at turns amplifies and complicates Wilson's own theories about race, representation, and political power as they took shape in his periodical correspondence in the 1850s. Taking inspiration from periodical reviews of art exhibitions as well as the urban sketch, a popular genre that offered readers glimpses into the grittiness and glamour of city life, the Picture Gallery was both deeply embedded in the world of antebellum newspapers, and a world apart from it. Indeed, the series becomes increasingly speculative and harder to define as it proceeds, taking off into flights of fancy and eventually transforming into a fantasy fiction untethered from the interior space of the museum. In lieu of the ordered gallery tour that opens the series, later installments are more plot-driven and include dramatic tales of fugitive escape and violent retribution taken against enslavers and slave-catchers in the wake of the Fugitive Slave Act.

But before we get to how Wilson uses the Picture Gallery as a platform to play out elaborate fantasies about torturing enslavers, let's return to the series' more genteel beginning. The first installment of the Picture Gallery opens with a warm invitation into a mysterious, little-known museum tucked away someplace in the author's Gotham City. Absorbing readers into the world of the text through a lush description of interior space, Ethiop promises a gallery tour that will be an immersive, sensory experience: "Let the reader, with me enter into this almost unknown Gallery. Well, here we are, and looking about us."[6] Ethiop begins with a quick scan of the gallery's collection, an impressive set of "pictures" that "vary according to the fancy or skill of the artist. Some are in oil, some in water colors, and India Ink shadings, a few statues, statuettes, and a few Crayons and Pencilings possessing a high degree of merit; others are mere charcoal sketches and of little worth beyond the subjects they portray." The gallery is introduced as a space of radical equality: Some objects in the collection are deemed valuable because they are "finely executed," while others, "mere rough sketches," are valuable because their subjects are interesting and worthy of study.[7] It seems that all art objects, from the amateur sketch to the finest oil painting, are welcome in this space as are all subjects, irrespective of color or station. (Later in the series, Ethiop's young assistant, Tom Onward, brings in a portrait of himself and asks to have it hung up. Ethiop complies.)

Ethiop has a complex and at times ambivalent relationship to the Picture Gallery's publicness. At the beginning of the series, he tries to stave off the hostilities and indignities of the outside world with the order and beauty of a quaint gallery of pictures. Depictions of the slave trade and scenes of plantation slavery are present, but they are carefully kept within the frame. While Ethiop says that the quiet, out-of-the-way gallery has "become one of my dearest retreats," he also holds out hope that it might have a busier future, with the help of the *Anglo-African Magazine*'s powers of publication and amplification. He makes this direct and "humble petition" to readers: "The walls are spacious, and contain ample room for more, and, in many instances, better paintings; and many niches, yet vacant for busts and statues; and just here, let me make an humble petition in behalf of this our newly discovered Gallery.—It is that generous artists, will, at their convenience, have the goodness to paint an occasional picture, or chisel a statue or a bust, and we will be sure to assign it to its appropriate place."[8] This moment is a canny invitation for readers to imagine themselves either as would-be visual artists, contributing to the future of Black art through the making of an "occasional" painting or statue, or as would-be writers who might send their own sketches to the *Anglo-African*. This is just one of many moments where Ethiop uses visual metaphors to provide a metacommentary on the *Anglo-African* and the periodical sphere in which it was embedded.

Ethiop also wants readers to know that he, perhaps like the ideal editor he imagines for his own writing, is a curator with a light touch. Indeed, this is one of a few moments where Wilson appears to be gently ribbing his editor, Thomas Hamilton. Wilson's gallery is a casual and picturesque space that shirks curation-as-surveillance. The gallery's works instead have an "unstudied arrangement," similar to how pictures would be put up in the private interior of someone's home. The pictures "seem . . . to have been put up out of the way, many of them, than hung for any effect," a statement that signals the accessibility of the space and asks readers to imagine filling up the empty spaces on the gallery walls with their own contributions.[9] By pointing to still-vacant pedestals and empty wall space, Ethiop also emphasizes the unfinished, improvisatory, and dialogic nature of the text itself, a periodical series that is revised and transformed by readers and editors through the process of serialization, publication, and readership over time. Thus, from the outset, the Picture Gallery series departs from the genre of the art review or gallery tour even as it partakes in it: This is a space that privileges process over product, autodidacticism over formal training. It is a place where amateurs should feel free to try their hand.

Even among the many striking publications featured in the *Anglo-African*, the Picture Gallery stands out. The formal experimentation of the series, the liveliness of its prose, and Wilson's use of a biting satire to expose the degraded status and ideological function of fine art in a slaveholding nation work together to make a unique contribution to early African American—and American—fiction writing. The series participates in the genre of the periodical art review and resonates with the ekphrastic descriptions of visual art that populate antebellum American literature, from Nathaniel Hawthorne to Walt Whitman. But this speculative text also reads like a work of postmodern fiction: The narrative constructs art objects mostly out of existing print sources, including frontispieces and illustrations that appeared in books, pamphlets, and broadsides. It further elevates those images from the print sphere into fine art objects through ekphrastic description and techniques of textual collage. Anticipating theories of the image in industrial modernity from the French photographer Félix Nadar to the Frankfurt School philosopher Walter Benjamin, the Picture Gallery theorizes as it constructs: It reflects on the meaning of the "original" and the "copy" for the representation of Blackness in modernity, while suggesting that racial slavery profoundly shapes and haunts an increasingly commercial sphere of artistic production.

Building on important book chapters and essays by Ivy Wilson, John Ernest, Derrick Spires, Rian Bowie, Leif Eckstrom, and Radiclani Clytus, this is the first book-length study of Wilson and his Picture Gallery.[10] It contributes to a growing body of scholarly and curatorial work seeking to restore Wilson and his writing to historical memory. To that end, the book includes an appendix that reproduces the full text of the Picture Gallery with an eye to making this early African American text more accessible for teachers, scholars, art workers, and general readers.

In addition to providing a deep analysis of the Picture Gallery itself, this study situates the series within several contexts, including Black cosmopolitanism and bohemian cultures in antebellum Brooklyn, the consolidation of Black political power in the antebellum urban Northeast, and the coming of the Civil War. The project contributes to scholarly conversations in the field on the diverse cultural work of early African American print cultures, the material circuits of Black print and image production, Black paratexts, and the origins of African American visual culture.[11] Wilson's own text is cannily reflexive about the ephemerality and vulnerability of African American print, especially periodicals, even predicting its own future status as a neglected text. In this way, the Picture Gallery speaks to ongoing conversations about the politics of recovering and republishing lost or otherwise neglected works of African American literature.[12]

I argue that the "Afric-American Picture Gallery" offers a unique vantage onto the origins of African American literary *and* visual culture. As a visually attuned text without images, the Picture Gallery explores the politics of visibility for Black subjects from positions that range from enthusiasm to caution. In this way, it reflects the deep ambivalence that attended debates about race and visuality amid the rise of a scopic regime of racial formation that increasingly tied race to the terrain of the visible and to the body itself, as chronicled by Nicholas Mirzoeff, Sarah Lewis, and others.[13]

At the same time as Wilson argued for the importance of visual representation for the uplifting of his race, his periodical writings suggest that he felt more confident about the power of rhetorical authority, which he flexed across his career, often in wide-ranging and experimental dialogue with his primary interlocutor, the New York–based physician, activist, and writer James McCune Smith. I further argue that the Picture Gallery, deeply embedded within the dialogic networks of Black intellectual exchange and artistic production in the period, emerged out of a turn in the late 1850s toward more experimental, and less transparently instrumental, forms of writing by African American writers. Wilson's textual museum was part of a more avant-garde aesthetics that was emerging in the years leading up to the Civil War, in which Black texts did not always have to be beholden to the imperatives of abolition, even as its writers were deeply involved with political struggles and organizing on the ground.

Wilson's text also suggests that we still have much to learn about the late antebellum period. Although the Picture Gallery was published in February to October 1859, during the months leading up to John Brown's raid on Harpers Ferry and amid an intensifying sectionalist crisis, the text registers the nation's headlines in complex and sometimes oblique ways. Ethiop is a flaneur and a dandy figure who moves, reads, and even *looks* slantwise from the dominant political grammar of his time. In this way, he wields the power of what bell hooks calls "black looks" and what Mirzoeff calls "the right to look."[14] Furthermore, a kind of queer hesitance marks the text, one that suggests a form of politics that differs starkly from the muscular immediatism of a Frederick Douglass or a Martin Delany. Wilson's caustic suspicion about art produced for an interracial audience ultimately glimpses a genealogy of African American artists and activists whose politics cannot be accommodated easily within current historiographies of abolition.

In what follows, I begin by delving into the history of early Brooklyn and the place that Wilson, his family, and his community played in its political and artistic development. From there, I argue that what Carl Plasa, James E. Ford III, and others have called "Black ekphrasis" is a mode that is especially useful for apprehending and navigating the visual binds of racial representation in an age in which race was increasingly being tied to regimes of the visual.[15] I then turn to consider the flamboyance and even queerness of the Picture Gallery, connecting the series to cultures of bohemianism and dandyism in an age of Black slavery, freedom, industrialization, and the birth of modern consumerism. I close with a map of the book's chapters, which track alongside Ethiop's own meandering perambulations and thus require some orientation for the reader.

Wilson's Brooklyn

William J. Wilson became known to readers though his witty and often sardonic contributions to periodicals edited by African Americans in the 1850s and 1860s, including *Frederick Douglass' Paper*, the *Anglo-African*

Magazine, and the *Weekly Anglo-African*. Wilson was a proud Brooklynite, and as the Brooklyn correspondent for *Frederick Douglass' Paper*, he not only reported on happenings and politics in the city that were of interest to Black readers but also helped write Brooklyn itself into existence at a time when the city was transitioning from a rural outpost to an industrial hub of commerce and trade.

Indeed, the gentrified Brooklyn that is recognizable to us today has its roots in Wilson's moment. Both Williamsburg and Bushwick were annexed in 1854, "making Brooklyn one of the five largest cities in the nation and a key commercial center in its own right."[16] Developers, including Brooklyn landowners whose families had controlled the island's land and wealth since the colonial era, aggressively developed Brooklyn's shoreline and used the city's lower taxes and available land to attract business owners away from Manhattan across the East River. The slave economy was also thriving in Brooklyn: From the mid-1850s through the Civil War, Brooklyn was one of the world's largest slave ports. Slave ships were outfitted and unloaded in broad daylight; sugar and cotton from the slave South filled Brooklyn warehouses. The sugar refining business grew to startling prominence among Brooklyn's industries in the 1850s, and Brooklyn "sugar lords" glutted the Northern market with refined sugars and syrups. Sugar refineries themselves were a dominant and haunting presence on the Brooklyn-Williamsburg shoreline: They were a central part of the landscape that Wilson traversed and wrote about.

Readers should keep in mind that William J. Wilson lived in a Northern city that was actively engaged in the slave economy and that it continued to do so into the beginning years of the Civil War. When sugarcane ceased to be easily available from Southern ports during the war, Brooklyn sugar lords turned to the plantations of the Caribbean. Kara Walker's *A Subtlety*, her epic 2014 installation of melting sugar statues in Brooklyn's old Domino Sugar Refinery, should remind us that the commodities of the slave trade were literally Wilson's surround. The sickly sweet smell of sugarcane hung in the air. To follow Christina Sharpe, in William J. Wilson's Brooklyn, slavery was the weather.[17]

Given this context, in which Brooklyn was emerging as a bustling site of industrial labor, manufacture, trade, and where the air smelled of exploitation and brutality, it is notable that Wilson was depicting Brooklyn as a space of quiet serenity and intellectual contemplation. In his very first column as Brooklyn correspondent for *Frederick Douglass' Paper*, he writes, "New York is a great city. When I say New York, I of course include its environs.—New York, proper, may be considered the body, of which the adjacent towns around it, are the limbs, or members thereof. Brooklyn, from its quietness, serenity, morality and intellectuality, may be regarded the head."[18] Here Wilson is seeking to draw attention to Brooklyn's growing status, portraying it as New York's intellectual and moral "head," and thus also as the city's center of culture. In writing Brooklyn as New York's privileged site of cultured "quietness, serenity, morality and intellectuality," we see a late antebellum Black writer working to decelerate the pace of industrialization and the urban chaos that surrounded him. This intentional tranquility, I want to argue, links up to the aesthetics of Black ekphrasis that can be found in the Picture Gallery: the idea that a studied and careful interpretation of a work of art can, even if only for a moment, take one away from the logics and grammars of the dominant world and, in so doing, help to recalibrate one's relationship to the political. In the March 25, 1853, issue of *Frederick Douglass' Paper*, Wilson observed, "All is tranquil in Gotham, and around the Heights, at least, within the *black world*." That such an autonomous Black world exists in Wilson's Brooklyn is notable, as is his comment that it is a space of intellectual calmness and even rest, not industrial clammer and chaos. Across his work and writing, Wilson was interested in how Black enclaves—spaces of retreat, rest, and contemplation—might be carved out amid the processes of industrialization and urbanization that surrounded his community. In other words, his writing here suggests that all was not tranquil in the *white* world.

Although Wilson identified as a proud Brooklynite, he was himself a migrant to the city. Born around 1818 near Shrewsbury, on the northern coast of New Jersey, he held free status, but this did not exempt him from frequent experiences of discrimination and even humiliation. His 1878 obituary in the *People's Advocate* noted that as a youth he attended a common school where his "presence was regarded as a practical joke."[19] It's not clear whether Wilson was the first generation of his family to have escaped the bonds of slavery, but it's certainly the case that the shadow of slavery loomed large over him and his home community. Slavery was outlawed in New Jersey in 1804, but only through a gradual manumission process, and small numbers of people remained enslaved until 1865. Wilson's own father was born on Virginia's Eastern Shore in Accomack County, a place where enslaved people frequently intermingled with the region's significant free Black population.[20]

As soon as he reached adulthood, Wilson struck out for New York City in the hopes of finding more job prospects and a larger community. He landed first in Manhattan, where he met his future wife, Mary Ann Garret Marshall, opened a boot-making shop, and became connected to a number of prominent activists and community leaders in the city, including James

McCune Smith, James Pennington, Phillip A. Bell, Henry Highland Garnet, and George T. Downing.[21] But Wilson's 1854 short story "Terance Ludlam" suggests that he initially found New York unwelcoming; he also struggled to find gainful employment and was shocked by the various forms of discrimination and indignities experienced by Black workers in the city. This early experience may have contributed to his decision to join the American League of Colored Laborers and an emerging American labor movement.[22]

An announcement of Mary and William's wedding appeared in the *Colored American* in November 1837.[23] The pair were married by Rev. Peter Williams, the prominent abolitionist and Episcopalian pastor of St. Philip's African Church in Lower Manhattan. St. Philip's was the congregation of Manhattan's best-connected and most prominent Black families.[24] Wilson's early connections to Black leaders and activists in the city may very well have been enabled by Mary's social connections. After all, it was she who had been born and raised in New York. Before settling in Brooklyn, William and Mary moved from Manhattan to Newtown, Long Island (present-day Queens), and lived there for a short period of time. News coverage of Newtown's African American community reveals that only a few years after his arrival in New York, Wilson was already highly active in Black politics, organizing circles, and the fight for suffrage and abolition.[25]

The Wilsons can be found in Brooklyn city directories beginning in 1842. That year William was appointed principal of Brooklyn's Colored School No. 1, one of the city's three public schools designated for Black students.[26] Wilson would quickly become a central figure in education in Brooklyn; Mary also taught at Colored School No. 1 and served for a short time as principal of its primary department.[27] William and Mary had one daughter, a girl they named Ann and called Annie. Census data and city directories show Wilson and his family living at several addresses in Brooklyn in the 1840s and 1850s, including residences on Chapel Street, Nassau Street, and Atlantic Street. The Nassau Street residence places the Wilsons around the corner from Duffield Street, a famous street of Black abolitionist activity that included homes of activists known to shelter fugitive slaves. Prithi Kanakamedala notes that in 1852, Mary opened a crockery store along the waterfront on Atlantic Street, in the heart of a "fashionable shopping district" in the city. She writes, "Mary was part of a long history of entrepreneurial Brooklynites fulfilling their neighbors' every dining needs. Crockery, particularly china, once a luxury for the rich, was especially in demand by middle- and upper-middle-class New Yorkers and Brooklynites in the mid-nineteenth century."[28]

Kanakamedala reminds us that even though their presence is not always reflected in the archive, Black women like Mary were at the "center of radical community building" in the city.[29] Mary and William also both contributed to efforts to build and sustain the autonomous Black institutions that Craig Steven Wilder has chronicled in detail.[30] Indeed, Brooklyn city atlases from the period register a surprising number of such institutions in their mapping of the city, including the African Church and the city's Black schools, including Colored School No. 1.[31] What comes as a surprise regarding these institutions is not their existence as much as that they were allowed a prominent presence in official records of the city. Indeed, it's hard to imagine city maps today affording such priority of place to Black spaces and institutions.

Black Brooklynites worked to carve out and name Black space in and against growing Irish immigration and labor competition, anti-Black sentiments and violence, and a casual proslavery agenda that viewed abolition as a threat to business interests and trade in the city. The official recording of African space in antebellum Brooklyn is notable, as is the insistence with which Black people named their institutions "African" in a moment of active experimentation with different forms of racial nomenclature, including both Hamilton's "Anglo-African" and Wilson's "Afric-American." (The latter had roots in anticolonization organizing in the early 1830s.)[32] Even though this was a moment when the African American population in Brooklyn was declining in numbers, Black presence and political power was more visible than ever.

Census data on Wilson's family further reflects the complexity of family and housing arrangements for African Americans in New York. At the same time that the African American print sphere was idealizing the Black family and white periodicals were pathologizing public displays of Black collectivity and intimate relation, actual people lived together in ways that challenged the nuclear, heteropatriarchal family. And of course, such nontraditional living arrangements and alternative forms of kinship were deeply tied to the disruptions and dislocations produced by slavery itself. For example, the 1860 US census suggests that the Wilsons had welcomed a twelve-year-old named Mary into their home, a young woman who is listed as a student and likely attended William's school. Another family is listed as living at the same address. The Bruce family, labeled "M." for "mulatto," included George Bruce, a thirty-five-year-old man; his wife, Elizabeth; a two-year-old named William; and a fifty-nine-year-old woman named Jane Redding (possibly Elizabeth's mother). George is listed as having no real estate, having been born in Virginia, and working as a steward, so it seems likely that he was a former slave. The presence of a mixed-race family with a possible past in the plantation South in Wilson's own home again highlights the material and, indeed, intimate presence of Southern slavery in the lives of Black Brooklynites like the Wilsons who were born nominally free.

The semiregular moves of Wilson's family in Brooklyn either reflect housing insecurity and Black itinerancies in the city or possibly track alongside increased financial security. Indeed, each move corresponded to a move closer to the homes and businesses of Brooklyn's Black elite.[33] Kanakamedala hypothesizes that it may have been the success and ultimate sale of Mary's business that allowed the Wilsons to become more upwardly mobile and financially secure in the 1850s.[34] By 1859, the year the Picture Gallery appeared in print, Wilson and his family were living at 4 Greene Avenue, in the Fort Greene area of Brooklyn. Carla Peterson notes that Fort Greene was a vibrant hub of Black social life and entrepreneurship: "Entrepreneurs rather than artisans and tradesmen, Fort Greene residents counted real estate agents, restaurateurs, and undertakers among their ranks. They too established their own churches and schools. To a greater extent than Blacks in Weeksville and Carrville they formed social clubs and literary societies similar to those across the East River."[35] It was in Fort Greene, in this milieu of Black elitism and cultural avant-gardism, proximate to Walt Whitman and other Brooklyn bohemians, that Wilson conceived his Picture Gallery.

Although Wilson did not have the national reputation of a Douglass or a Delany, he was active in several local and state-level struggles, including the battle over suffrage in New York. He was part of a group that in 1855 petitioned the New York state legislature to remove the property qualifications that had been put in place to limit African Americans' access to the franchise.[36] He attended meetings of the National Colored Conventions and served as both a press correspondent and as a secretary for some of those proceedings. He also became a member of the Committee of Thirteen, a group of leaders and activists in New York who came together to strategize and challenge the Fugitive Slave Act of 1850. The group held a strong anticolonization stance, arguing that colonization was a malicious scheme intent on removing antislavery influence from the nation. They also worked to shelter and protect fugitives who arrived in New York.

While this was a period of increased immigration into New York, especially from Ireland, it was also a time of dislocation and migration for African Americans *within* the city and its boroughs. For example, Black Manhattanites moved from Lower Manhattan to Brooklyn in the mid-1850s after the historic Seneca Village was destroyed so that Central Park could be put in its place. As Derrick Spires notes, "This land grab not only displaced a well-established Black community but also eroded that community's political power, because the state's payment was not enough to allow them to reestablish themselves in the city."[37] In the 1850s, Brooklyn, Harlem, and Queens also became attractive sites for resettlement as activists were advocating for migration out of urban centers in favor of subsistence farming as a path toward elevation.[38] These were also places where land could still be purchased so that Black New Yorkers might qualify to vote. Property ownership for Black New Yorkers was not only about putting down roots; it was also a practical means to secure voting rights. In 1863, in the middle of the war, New York's Draft Riots initiated another round of traumatic displacements for Black New Yorkers, again often from Manhattan to Brooklyn. Donald Yacovone says that around this time Wilson was pushed out of his principal position by the city's board of education because he had delivered a series of lectures endorsing Lincoln's Emancipation Proclamation at the Cooper Institute.[39] We know that Wilson and his family were among the teachers who left New York during the war to provide education and aid to former slaves in the South, but it's also likely that Brooklyn's rising anti-Black violence and tense political atmosphere contributed to William and Mary's decision to leave the city for good.

Late Antebellum Black Aesthetics

Despite their tireless organizing efforts, Black New Yorkers struggled to both access and maintain citizenship rights. In the face of an attenuated citizenship, many turned to other venues for representation, including writing and the visual arts. Ivy Wilson has argued that in a period before formal political representation, African Americans used "representation in art as a proxy for their desired representation in politics."[40] He is particularly interested in how "Black Americans used rhetoric and ekphrastic writing to articulate the meanings of their own personhood in opposition to the definitions imposed upon them by the far reach of slavery, even if one were not a slave. Such a focus on cultural production is especially necessary to recover the African American presence in political debates before the ratification of the Fourteenth and Fifteenth Amendments."[41] For Ivy Wilson, the Picture Gallery stands as a superlative example of ekphrastic expression operating as a form of political surrogacy for antebellum Black Americans.

Ekphrasis can be found across Black antebellum writing, but it is not always a wholly celebratory or even confident modality; works like the

Picture Gallery series also embody what W. J. T. Mitchell calls ekphrastic ambivalence.[42] *Ekphrasis*, in the broadest terms, is a written description of a work of art. In ancient Greece, ekphrasis was a popular rhetorical exercise for students. While ekphrasis is traditionally defined as the representation of visual art in written form, in this project I broaden its definition to highlight the specificities of the visual field for Black subjects subjected to an increasingly visual regime of racialization in the nineteenth century, and to account for the material constraints on image production for African Americans. To produce public work, writers need writing materials and printing presses; painters need canvasses, paint, and exhibition space; photographers need cameras, chemicals, and studios. These materials and technologies were not easily accessible to most Black creatives in the period. Thus, when Black writers created ekphrastic accounts of art objects that didn't exist, they were also pointing to the infrastructural conditions and economic inequalities that suppressed their creative production.

In this way, the ekphrastic mode in Black antebellum aesthetics did more than simply uphold the primacy of the visual or forward the idea that aesthetic representation is the equivalent of political representation. Black ekphrasis was deeply attuned to the dangers of ocularcentrism in an age where race was being increasingly tied to visual signifiers and regimes of racial surveillance. Thus, rather than ossifying the visual, these works traffic in what Tina Campt talks about as the *hapticity* of Black art, an orientation that privileges multisensory connection and invites "feeling across difference and precarity."[43] It is also a mode that invites alternative ways of viewing and relating to art. Writing about her own method, Campt notes, "Rather than writing *about* artworks, I spend most of my time at exhibitions and galleries sitting with and writing to them. I write to them about the feelings they solicit, the forms of discomfort they evoke, the emotional work they require and often demand, and the potentially transformative effects they have when we allow ourselves to inhabit those feelings and responses."[44] Ethiop has a strikingly similar relationship to the art objects in the picture gallery, standing or sitting before them, "sketching" his reflections on the works and the emotions and responses they elicit from viewers. The texts that are of concern in this study all engage with Black art's haptic orientation: They rewire the relationship between race and representation, denaturalize our understanding of the relationship among the senses, and refuse a hierarchy among different forms of media. Given the historical surveillance and suppression of Black art, in this book I widen ekphrasis to include literary descriptions of art works that may have never existed.

African American writers had to be incredibly creative and resourceful in the face of such conditions of material scarcity and a pervasive racism in the print spere. Throughout this book, I rethink the late 1850s as a moment of profound experimentation in Black writing, and in Black creativity more generally. The years leading up to the Civil War were a period of profound instability, and the anarchism of the moment was unleashing energy that moved Black writers to produce experimental texts with which we have yet to fully reckon. What kinds of aesthetic forms, I ask, are produced when a society is on the cusp of collapse?

It has been difficult to identify the emergence of Black experimental writing in the late 1850s in part because the mainstream abolition movement and the coming of the Civil War have often operated as historical steamrollers that swallow up everything else that happened in the decade. This deeply collaborative and dialogic genealogy of writing has also been obscured by scholarly reluctance to think about nineteenth-century literary production beyond the production of single authors and single works. Zooming in on what Elizabeth McHenry calls the "workspaces" of African American literature, we might instead become closer attuned to the vibrant networks of Black cosmopolitanism, queer bohemianism, and periodical exchange that Wilson belonged to.[45] Paying attention to *networks* of writing shows how Black writers in this moment were goading each other on, extending and fulfilling each other's calls, and engaging in a vigorous debate—in and through their work—about the nature and meaning of Black aesthetics. These debates could not be captured by the instrumentalism of abolitionism, and for this reason they have often been neglected in scholarship. While scholars have capably elaborated how white abolitionists framed and co-opted Black narrative throughout the period, African American writers were also working to cultivate an autonomous domain of creative expression in the very same moment that they were deeply enmeshed in interracial politics, intersectional alliances, and coalitional struggles.

These writers were also invested in a set of affects and forms that resist historical memorialization. When Douglass launched into his diatribe against racial science in his 1854 speech "Claims of the Negro, Ethnologically Considered," he began by stating his hesitance: "There are three ways to answer this denial. One is by ridicule; a second is by denunciation; and a third is by argument. I hardly know under which of these modes my answer to-day will fall. I feel myself somewhat on trial; and that this is just the point where there is hesitation, if not serious doubt."[46] This study explores how Black antebellum ressentiment, hesitation, ambivalence, and even exasperation produced an alternative theory of Black aesthetics on the cusp of the Civil War. My argument is not that these writers were detached from politics; indeed, the book is filled with figures who were prominent antislavery activists. William J. Wilson himself was a committed race man and was deeply engaged in politics. As noted above, he was a member of the Committee of Thirteen, an anticolonization group formed after the passage of the Fugitive Slave Act; he also participated in Black state conventions in New York and served as a delegate to the National Colored Convention held in Philadelphia in 1855. While serving as principal of Colored School No. 1 in Brooklyn, he advocated for many years on behalf of his students in a racist and violent city that often targeted youth. This is all to suggest instead that at the same time as writers like Wilson were organizing locally, agitating at the level of the state legislature, and engaging in robust local and national debates about Black emigration and colonization, they were also experimenting with rhetorical forms and expression in ways that are not reducible to their political activities. Indeed, Black aesthetics in the late 1850s is marked by a surplus that can't be read in terms of the political pragmatism of the moment. In the simplest of terms, this project questions the desire to make Black literature and activism isomorphic.

Literary scholar Derrick Spires notes that in the two years preceding the Civil War, a literary explosion was occurring in Black periodicals and magazines, "where writers were producing fiction, poetry, and essays at a blistering pace."[47] He notes that this uptick in literary production on the eve of the Civil War—as well as the crucial theorizing being done in this work—"often gets overshadowed by what comes after in much the same way that *Dred Scott v. Sandford* overshadows events of 1856, including 'Bleeding Kansas' and Margaret Garner's killing of her daughter."[48] By delving into the landscape of Black letters right before the beginning of the Civil War, Spires is interested in capturing "the tensions between possibility and disappointment from this prewar perspective—as if emancipation and the Reconstruction amendments had not and perhaps would never happen—and from a moment when all signs pointed toward the permanence of enslavement and increasing racism."[49] This moment just before the Civil War witnessed an increase in published Black writing, and also marked a shift toward an increasingly experimental Black aesthetics. Writers like William J. Wilson, James McCune Smith, Harriet Wilson, and Harriet Jacobs were developing literary forms and tropes that departed from the propagandistic and documentary imperatives of Black narrative that had defined the 1840s and the earlier 1850s under the directive of abolitionist demands and priorities. By the end of the 1850s, Black writers continued to excoriate the nation for the suffering of their people under the lash and through broader regimes of racial surveillance and terror, but their writing is also marked by a kind of frustration and even exhaustion about being asked to fight, relentlessly, in a white supremacist nation that seemed unlikely to ever leave behind its reliance on enslavement and exploitation.

Writers like Wilson and McCune Smith also resented how anti-Black racism and the imperative to be politically expedient narrowed the horizon of Black expression. In other words, antislavery gains—as well as demands that African Americans be "practical" and fight for a freedom that had already been guaranteed to them during the Revolutionary War and then betrayed—occurred at the detriment of the development and advancement of Black aesthetics and intellectual freedom. As literary flaneurs, slowly and performatively parading about town (and writing about what they saw as they strolled), Wilson and McCune Smith's writing refused hegemonic political grammars, especially those that involved a kind of accelerationism and the narrowing of experience and politics around single-issue causes and priorities.[50] Indeed, at several points in their periodical correspondence, Wilson and McCune Smith complain about the Garrisonians because of how they instrumentalized the struggle—and exploited Black suffering and enslavement—in order to drive their own political agendas.

In opposition to the documentary demand placed on Black writing (that all writing by African Americans, even fiction, be true, verifiable, respectable, and not deviant), Wilson and McCune Smith experimented with alternative forms of address and rhetoric. They refused to allow any outside force to limit the range of creative expression, and their writing displays a virtuosic relationship to topic, tone, and style. McCune Smith, for example, was known for sprinkling Latin phrases and classical references into his writing. Doing so reminded readers of his cosmopolitan commitments and elite medical education in Scotland, but it was also a tactic that forced readers to slow down rather than skim the newspaper. Ultimately, Wilson and McCune Smith rejected an attenuated definition of Blackness as a political category; they instead defined Blackness as an aesthetic category, or what McCune Smith calls "our essentially aesthetic or art-nature."[51]

Even though prominent leaders like Douglass and Delany threw their weight behind mobilizing soldiers and support for the Union cause, others continued to organize alternative plots and plans. Indeed, some African Americans remained hesitant about the war effort and continued to put together plans to jump ship from a sinking nation. Some even continued to organize emigration support and missions during the war. Spires points to the radical possibilities—and forms of radical imagination—that were actually foreclosed by the Civil War. In his Picture Gallery, Wilson sometimes seems to be already lamenting the narrowing of Black radicalism into a series of reforms, laws, and amendments during the Reconstruction period. My turn to a microperiodization, focusing here on roughly 1859–61, aims to help us tune into the grammars of hesitance, political restraint, and experimental noninstrumentalism that characterized Black aesthetics during a brief yet significant historical flashpoint. By looking closely at specific desires, polemics, and theories being developed by Black intellectuals, activists, and writers right before the Civil War, we glimpse the beginning of a Black avant-gardism that was forestalled by the pragmatism and masculine militarism of war politics and priorities.

Dandies, Bohemians, and Antebellum Afropolitanism

In her foundational study *Slaves to Fashion: Black Dandyism and the Styling of Black Diasporic Identity*, Monica Miller traces how the figure of the Black dandy emerged in the context of the rise of conspicuous consumption alongside the explosion of the slave trade in the eighteenth century, especially as planters and merchants sought to show off their wealth through the possession and display of fashionable, "luxury" slaves. But dandyism was not just foisted on captives. The sartorial displays, gestures, and wit of the dandy, she argues, were also wielded by people of African descent to challenge violent limits placed on their selfhood and to refashion social and political possibility.[52] The Black dandy was also viciously satirized in popular culture in the antebellum United States. In cartoon series like Edward Clay's *Life in Philadelphia*, African American men were lambasted as lazy fops who dressed up in finery and tried to pass as civilized gentlemen. A dandy figure named Zip Coon, along with Dandy Jim, were frequent targets of derision on the minstrel stage (figure I.1). These pervasive anti-Black images mocked both enslaved and free people for their aspirations to freedom and dignity and for their audacity to look and act like citizens of the nation. According to Richard Powell, "In a society that sought comfort in clearly defined social roles and a spatially predictable landscape (despite idealistic claims of a broad-based democracy and upward social mobility), the Black dandy's striking, audacious appearance on America's street corners disrupted the white majority's false notions of social order, racial homogeneity, and cultural superiority."[53]

At the same time, popular depictions of Black dandies registered white anxieties about the growing political power of African Americans. As Black communities in places like New York became more organized, figures like William J. Wilson embraced dandyism as a way to establish their status, wealth, and cosmopolitanism, as well as their intellectualism. As Miller notes, the dandy was also a global figure, one that allowed former slaves and free people in the United States to connect to diasporic solidarities. She understands Black dandyism as being a sign of an "early Afro-diasporic identity" and a cosmopolitanism "that African subjects did not choose but from which they necessarily reimagined themselves."[54]

Miller's and Powell's nuanced accounts of early Black dandyism help to bring into view the flamboyances and flourishes that characterize Wilson's writing as Ethiop and appear throughout his periodical correspondence with McCune Smith. I agree with Radiclani Clytus that scholars would do well to pay attention to a vibrant Black masculine belles lettres tradition as it takes shape in periodicals like *Frederick Douglass' Paper*.[55] However, in seeking to establish the centrality of republican values in an emerging culture of Black belletrism, harking back to the epistolary cultures of the Revolutionary era, we risk missing the performativity as well as the queerness of these exchanges. Wilson and McCune Smith were working to establish something like their own literary vanguard in the 1850s, and they did so through a flexing of intellectualism, countercultural references, and a rhetorical playfulness that seems worlds away from the ideals and rhetoric of American republicanism.

It is my wager that while Wilson and his cohort certainly drew on the rhetoric of republicanism to make their views legible within the civic sphere, their actual commitments—to the terrain of culture, cosmopolitanism, and aesthetics—feel closer to the bohemian homosociality of Walt Whitman and his own cohort in 1850s Brooklyn. James Smethurst has located the emergence of a Black bohemianism in the late nineteenth century in the writings of Paul Laurence Dunbar, predating American countercultural movements and avant-garde aesthetics by several decades.[56] This study draws the timeline of Black bohemianism even further back, to include the networks of Afropolitans in antebellum New York that Peterson traces in *Black Gotham* and that come into view through Wilson's Picture Gallery and his periodical correspondence with McCune Smith in *Frederick Douglass' Paper*.

The queerness and bohemianism of Wilson's writing inheres perhaps most powerfully in its articulation of both space and movement, especially its interest in strolling and other forms of wayward movement as a form of freedom. In "Terance Ludlam," Wilson's narrator recounts a recent trip he

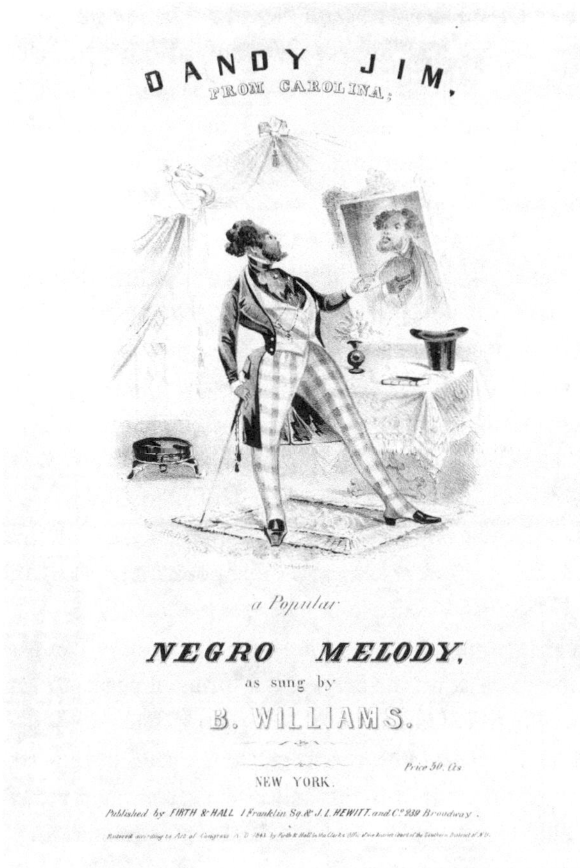

I.1 *Dandy Jim, from Carolina; A Popular Negro Melody as Sung by B. Williams* (New York: Firth & Hall, 1843). Consolidating white fears about Black freedom, wealth, and sexuality, the dandy was a common figure in antebellum minstrelsy.

took to a village north of New York, possibly upstate to Washington Irving's Hudson Valley. (Irving was a formative influence on Wilson and Wilson's story is Irvingesque.) Setting out on this journey, the narrator says that "the pleasure of the undertaking lies in the absence of any arrangement how or where to go, time and liberty being the only requisites."[57] Strolling and wandering give Wilson's narrator occasion to comment on a changing, industrialized landscape based on his own observations on the ground. Recalling a familiar language of queer movement and practice beginning in the twentieth century, Wilson's narrator refers to his retreat upstate as a country "cruise."

Indeed, given Wilson's sardonic wit, his dandyism, and his interest in dragging and "reading" his closest friends in print, we might also place Wilson's writings within the beginnings of a Black queer aesthetic that is often dated to the New Negro Renaissance but that we can start to see emerging in this crucial historical turning point in the late 1850s.

Both Wilson and McCune Smith also deployed wry humor and even caustic critique as a way of establishing a critical distance—and creating a zone of self-defense—from the racism of the US public sphere. Here I'm thinking about Gabrielle Foreman's idea of how sentimentalism could operate as a cover for Black women writers and intellectuals: Black women's sentimentalism was less about the earnest belief in sentimental values than about how it could be used as camouflage.[58] Something similar could be said about how Black masculine writers in the period deployed republicanism and used it as a cover for the expression of alternative ideas and desires. Wilson and McCune Smith's multiyear correspondence in *Frederick Douglass' Paper* is sometimes cantankerous; at other points, it revels in a playful homosociality. Wilson, for example, emphasizes the "luxury" of homosocial comradery in his account of an 1855 soirée held in honor of Douglass at the Broadway Tabernacle, which he praised as a "brilliant pageant": "I found myself comfortably seated in one of the luxuriating chairs of the gorgeous apartments of the Sybarites, with Frederick Douglass on the one side, and Communipaw on the other."[59] In this and other such moments in Wilson and McCune Smith's correspondence, homosocial exchange intermingles with commodity fetishism ("luxuriating chairs"; "gorgeous apartments"). In this regard, see also McCune Smith's description of a formerly enslaved dandy in New York in these terms: "That memorable walk! His blue cloth coat and double gilt brass buttons! And the silks that rustled by his side!"[60] Wilson, too, turns his eye to the extravagant sartorial displays of young Black men in the city. Marx famously called the commodity "a queer thing"; Wilson and comrades add to this that the commodity is especially "queer" when it is you, your friend, or your family member that has been commodified and circulated as an object.

This study also connects the Picture Gallery to later histories of the avant-garde and countercultural writing as a way of pushing back against the fetishization of circulation in early African American literary studies. Scholars of the period tend to privilege circulating texts and make arguments that depend on assumptions about circulation, sometimes without concrete knowledge about the actual distribution, circulation, and readership of texts, all of which can be incredibly hard to pin down. What, for example, to do with copies of slave narratives in the archive that were clearly never opened and read, but instead displayed in a parlor to show off one's own sympathies with the situation of enslaved people? Ultimately, we need to drill down into the facts of readership and circulation if we want to make arguments about readership and circulation. At the same time, we need more methods and frameworks that allow us to take noncirculating African American texts seriously.[61]

In this project, I make an argument for the centrality of a text that barely circulated and that left almost no trace of reception in the nineteenth century. I do so because it is a singular text that speaks not only to the problem of Black aesthetics in the late 1850s but also to many of the most pressing conversations about Blackness, art-making, and the politics of institutions today. The *Anglo-African Magazine* had only five hundred subscribers, though they reached beyond New York City and likely included a broad swath of prominent Black intellectuals and cosmopolitans as well as white abolitionist-leaning readers. At this point, I can verify three readers of the text: Thomas Hamilton, editor of the *Anglo-African*; William Wells Brown (who cites from the Picture Gallery in his 1863 collective biography, *The Black Man*); and William J. Wilson himself. The "Afric-American Picture Gallery" nonetheless warrants our attention even though and perhaps even *because* it seemed to have little influence in its own moment of publication. Scholars in performance studies have long argued for the importance of attending to ephemeral forms and other works and contexts that refused or never reached an audience.[62] Indeed, Wilson's Picture Gallery thematizes the question of audience throughout: And when Ethiop chases gallery visitors back out the door of his beloved gallery "retreat," it actively refuses one.

Wilson's Picture Gallery is indeed only one text, and one that did not shape history or literature in an obvious way, but it warrants a full book because it is fascinating on its own terms, and with further circulation and study it might make a mark on our own moment. As in my past collaborative work on the statistical graphics that W. E. B. Du Bois and his students at Atlanta University created for an exhibition at the 1900 Paris Exposition, scholars can help to further the transmission of archives and texts that remain hidden or inaccessible because of historical neglect, racism, and inattention to the preservation of Black archives. In the case of the Du Bois infographics, the housing of the contents of the American Negro Exhibit from the Paris Exposition in the Library of Congress kept these crucial images out of the hands of the communities they were meant to both represent and serve for over a hundred years.[63] The Picture Gallery might also take on a new life today, especially given its deep connections to current conversations about the politics of race and museums, Afrofuturism, and the politics of Black archives and collections.

Chapter Overview

While census data, newspapers, convention records, and other documents help fill out the shape of Wilson's biography, they do not offer many details about Wilson's personality and temperament. Luckily, William Wells Brown includes William J. Wilson in *The Black Man: His Antecedents, His Genius, and His Achievements* (1863), alongside leaders and creatives ranging from Benjamin Banneker and Placido to Henry Highland Garnet and Frederick Douglass. As in the Picture Gallery, Wells Brown's biographical entries are not just characterological descriptions of Black leaders; they are also ekphrastic sketches. Of Wilson, Wells Brown notes, "In personal appearance he is under the middle size; his profile is more striking than his front face; he has a rather pleasing countenance, and is unmixed in race."[64] Wells Brown was himself part of the illustrious group he featured in *The Black Man*, and the book was published by none other than Thomas Hamilton. The book likely bears the traces of Hamilton's editorial input and contributions.

Wells Brown deepens one's sense from Wilson's newspaper correspondence that there was something both idiosyncratic and extravagant about the way he carried himself in the world. Wells Brown hints at the view of Wilson-as-libertine that I have sought to draw out at the fringes of the respectability politics of Black print in this period. He says Wilson is known for writing some of the "raciest" essays found in "public journals in the country" and goes on to reproduce Wilson's bawdy poem "The Teacher and the Pupil" in its entirety from the *Anglo-African Magazine*.[65] He goes on to highlight Wilson's unique capacity to use writing to stimulate the senses and the imagination. Wells Brown writes, "With acute powers of conception, a sparkling and lively fancy, and a quaintly curious felicity of diction, Mr. Wilson wakes us from our torpidity and coldness to a sense of our capabilities."[66] In what follows, I want to hold on to the "sparkling" dimensions of Wilson's correspondence and fiction writing as they are described by Wells Brown, including this idea that his powers of conception—and "felicity of diction"—have a stimulating and enlivening effect on readers, "wak[ing] us from our torpidity and coldness to a sense of our capabilities."[67] Indeed, Wilson's writing refuses to be pinned down; it moves and puts readers on the move. It participates in the flaneur culture of urban dandyism and the perambulatory epistolatory networks of New York's periodical culture, while at the same time recognizing that Black movement was constantly being surveilled and contained. Wilson's is a dynamic, life-making kind of writing that attempts to vivify in the face of slavery's necropolitics.

This book would not be possible without a rich scholarship on Blackness and visual culture as well as theories of race and visuality, especially as they intersect with histories of slavery and abolition.[68] I have benefited tremendously from this work. But instead of reading the Picture Gallery solely through the lenses offered through theories of race and visuality, I ask how a textual museum such as Wilson's asks us to *see* differently. Through Ethiop, Wilson uses narrative both to insert himself into a visual sphere and to raise philosophical, social, and political questions about the limits of a knowledge and a politics rooted in visibility. In this way, we might understand ekphrasis as a kind of fugitive visual practice, one that evades capture at the same time as it explores the complex terrain of race and vision in an age in which the two were becoming inextricably linked to one another. Across the book, I take seriously the ways African American commentators on the visual in the period were often relying on rhetorical—rather than visual—authority to make their arguments.

Indeed, Wilson, McCune Smith, Douglass, and their cohort luxuriated in the powers of verbal and textual rhetoric. To that end, I begin with a brief reading of the ekphrastic description of a slave ship that inaugurates Ethiop's gallery tour. Upon entering the gallery-text of the "Afric-American Picture Gallery," visitor-readers are immediately confronted with a large painting of a slave ship hung near the museum's entrance and titled "Picture Number 1.—The Slave Ship." Wilson encourages readers to interpret the museum's holdings, and the rest of the text, through the lens of the Atlantic slave trade and the horrors of the Middle Passage. In that same spirit, I position Wilson's ekphrasis of the slave ship as a frame for the rest of this study, a reminder that slavery's mark is everywhere in the Picture Gallery, as in the world outside it.

Chapter 1 reads the Picture Gallery as a text that theorizes Black art in an industrializing society structured by slavery and racial capitalism. What, Wilson asks, is the status of the work of art in an industrializing, slaveholding society? How must philosophies of the image take into account racial capitalism's deforming and degrading influence? To do so, I place the Picture Gallery in conversation with Walter Benjamin's *Arcades Project*. Wilson and Benjamin, situated in two moments of historical transition in the history of capitalism, are both interested in the status of the work of art in regimes that are increasingly defined by the commodity form and by individual acts of consumerism. The second half of this chapter explores the curious status of photography in the Picture Gallery. The Picture Gallery suppresses photography as a signifier at the same time as it is deeply shaped by this new visual technology and its transformation of the visual field. I argue that the Picture Gallery's repressed photographic unconscious signals Wilson's participation in the elevation of photography into a field of fine art; it also marks an ambivalence regarding the move to capture and submit to the camera in the name of making African Americans visible and legible as citizens.

Chapter 2 situates the Picture Gallery within the broader landscape of African American aesthetics in what I conceptualize as a late antebellum period. The Picture Gallery is, among other things, part of what Nafissa Thompson-Spires calls the nineteenth-century "black sketch tradition."[69] I am interested in how "sketching" by African American writers in the period privileged provisional experimentation over elegantly completed masterpieces, and favored active (if sometimes cantankerous) intellectual collaboration over the singular productions of individuals. Focusing on the multiyear periodical correspondence between James McCune Smith and William J. Wilson in the pages of *Frederick Douglass' Paper*, I consider the deep dialogism of Black writing in the 1850s and how McCune Smith and Wilson were themselves forging a theory of Black aesthetics through their exchanges. I argue that Wilson created the Picture Gallery as a contribution to the dialogic and collaborative cultural production that was happening within coteries of Black writers and artists in the 1850s.

Chapter 3 pauses to consider the significance of Wilson's installation of Phillis Wheatley's portrait in the center of his imagined gallery space. It takes seriously the possibility that when Wilson was writing as Ethiop, he was paying homage to and perhaps even writing in a kind of drag as the enslaved poet Phillis Wheatley, who, like Wilson, used writing to connect to other working Black artists and writers in her community. More broadly, the chapter considers the Picture Gallery's investment in reclaiming Black heroes from the Revolutionary era, concluding with an analysis of Ethiop's description of a portrait of Crispus Attucks, martyr of the Boston Massacre. The Picture Gallery contributes to a broader culture of Black memorialization in the 1850s, which sought to make sacred communion with Black heroes and artists across time and space. This was a radical act in a white supremacist society that continually worked to disrupt connection and solidarity among people of African descent.

A final chapter turns to the Black Forest fairy tale that comes to preoccupy the plot of the Picture Gallery, transforming the series from a gallery tour to a work of fantastic flight and speculative fiction. Halfway through the seven-part series, readers are asked to leave the picture gallery to follow Ethiop on a journey to visit a Black artist living deep in a mysterious forest. I am interested in how the seemingly nonpolitical dimensions of a quest fantasy allow Wilson, in a moment of abolitionist immediatism and political agitation, to sit with feelings of ambivalence. In general, political propaganda does not allow for messy feelings or uncertainty. I argue that the Picture Gallery—like the Black antebellum epistolatory cultures to which it was deeply connected—becomes political insofar as it seeks to be a space where contradictory views, half-formed positions, and deep ambivalences can be held without neat or easy resolution.

The book's conclusion returns to questions of aesthetic experimentation and vanguardism in order to better understand how the Civil War and Reconstruction both augured new Black futures and obscured others that were being actively constructed by Wilson and his Afropolitan cohort in the late 1850s. Writers like Wilson and Harriet Jacobs, along with other Black educators and activists, left New York City during the Civil War, committing themselves to educating and caring for former slaves in the South. I pause to think about how these migrations left absences and forms of grief in their wake in postbellum New York. The spectral presence of Wilson's departure can be felt in a curious and stunning archival trace: A notice in the *Brooklyn Daily Eagle* from 1865 notes that mail has been waiting for him at the post office for three months. Given Wilson's embeddedness within Black epistolatory networks of exchange, this cache of waiting mail—letters never received and never to be answered—bears a haunting weight that might tell us something about aesthetic genealogies that are present to us only as absences. Wilson's Picture Gallery gives us an important origin point for a Black queer aesthetics that would continue to proliferate in the shadows across the nineteenth century, ultimately flourishing in the New Negro Renaissance. I ask what it might mean to place Wilson at the origins of a Black queer aesthetics that could be glimpsed, often only intermittently, across the nineteenth century.

Finally, a word on method. This project takes much inspiration from the Picture Gallery's expansive visual imagination, including the work it does to carefully describe a visual field in the absence of actual images reproduced on the page. Throughout the book's chapters, I often pause to study a particular object of ekphrasis in the text, contextualizing it within relevant art-historical contexts, political history, and, when relevant, the world of antebellum print and periodical culture in which the Picture Gallery was embedded. In so doing, I seek to illuminate the specific ways Wilson was situating his work within debates about both print and visual culture in the period, and the various ways he was speaking back to the world of fine art, especially portraiture and landscape painting, to make visible how American aesthetics participated in grammars of both slavery and Blackness in America. In other words, this book includes many of my own descriptions of Wilson's ekphrastic descriptions. I work to excavate and disentangle multiple layers of citation and meaning as they are combined and condensed within individual objects in Wilson's gallery. I have found that my own experiments in ekphrasis often work, as in the Picture Gallery, as freeze-frames that ask readers to pause, decelerate, and shift their focus to a single work of art, static and still in appearance but vibrating with a rich palimpsest of meaning. The book also includes several images, some of which are direct inspirations for Wilson's word portraits; others are visual objects that are meant to supplement and further expand the visual imagination of the original text.

Following the Picture Gallery's exhilarating refusal of historical chronology and understanding that history only ever reaches us mediated by narrative, the chapters that follow are willfully experimental, at times playfully so. Historical context is given when and where it helps to illuminate some aspect of the text, which I want to keep at the center of my view and attention (inasmuch as a text such as this one allows it: more on the politics of aesthetic absorption and distraction in the Picture Gallery later). I take some leaps of faith in the hopes that they will encourage further study and thought on this unique work written in a period of profound political and cultural transformation. In this way, these chapters are not intended as definitive interpretations of the text; rather, they are offered—humbly—as preliminary starting points for future thought and study. From delineating the source materials and works of art that inspired represented objets d'art in the gallery to illuminating Wilson's complex relationship to the politics of emigration and colonization, there are countless ways into this text, and countless ways out of it. There is nothing definitive about the Picture Gallery itself: It's a work that refuses to be pinned down and that aims to spark the imagination. I thus write about it in adherence to its own spirit of evasiveness and refusal of capture. I also take inspiration from Wilson's own commitments to a dialogical aesthetics. Writers like Wilson and McCune Smith composed what they called "outlines" and "sketches" because they wanted others to further flesh out their writings and ideas. This book thus also stands as an invitation for future work on the Picture Gallery, Wilson, and his milieu.

Picture Number 1

THE SLAVE SHIP

Upon entering the gallery-text of the "Afric-American Picture Gallery," visitor-readers are immediately presented with a large painting hung near the museum's entrance and titled "Picture Number 1.—The Slave Ship." William J. Wilson's avatar, Ethiop, infuses his description of the piece's location and lighting with his characteristic wit: Nodding to geographies of enslavement in the antebellum South, he says that the painting hangs on the "south side of the Gallery." Hinting at the horrors of the slave trade, and perhaps also at abolition's increasing success at swaying public opinion, he goes on to say that the painting appears in "rather an unfavorable light."[1]

The slave ship became central to the visual propaganda of abolition in the late eighteenth century. In 1788, the Plymouth Committee of the Society for Effecting the Abolition of the Slave Trade in England published a detailed broadside depicting the plan of the Liverpool-based slaver *Brooks* and titled *Description of a Slave Ship*. The engraving relied on measurements and a firsthand account from a young abolitionist named Thomas Clarkson. Along with the dimensions of the *Brooks*, it showed hundreds of captive Africans depicted as identical figures tightly packed into the hold of the ship (plate 1). This image immediately struck a chord: It was reproduced widely in England and the United States, and it circulated across the Atlantic world through the same routes that transported millions of African captives to the Americas. The *Brooks* engraving would become an iconic abolitionist image reflecting the systematic nature and inhumanity of the slave trade, part and parcel of a world of commodities and trade built on the traffic of human beings. It also served as crucial evidence in the court case that led to England's abolition of its slave trade in 1807.[2]

The *Brooks* image would continue to occupy a central location in the transatlantic abolitionist imaginary and its visual campaign into the nineteenth century.[3] But here, in "Picture Number 1," Wilson doesn't seem to be recalling the mathematical and architectural hold represented in *Description of a Slave Ship* as much as he references a tradition of representing the slave ship through a Romantic aesthetics of sublimity, awe, and terror. J. M. W. Turner's famous painting of the 1781 *Zong* massacre, *Slave Ship* (1840), is perhaps the best-known example of this kind of Romantic abolitionist aesthetic (plate 2). Originally titled *Slavers Throwing Overboard the Dead and Dying, Typhoon Coming On*, Turner's frenzied storm of red, yellow, and blue mixes sea and fire elements to portray the world-destroying power of human greed; a starkly painted leg, fed upon by fish, in the painting's right foreground, portrays slavery as a grotesque and monstrous enterprise. While the complicated provenance and semiprivate history of the painting makes it difficult to imagine Wilson himself viewing Turner's *Slave Ship*, the piece is representative of a broader Romantic aesthetics of Atlantic slavery that traversed visual culture, prose, and poetry in the early to mid-nineteenth century.[4]

Like many objects of ekphrasis in the "Afric-American Picture Gallery," Ethiop's "The Slave Ship" also deploys both the gothic and the category of "ugliness" to portray a world degraded by slavery: This ship, Ethiop notes, is "Dutch-modeled and ugly, even hideous to look upon, as a slave-ship ought to be." Next we learn that the painting depicts the first group of captive Africans forced onto the shores of an American colony, arriving at Jamestown: "On the shore is a group of emaciated *Africans*, heavily manacled, the first slaves that ever trod the American continent." Ethiop next draws the mind's eye back to the "fierce and angry waters of the bay," where we see "a small boat containing another lot of these human beings, just nearing the shore." Zooming out from the shore to the bay, Ethiop's description suggests a monstrous procession and a horrifying cycle: Africans on shore, heavy with chains, are followed by the transport of more captive souls by boat, to be followed by more ships, more boats, and more humans pushed into bondage. This moment in the text echoes both Marcus Rediker's description of the slave ship as a floating factory and Stephanie Smallwood's account of the terrifying seasonality of slave ship voyages, wherein enslaved people, especially those who had experienced the Middle Passage firsthand, dreadfully awaited the annual return of the slave ships to American shores.[5]

From here, Ethiop guides readers to a detail in the painting, forcing us to confront the Africans in chains in their individuality, rather than as a depersonalized mass (as on the *Brooks* broadside and in other pro- and antislavery visual propaganda): "The small boat struck by, and contending with a huge breaker, is so near the shore that you can behold, and startle as you behold, the emaciated and death-like faces of the unfortunate victims, and the hideous countenances of their captors."[6] If the leg in Turner's painting is for most viewers what Ronald Barthes calls the *punctum*, in Wilson's "The Slave Ship" the "death-like faces" are; Ethiop says they are the painting's "crowning point."[7] Most dramatically, Satan himself lords over the whole terrifying scene, watching the poor souls being transported to shore: "High and above all, perched upon the stern, with foot, tail and horns, and the chief insignias of his office, is his Satanic Majesty, gloating over the whole scene."[8]

Ethiop concludes the first stop on his gallery tour with this haunting query: "What is more truthful than that the devil is ever the firm friend and companion of the slave ship?" While Wilson's Satan may have been inspired by specific cultural images of the devil in the period, "Satanic Majesty" also feels Miltonic, pulled from the pages of *Paradise Lost*. Wilson also wrote poetry, and at several points in the Picture Gallery, we can feel his poetic interests and reading of poetry coming to bear on his prose. For example, in his ekphrastic description of Wheatley's portrait, Wilson offers details from Wheatley's biography that echo lines from her own poems. Wilson pens his own short poetic ode addressed to Wheatley in that same section of the text. Here, in "The Slave Ship," a Miltonic Satan lends a sense of terror to the scene. Filtering a scene of the slave trade through the lens of *Paradise Lost* further reminds readers of the evils of humanity in a fallen, unredeemed world while lending an epic timescale and frame to the history of the Atlantic slave trade.

In her magisterial history of the "slave ship icon" from its original publication as an abolitionist print in 1788 to its circulation in contemporary artistic practice, Cheryl Finley says that the *Brooks* image began to be reappropriated and repossessed during the New Negro Renaissance by "the descendants of those who were the subject of the image, by diasporic Africans, that is, by black Atlantic artists and their allies" (see, for example, plates 3 and 4).[9] She further argues that visual representations of the slave ship by Afro-diasporic artists engage in a practice of mnemonic aesthetics, a ritualized practice that uses "memory as an aesthetic tool and organizing principle to emphasize recurrent themes that have shaped the African diaspora."[10] Seeking a "spiritual conversion of the icon," these artists also understand that this work comes with a great responsibility: "to create works that recall the history of the artists' African origins and to ensure that this history's significance is never forgotten."[11]

Wilson's "Picture Number 1" made an early contribution to the long diasporic tradition of visualizing the slave ship that Finley describes, but it does so through text rather than visual art. While the *Brooks* image has had undeniable currency as a visual metonym for the terrors of slavery, its power has, from its very beginnings, also derived from narrative. Indeed, Carsten Junker argues that the relationship between text and image was central to the image's affective power and political effectiveness. Noting that "there was never a moment in time when [the image] caused affective results without the contextual knowledge that the accompanying text provided," Junker questions the presumption, repeated by commentators since 1788, that it was the *image* of the Brooks that shocked the reader.[12] For example, while Clarkson said that there was instantaneous horror when spectator-readers viewed the visual diagram, it was the broadside's accompanying narrative that actually conveyed the gruesome horrors of the Middle Passage. Moreover, the original broadside did not signal an "image," "diagram," or "depiction," but was instead titled *Description of a Slave Ship*.

But what about representations like Wilson's that eschew the visual altogether? For one, Ethiop's ekphrastic rendering of the slave ship intervened in the hegemony of the *Brooks* slave ship image as it continued to circulate across transatlantic popular culture into the late 1850s. It also does something similar to how Carl Plasa describes Elizabeth Alexander's poem "Islands Number Four" (2001), itself an ekphrastic account of the famous *Brooks* slave ship image: "Alexander contests the primacy of the visual mode, placing an imaginative counter-faith in the ability of the written word to act as an effective conduit of historical memory."[13] Here, narrative accounts of the slave ship operate according to the principles of mnemonic aesthetics that Finley describes in her visual history. Writers like Olaudah Equiano and Phillis Wheatley also complicated the abolitionist iconography of the slave ship through phenomenologically rich narrative accounts that were, in some ways, better able to better capture the horrors of the passage. It's significant in this regard that the abolitionists responsible for *Description of a Slave Ship* sought a statement from Equiano verifying that their representation was truthful.

Wilson's ekphrastic depiction of the slave ship points to the *narrative* origins of African American visual culture, while suggesting the limits of an abolitionist ethos grounded solely in sight. Through his description of an ominous image of the beginnings of the slave trade on North American shores,

Wilson also presents slavery as an undeniable—and haunting—presence in both American history and American art. Positioned as a work that readers of the Picture Gallery must pass through to read the rest of the gallery, this painting within the text also becomes something like the door of no return, the literal and metaphorical passage through which Africans were transformed into captives.[14] By beginning his gallery tour this way and by hanging "The Slave Ship" at the gallery's entrance, Wilson asks readers to interpret the rest of the gallery's collection through slavery's original traumas and ongoing horrors. Following Wilson's lead, I too position the slave ship as a frame, and portal, for this study.

1

"He Thinks He Will Submit"

THE WORK OF BLACK ART IN THE AGE OF RACIAL CAPITALISM

If an ever abiding love for any branch of *Art* is indicative of a fitness to pursue it, then I should have been a painter.

Ethiop, "Afric-American Picture Gallery," *Anglo-African Magazine*, February 1859

William J. Wilson was among the first theorists of Black visual culture in the United States. He believed strongly in the unique capacities of visual representation to build political power. Prominent figures like Frederick Douglass, William Wells Brown, James McCune Smith, and others in Wilson's cohort were also interested in self-representation as a crucial pathway to self-determination. As many have chronicled, Douglass was especially interested in photography's potential for democratizing image-making by allowing nonelites to have control over their own image and for African Americans to be represented truthfully without the distortion of caricature.[1]

Whereas Douglass promoted photography's significance for the race and for the movement, Wilson was focused on questions about racial representation within the sphere of fine art. He argued for the importance of seeing Black Americans represented not just within but also *across* visual mediums, including painting, sculpture, and print, and to seeing such works produced by African Americans themselves. Writing in the March 11, 1853, issue of *Frederick Douglass' Paper*, he recounted his visit to two small galleries with art hanging for purchase, where he was disappointed to find a glaring absence of Black portraiture: "There stood Franklin and Adams, Lafayette and Jefferson, and Clay and Webster; the gods and goddesses were there, and the Queen of England was there, and so was the emperor of France; but I found not the Emperor of Hayti, nor of D[a]homey, nor the President of Liberia, nor any other distinguished *black*." He goes on to say that he "demand[s] not caricatures but correct emanations," and that such work is about loving and acknowledging Blackness in all its many forms. In this future of Black art to come, he writes, "we must . . . acknowledge and love our own peculiarities if we have any." Wilson longed for a world of art that reflected the demographic realities of the city he lived in, and where common folks could decorate their walls with images of Black revolutionary leaders rather than enslaving Founding Fathers. Moments like this one resonate, in a much later context, with the popularity of images of Barack Obama in Black homes and other spaces during and after his election as president of the United States. In his own moment, Wilson was entering into a conversation about the importance of public portraiture and its role in reimagining the nation.

Wilson insisted over and over that African Americans needed two things: power over their own image and access to capital. He believed that the accumulation of wealth was crucial to the building of Black political power.[2] More than that, he understood that money and images were deeply connected, and increasingly so amid the intensification of both capitalist exploitation and consumerism. Thus, Wilson's advocacy of Black representation was neither naive nor ungrounded in the material transformations that surrounded him. He was keenly aware that art was being pulled into a widening economic sphere, and that works of fine art—like people of African descent in the United States—were being subjected to intense forms of commodification. In other words, Wilson was working to understand the nature of fine art, and its shifting role in society, in a capitalist system that was consolidating around him.

This chapter positions Wilson as a prophetic theorist whose work anticipates later philosophies of the image, especially Walter Benjamin's writings on the role of the image and the image of history in industrial modernity. A canny theorist of the work of fine art in a society defined by slavery and capitalism, Wilson both anticipates and complicates Benjamin's understanding of the work of art in the age of mechanical reproduction. Wilson was a forward-looking, even futurist writer—anticipating and dreaming a Black art still to come—while Benjamin was concerned with looking backward to the nineteenth century to excavate the buried origins of commodity capitalism as well as what Foucault called a "history of the present" from the vestiges of nineteenth-century commodity culture that had survived into the early twentieth-century: trinkets, souvenirs, "archaic images," and the Paris Arcades, still standing but no longer in their nineteenth-century consumerist glory. Across the "Afric-American Picture Gallery" series, as well as in his correspondence with James McCune Smith, Wilson announces the beginnings of an Afromodernism from his vantage in the late antebellum period. Benjamin, on the other hand, reconstructs his own modernity by looking back to the relics and concrete object-worlds of the previous century that were still materially visible, often as vestiges, traces, and antiques, in the early twentieth century. Benjamin's moment, we should not forget, was also the moment of Black modernist cultural and artistic production that we now call the Harlem Renaissance and that was in its own moment called the New Negro Renaissance. In this way, I wonder whether we can imagine Wilson and Benjamin exchanging looks from two distinct yet overlapping historical vantage points.[3] The two also shared geographic imaginaries: Benjamin dreams of nineteenth-century Paris while writing there in exile; Wilson conjures a global Black cosmopolitanism as he sits in his "rooms" in Brooklyn. He writes Ethiop from a position of being cloistered in a New York gallery that he says is maddeningly disorganized but that also feels like a protected respite from the busy New York streets and a racist public sphere.

Both the Picture Gallery series and Benjamin's *Arcades Project* are kaleidoscopic texts that theorize a new regime of image and knowledge being produced by the turbines of industrial modernity. Wilson contributes to modern philosophies of the image by emphasizing how images are produced and circulated within a regime of *racial* capitalism, the ongoing terrors of slavery, and a representational system predicated on anti-Blackness. In what follows, I begin with Benjamin's concept of the dialectical image and suggest how Wilson prefigures that idea in the Picture Gallery. I go on to think about the Picture Gallery in the context of the rise of the modern art museum and a revolution in visual technologies in the middle of the nineteenth century, focusing on the complex place that photography plays in the series. Although photography is suppressed as a signifier in the Picture Gallery, its influence on the text—as on the broader US culture in the 1850s—can be felt nearly everywhere. I argue that the Picture Gallery's repressed photographic unconscious signals Wilson's participation in the elevation of photography into a field of fine art in the period. It also marks an ambivalence regarding the move to capture and submit to the camera in the name of making African Americans legible as citizens. Despite his enthusiasm for the broad representation of African Americans in the public sphere, Wilson also knew that visibility in a white supremacist society came with real risks. Finally, I consider the fact that although the Picture Gallery relies on sentimental cultures of photography as well as domestic constructions of space, women are largely absent from the text. Among other things, the elision of Black women as figures of political and artistic agency point to some of the limits of Wilson's speculative imagination.

The Dialectical Image from the Paris Arcades to the Picture Gallery

William J. Wilson and Walter Benjamin were both interested in tracing the status of art, and the image more generally, under the deforming pressure of industrial capitalism and the commodity form. But Wilson goes one step further by focusing on the production of the image within regimes of *racial* capitalism and the ongoing terrors of slavery and anti-Blackness. If Benjamin's modernity is haunted by earlier moments of history and cycles of capitalism that pass themselves off as eternal myth, progress, and even nature itself, Wilson's modernity—and its production of images—is always haunted by the traumatic memory of the slave trade. Most poignantly, in "Picture IX," an ekphrastic depiction of Mount Vernon, Wilson establishes the degraded status of fine art in an enslaving society by portraying the estate of the nation's "father," George Washington, in a state of total "dilapidation and decay."[4] As in many other pictures in the gallery, "Picture IX.—Mount Vernon" finds Wilson once again returning to the early days of the American Republic to remind readers of the nation's original sin and how the betrayals of the Revolutionary era continued to echo into the present. The Picture Gallery's sketch of Mount Vernon places slavery at the center of our consideration of Washington and of the nation's founding.[5]

Ethiop's entry opens with a note on the contemporary craze for all things Mount Vernon and directly links this frenzy to an emerging market, where the memory of Washington has been commodified and sold to the consuming masses for their pleasure and entertainment: "Mount Vernon just now enters into everything. It has something to do with every spring of the machinery of American society. . . . The boys in the streets busily cry out Mount Vernon; the fashionable young belle simpers Mount Vernon. Mount Vernon exclaims the breastladen patriot; Mount Vernon echoes the good old ladies, Mount Vernon is piped, Mount Vernon is harped; Mount Vernon is danced; Mount Vernon is sung. Even men walk by the aid of Mount Vernon canes, manufactured from some of its decaying relics."[6]

Ethiop describes the creation of a whole culture industry around Washington's estate, similar to the "Tom mania" that cropped up after the publication of *Uncle Tom's Cabin* in 1852.[7] Mount Vernon, Ethiop notes, is quite literally commodified through the production of canes manufactured from "decaying relics" stolen from the estate itself. Thus, right from the beginning of his description, Ethiop points to the predatory, vampiric quality of an emerging consumer capitalism and to how the transformation of the world into a market tarnishes the nation's republican ideals.

Picture IX also reflects a historical fact: By the 1850s, Mount Vernon had fallen into disrepair because of its neglect by Washington's heirs, who did not have the financial means to keep up the estate. The public and the press decried this tragic state of affairs, calling it a disgrace to Washington's memory. The dilapidation of the first president's home also served as a ripe metaphor for a nation whose house seemed to be collapsing under the weight of sectionalist division. But Ethiop goes further by suggesting that it is slavery that rotted and continues to rot Mount Vernon. "Decay," Ethiop notes, "is written by the Artist's pencil" everywhere, on the housetop, doorsill, chimney, gable, and eaves. On "every old slave hut," he says, "like so many spectres shadows forth decay."[8] Ethiop's description reminds readers that the Founding Father and first president was also an enslaver. As "consuming fingers" of decay creep across the entirety of Washington's estate, picture IX suggests that the institution of slavery degrades both the nation and the work of art.

While genre and landscape paintings in the antebellum period typically depicted enslaved people as happy and lively affordances to the scene at hand, picture IX conjures a frightening and haunting image of the people Washington presumed to own. Unlike the depiction of cheerful slaves in Eastman Johnson's 1859 painting *Negro Life at the South* (plate 5), Washington's Virginia slaves appear in the center of the work about to be sold off—a scene of gothic horror and repulsion. Ethiop says, moreover, that a "living slave of to-day stands, with the *bones* of Washington gathered up in his arms, and labelled 'For Sale' 'Price $200,000; this negro included.'" Next to the tomb stands Washington's "faithful old slave and body servant" William Lee, depicted here as a ghost watching over the sale of his former master's remains and estate, including the humans he held in captivity. Lee's presence is an especially important part of Wilson's critique of the status of the work of art in an enslaving society: He appeared next to Washington in multiple portraits during the Revolutionary Era. Although a ladies association purchased Mount Vernon in 1858 with the goal of fixing up and preserving the estate, picture IX suggests that the blight of slaveholding and the traffic in captives has irreparably damaged Washington's home as well as his legacy. Through Ethiop's eyes, readers are asked to see how a market economy desecrates and then consumes everything in its path. With the Potomac "sluggishly" gliding by Washington's tomb, the blight of slavery turns the American landscape into a gothic nightmare.

The Picture Gallery navigates the question of image-making in an age of slavery not only through representation, as in the ekphrastic depiction of Mount Vernon, but also at the level of form. It is my wager that the "Afric-American Picture Gallery" is a vital document of nineteenth-century African American visual culture, yet it reproduces no actual images. How do we make sense of this paradox? Benjamin's *Arcades Project* has a similarly impossible status. As the "unfinished, major project of Benjamin's mature years," Susan Buck-Morss notes that it is a book that does not exist, a "never-written work": "Instead of a 'work,' he left us only a massive collection of notes on nineteenth-century industrial culture as it took form in Paris—and formed that city in turn. These notes consist of citations from a vast array of historical sources, which Benjamin filed with the barest minimum of commentary, and only the general indications of how the fragments were eventually to have been arranged."[9]

Here and elsewhere in her study, Buck-Morss conjures an image of Benjamin as a "filer" and as otherwise engaged in a kind of secretarial labor. Ethiop's role is similarly secretarial: taking notes, organizing information, filing sketches, and performing administrative work for the gallery. At one point, Ethiop complains that the Picture Gallery is in disarray and should be better organized. Wilson himself served as secretary for organizations and committees working to expand rights and autonomy for African Americans. In *Frederick Douglass' Paper*, Wilson even calls abolition "office-work." In calling it such, he frames abolition as a necessary labor, but also as a kind of drudgery he seems reluctant to take on. Wilson and Benjamin both posit the secretary-philosopher as a new model for the thinker in an age of reproducibility and commodification: one who is more oriented to collecting, arranging, and juxtaposing images and images of thought than to producing "original" theories. But the secretary-philosopher also suggests that even the thinker is alienated from their labor in a world where everything is assigned a value and put on the market for sale.

Buck-Morss's *The Dialectics of Seeing* is a meticulous reconstruction of Benjamin's project that also understands how loss, fragmentation, and tragedy (as a genre, as an affect proper to capitalism's cataclysmic destruction, and as a way to understand the conditions of Benjamin's own life) must infuse any analysis of the *Arcades Project*. Loss haunts the fragments that compose Benjamin's project, as well as any critical engagement with that work/non-work. Later, in her own "picture book of philosophy," Buck-Morss reminds readers, "Now, it must not be forgotten that there is no *Passagen-Werk* [*Arcades Project*]. We are in a real sense confronting a void."[10]

A sense of loss similarly marks the "Afric-American Picture Gallery," emerging from the ephemerality and fragmentation that is constitutive of periodical production in general but that was especially profound for African American print culture during this period. The loss that haunts the Picture Gallery also emerges from the silences and destructions of the slave archive ("We are in a real sense confronting a void"). Ethiop is at pains to show how the brutal separations and displacements of the Middle Passage continue to ripple through the domestic slave trade and expanding slave system in the United States. He does this by alternating views of the Middle Passage and the African continent with pictures that focus on slavery in the US South. At other moments, the series displays a strange aporia around slavery itself. The series takes the crime of enslavement head-on in paintings like "The Slave Ship" and in showing the dilapidated state of Washington's Mount Vernon, a visual metaphor for the degradations wrought by slavery as well as the nation's fall from grace since its founding. But at other points, Ethiop, shut up in his gallery, suggests something about the geographic and felt distance between nominally free Black communities in the US North and enslaved people down South, especially in the Deep South. In other words, fugitive slaves/refugees appear as a kind of return of the repressed throughout the Picture Gallery. Fugitives had a similar status in Wilson's Brooklyn. When runaways found their way into Black communities and abolitionist circles in the North, they became embodied signs, even metonyms for the slave system itself, a terrifying reminder of the millions held in chains down South, and of the various ways that Northerners depended on and profited from slavery.

Absent images also haunt both the *Arcades Project* and the Picture Gallery. Buck-Morss notes that Benjamin originally planned to include images in the *Arcades Project*, much like in his early experimental publication *One-Way Street* (1928). While we can't know for sure whether Wilson would have liked actual images to be included in his Picture Gallery, it seems more than likely that he did, especially given his repeated calls for the growth of a Black visual sphere—produced by and for Black people—in his newspaper columns. Leif Eckstrom and I have argued elsewhere that the Picture Gallery emerged out of the image-poor, text-rich contexts of the early African

American print sphere, in which access to printing technologies and funding for publications were limited.[11]

The technologies required to reproduce images, including engravings and photographs, were even more difficult to secure. Scholars such as Eric Gardner have meticulously documented the precarious nature of Black periodical production this period: These publications were often established and then quickly folded because of financial difficulties. Subscribers of all backgrounds were notoriously delinquent in paying for their subscriptions; appealing to solidarity and the righteousness of the cause could only get editors so far.[12] Countless early African American periodicals were forced to stop production after only a few issues. Abolitionist printers and editors also dealt with intimidation and attempts to suppress the circulation of antislavery and Black print by proslavery thugs and by competing white printers; in one spectacular case from the 1830s, the abolitionist Benjamin Lundy's printing press was tossed in the river by angry Philadelphians.[13] Such histories are a reminder of the miracle of Black publication in a society structured by racial terror and subjection.

Rather than fetishizing the material scarcities that shaped Black publication in the period—and thus reifying loss—Eckstrom and I think about the Picture Gallery in the way that Fred Moten talks about the underfunded institutional locus called Black studies as a source of wealth: an abundance that emerges within but also despite an institutionally produced scarcity of resources.[14] Moving beyond a view of Black image production solely in terms of economic scarcity, the Picture Gallery produces a textual plenitude, one that also characterizes the experimental aesthetics of other Black periodical fiction and creative nonfiction in the 1850s.

The experimentalism of the Picture Gallery also derives from the fact that the image itself has a complex, even philosophical status in the text. Wilson's ekphrastically presented images in the Picture Gallery are dialectical images that produce images of thought for understanding capitalist modernity. According to Buck-Morss,

> Benjamin believed [that] philosophical-historical constellations could be represented by a dialectical image rather than by dialectical argumentation. . . . In the present context it refers to the use of archaic images to identify what is historically new about the "nature" of commodities. The principle of construction is that of montage, whereby the image's ideational elements remain unreconciled, rather than fusing into one "harmonizing perspective." For Benjamin, the technique of montage

> had "special, perhaps even total rights" as a progressive form because it "interrupts the context into which it is inserted" and thus "counteracts illusion" and he intended it to be the principle governing the construction of the *Passagen-Werk* [*Arcades Project*]: "This work must develop to the highest point the art of citing without citation marks. Its theory connects most closely with that of montage."[15]

Benjamin's *One-Way Street* begins to theorize the dialectical image through the juxtaposition of aphorisms with a series of images; the *Arcades Project* meditates on the dialectical image solely through narrative, and through a method of "textual montage." Across the Picture Gallery series, Wilson elevates actually existing print objects—including frontispieces and other illustrations—into objects of fine art. He transforms engraved portraits from the print sphere into paintings. Wilson also deploys the genre of the art review to contemplate historical circumstances and to address more existential questions. In other words, the setup of an ekphrastic description of a particular work of art often gives license to completely different lines of thought. In some moments, the content of the artwork is beside the point. Black art rather becomes an occasion for—and that which authorizes—Black critical theory.

Across his writings, Benjamin seeks to excavate what he calls the dialectical image through textual montage. Wilson, like Benjamin, is also interested in the counterimages of modernity that are waiting to be excavated from historical images. Such excavations unveil the ideological sediments of capitalism that pass themselves off as common sense and as "natural history" rather than as a set of historical conditions that might be changed through organization, revolt, and revolution. In the *Arcades Project*, Benjamin says that it is in the nineteenth-century French genre of the literary sketch that writing is first subjected to the effects of montage: "Literature submits to montage as the *feuilleton*."[16] The New York urban sketch tradition to which Wilson contributed, and which was itself influenced by the feuilleton, similarly offered montage-like scenes of life in the city for curious readers.

The Picture Gallery uses textual layering and juxtaposition to create what Benjamin would call the dialectical image. The text collages together descriptions of images with text, including excerpts from biographies, periodicals, and other published works. Wilson's method here is close to scrapbooking, a popular nineteenth-century practice that allowed the maker to collect and preserve important visual and textual items. The scrapbook was also a dynamic space of arrangement and juxtaposition, where image and text could be remixed according to the will and whim of the maker. For example, Wilson's ekphrasis of the "Head of Phillis Wheatley" moves from the poet's face to a description of her life drawn from the 1834 memoir by Margaretta Matilda Odell. In describing the poet's experience of the Middle Passage, he conjures an image of the young Wheatley wearing an iron muzzle. Moving between and combining different images and texts, it feels here as if Wilson is working from a page of his scrapbook (which he referred to as his sketchbook). In referencing both Wheatley's frontispiece portrait (see figures 3.1 and 3.2) and one of the notorious images of torture devices used on enslaved people that were circulated widely by abolitionists, Wilson conjures a third—dialectical—object, one that collages together two different objects from the print sphere.[17]

Approaching the Picture Gallery through collage and scrapbooking helps to frame Wilson as a protomodernist who anticipates not only the writings of Benjamin but also the aesthetic assemblages of Afro-modernists like Romare Bearden, Jean Toomer, and, later, Betye Saar. This move is not just an exercise in being needlessly presentist. Approaching the Picture Gallery through its production of dialectical images and use of textual collage allows us to home in on the aesthetic experiments that were taking shape in Black writing in the late antebellum period, especially as they harnessed the material specificities of the periodical format. Notably, the Picture Gallery turns at several points to past essays in the *Anglo-African Magazine* as source material for its gallery text. In so doing, it replaces historical referents with the text of the *Anglo-African* itself, anticipating postmodern theories which have posited that "there is no outside to the text" and that history is itself discursive. When readers try to find the "truth" of history in the Picture Gallery, Wilson redirects them back to history's mediation—and re-mediation—by the field of discursive representation. In other words, the Picture Gallery's archive is not history, per se, but the *Anglo-African* itself.

The Picture Gallery and the Invention of the Modern Museum

African American writers and intellectuals were keenly aware of how transformations in both industry and commerce were transforming the terrain of culture. In his study of Black image-makers in the movement to end slavery and discrimination, Aston Gonzalez notes that "these activist producers of visual culture not only intended to change *what* people saw relating to race but also instructed *how* audiences should see it."[18] Their work also grew out of a visual revolution in the middle of the nineteenth century:

"Technological developments in imaging dramatically changed the very ways that people viewed and understood their world during the middle decades of the nineteenth century. More specifically, the creation of the daguerreotype, the proliferation of the lithograph, the revival of the moving panorama, the emergence of the illustrated newspaper, and the invention of cartes de visite enabled people in the United States to see and participate in social reform movements in new ways."[19]

The Picture Gallery appeared at the same time as these world-changing transformations in visual culture; it also emerged alongside the birth of the museum. The modern museum grew to cultural dominance in the nineteenth century as a space of visual display that was deeply connected to emerging regimes of scientific rationality, order, and classification.[20] The nineteenth-century museum, as Foucault famously argued, defined itself in opposition to popular exhibitions, especially the fair, those ephemeral and carnivalesque spaces of enjoyment, distraction, and disorder that would crop up seasonally on the outskirts of towns for the benefit of the working classes.[21] But the process of the modern museum's "emancipation" from the anarchy of popular entertainment was a long and uneven one. And it would be a long time before museums would contain only works of fine art. In Wilson's own moment, for example, natural history museums still served as important venues where regular people could view original pieces of art. American landscape paintings appeared alongside cabinets of curiosities, and natural history museums like Peale's Museum in Philadelphia were popular venues where patrons could see oil paintings of Founding Fathers alongside taxidermied flora and fauna from the West. From our twenty-first-century viewpoint, in a world filled with museums devoted to visual art, there's nothing particularly notable about Wilson's choice to fill his gallery exclusively with pictures. But in Wilson's own historical moment, the public display of art was still operating under other rules, logics, and principles of collection. In other words, in 1859, the modern art museum was inchoate, still only glimpsable in speculative forms like the Picture Gallery itself.

The Picture Gallery is also a bold experiment in imagining a modern museum that refused racist display practices and that challenged rather than upheld the racism of the public sphere. Wilson was certainly aware of P. T. Barnum's wildly popular and viciously anti-Black American Museum, situated as it was on his beloved Broadway and filled as it was with the kinds of gross caricatures and minstrel representations of the race that he railed against. One wonders whether he ever went inside Barnum's museum during his strolls, or walked by it in disdain. It's also notable that the Picture Gallery does not contain any natural history specimens or other objects of curiosity. In this way, Wilson distances the field of visual art from both the field of natural history and the racial taxonomies they produced and enforced. For example, when Ethiop describes Wheatley's head, he makes a somewhat surprising detour into the discourse of physiognomy, describing the poet as having a "facial angle" of "ninety degrees" and further emphasizing her physiognomic superiority this way: "The forehead is finely formed, and the brain large. . . . The whole make-up of this face is an index of healthy intellectual powers."[22] Wilson was certainly aware that physiognomy was a field that traversed both art and science. Thus, the stakes of Black portraiture were incredibly high. When Wilson railed against anti-Black imagery in the popular sphere, he was also challenging the visual codes of racial ethnology and craniology that buttressed the field of anti-Black representation.

I suggest that the Picture Gallery imagines a museum whose very modernity depends on its commitment to antiracist practices of curation and forms of expression. In this way it is an experiment in imagining a museum untethered from imperial principles of collection, display, and surveillance at the very moment when the museum was becoming a crucial arm of governance itself. Indeed, the modern museum was central to new forms of social control and management in the nineteenth century, including the regulation of movement itself. As a space of directed movement within a controlled environment, the modern museum instantiates a form of what Tony Bennett calls "organized walking" that was part of a broader concern with regulating the "performative aspects of their visitors' conduct."[23] The picture gallery registers the museum's enforcement of this new kind of "organized walking," but it also reminds readers that for Black New Yorkers, walking *outside* the museum was also a frequent site of surveillance and control. Wilson's own flamboyant strolling took place in the context of widespread vagrancy laws and other practices that surveilled and contained the movement of Black people in public space. Wilson's stylization of himself as a flaneur and commentator was an extravagant gesture in part because it was dangerous.

At the beginning of the Picture Gallery, Ethiop tells us that his love of art is directly connected to his love of exploratory walking and says that since he was a young boy, he loved to "ramble" to find a picture.[24] In addition to what he saw hanging up in galleries of various kinds, Wilson would have also seen a plethora of images in the windows of printers, booksellers, photography studios, and other retail establishments around the city. As a member of Brooklyn's Black elite, he may have also seen original paintings in private homes. An emerging popular print sphere afforded an additional space of spectatorship, one where looking was deeply entwined with the act of reading itself. Tellingly, when Ethiop recounts his early adventures in "picture hunting," his source is not a museum or gallery but a very particular object from the print sphere: "the old family almanac," taken down from his "mother's mantle piece."[25] Illustrated newspapers provided another important source of images, especially landscapes, portraits of people in the news, and visual renderings of current events. But such sources were fraught and compromised: For example, *Harper's Weekly* represented New York City as a city of white people. When African Americans appeared in its pages, they were depicted as slaves, servants, pickaninnies, and savages. In other words, in both the world of galleries and the world of print, Wilson and his cohort were constantly confronted with images that reinforced the stranglehold of white supremacy.

African Americans were also routinely excluded from spaces where art could be viewed by the public. Institutions like the American Art-Union in New York were crucial to making art more accessible to middle-class Americans, but its gallery was free only for subscribers, and the board was run by financiers, bankers, judges, and other white professionals—in other words, by the same social conservatives who were working to keep Black Americans on the margins of the city. Black art was also deemed a threat to art institutions. Richard Powell recounts that when the Black abolitionist Robert Purvis donated a painting of Cinque, leader of the Amistad Rebellion, for exhibition by the Philadelphia Artists' Fund Society, the society's president, American painter John Neagle, deemed it too incendiary for exhibition. Cinque was a metonym for Black rebellion and in that regard threatened to upset the sensibilities of a bourgeois viewing public: "The hanging committee have instructed me, most respectfully, to return the portrait you so kindly offered for exhibition—it being contrary to usage to display work of that character, believing that under the excitement of the times, it might prove injurious both to the proprietors and the institution."[26] Such stark examples of the surveillance of Black art speaks to the political power of a text like the Picture Gallery. In this way the Picture Gallery served as an ekphrastic *surrogate* for actually existing galleries in antebellum New York, where Black people could not expect to see themselves represented accurately if at all.

The 1850s also witnessed transformations in printing technologies that gave rise to the illustrated press, those periodical publications that featured handsome and large engravings of current events, landscapes, and portraits of political leaders and people making headlines at home and abroad. *Harper's Weekly* first appeared in Wilson's New York in 1857, and Wilson mentions additional pictorial news sources that he read, including *Gleason's Pictorial*, out of Boston, and transatlantic publications like the *London Illustrated News*.[27] The picture gallery was clearly created in conversation with the illustrated news sources that Wilson read regularly.

In this period, the city was itself being transformed by a world of print. As David Henkin chronicles, broadsides, advertisements, and other printed materials were everywhere in antebellum New York, plastered on posts and building walls, hanging in shop windows, and flying through the air.[28] In this world of paper, it became increasingly possible to read and view images in public. The *Anglo-African Magazine* was itself a part of the almost frenetic circulation of paper and print in antebellum New York. Transformations in both print and photographic technologies thus held out a promise that image-making might be made more accessible for nonelite Americans. However, even as the print and image sphere expanded, African Americans struggled to gain access to it and contribute to it. They rarely saw themselves reflected in it in nonstereotyped ways.

The "Afric-American Picture Gallery" thus appeared in a world increasingly defined by easy access to reproducible images, but control over the means of image reproduction still proved difficult if not altogether impossible for most African Americans. Given inequalities in access to both oil and photographic portraiture in the nineteenth century, Black intellectuals in the late 1850s and into the 1860s began proliferating "word portraits" of their communities as ekphrastic surrogates for actual portraits. In 1854, James McCune Smith published his "Heads of the Colored People" within his correspondence with Wilson in *Frederick Douglass' Paper*. Wilson's 1859 Picture Gallery was another experiment in ekphrasis of Black portraiture, clearly inspired in part by his reading of Smith's "Heads," although Wilson replaces McCune Smith's folksy portraits of the Black upper class with formal portraits of the race's most elite and distinguished members. And in 1863, William Wells Brown would continue this thread of narrative portraiture with his publication of *The Black Man: His Antecedents, His Genius, and His Achievements* with Thomas Hamilton's publishing house. As noted in the introduction, Brown's collective biography includes a word portrait of Wilson himself, describing his height, profile, and character. Brown's ekphrastic description is the closest thing we have to an image of Wilson. No photograph or engraving has yet been discovered—a haunting irony, given Wilson's enthusiasm for pictures, and his belief in their power to elevate and ennoble the race. On the other hand, given Wilson's own commitment to the powers of ekphrasis, it may be fitting that we can only see Wilson himself in and through words.

The Picture Gallery in the Age of Photography

From the twenty-first century looking backward, Wilson's Picture Gallery is a textual representation of a museum of fine art. But in the 1850s, picture galleries were any collection of pictures: They could be pictures in a museum, an exhibition, or even in a book. Photography studios were especially prominent picture galleries. The invention of photography had a profound influence on Wilson and his cohort. In the middle of the nineteenth century, the ability to capture an image of a "real thing"—something that had actually existed in a particular moment in time—would revolutionize not only image-making but the entire field of representation. Photography's referent, according to Roland Barthes, was different from "other systems of representation" because "the 'photographic referent' [is] not the optionally real thing to which an image or a sign refers but the *necessarily* real thing which has been placed before the lens, without which there would be no photograph. Painting can feign reality without having seen it. Discourse combines signs which have referents, of course, but these referents can be and are most often 'chimeras.' Contrary to these imitations, in Photography I can never deny that *the thing has been there*."[29] But photography's indexicality—the apparent presence of the "thing [that] has been there"—also produced a separation between the photograph's referent and the viewer, one that was especially pronounced in the representation of human subjects: "What I see has been here . . . and yet immediately separated; it has been absolutely, refutably present, and yet already deferred."[30] Photography's powers to document the real were thus always shadowed by an uncanniness, a feeling that, yes, I believe this moment existed and yet I feel alienated from it. Looking at one's own image could be an especially unsettling experience.

For these and other reasons, photography destabilized established theories of representation and identity in the period. When something is new and not yet understood, it is often rejected from the psyche through repression. But the act of repression does not mean that the new thing does not continue to work on the unconscious or on representation; it just means we need different tools for registering its field of expression. I argue that this is ultimately how we should understand photography's place in the "Afric-American Picture Gallery": as a force of profound but repressed influence. More broadly, even when Black writers in the 1850s did not address photography head-on, its popularization was profoundly shaping writerly and artistic practice.

Like many inventions, photography had multiple points of origin, impossible to pin down into one moment of individual discovery. In the 1820s,

Joseph Nicéphore Niépce was able to permanently capture images with a camera obscura through a process he called "heliography," or "sun drawing." In January 1839, Louis-Jacques-Mandé Daguerre announced his invention of the daguerreotype, a process whereby a likeness was reproduced on an iodized copper plate. That same month, William Henry Fox Talbot announced his own discovery of the photographic process; Talbot would call the results of his photographic experiments "calotypes," seeing them as experiments in "photogenic drawing." American newspapers began reporting on Daguerre's invention and process in the spring of 1839, and the American fascination with photography was immediate. Famously, long-awaited descriptions of the process arrived in the United States by way of newspapers carried on a transatlantic steamer into New York's harbor in September 1839.

By the early 1840s, the daguerreotype process had been enthusiastically embraced in the United States. Studios sprouted up in urban centers, and itinerant photographers took and sold likenesses as they traveled across more rural areas of the nation. People of African descent across the diaspora immediately understood the power of this new process; some eagerly became photographers themselves. Jules Lion, a free person of color who immigrated to the United States from France, was the first person to introduce the art of daguerreotyping to New Orleans in 1840.[31] Deborah Willis notes that in photography's first decade, there were at least "fifty documented Black daguerreotypists who operated successful galleries in American cities."[32]

Daguerreotypes were particularly popular in New York City. Claire McRee notes that by 1853, the city had more Daguerrean galleries than all of England.[33] Wilson's beloved Broadway was lined with daguerreotype studios; they were a major attraction for bohemians, workers, pleasure-seekers, and others who were drawn to Broadway for its art, culture, and entertainment (figure 1.1). Given his well-documented enthusiasm for the powers of visual representation, Wilson must have had his photograph taken, if not on Broadway, then in the studio of one of his friends or neighbors. Other members of Wilson's coterie did so, and some even became photographers themselves. For example, the educator, emigrationist, and photographer Augustus Washington circulated in Wilson's social networks. Wilson replaced Washington as the principal of Colored School No. 1 after he left the position to move to Hartford to open his first daguerreotype studio (figure 1.2). In 1853, Washington left the United States with thousands of other African Americans bound for resettlement in Liberia; he would set up another daguerreotype studio in Monrovia, where free people rushed to have their portraits taken as an indication of their freedom and success in their new

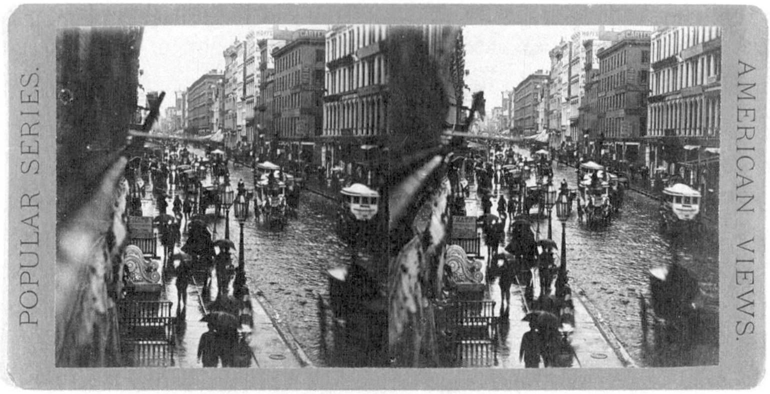

1.1 Edward Anthony and Henry T. Anthony, *Broadway on a Rainy Day*, 1859; stereoscopic view. Albumen silver prints from glass negatives, 3½ × 6⅞ in. The New York Historical.

homeland (plate 6).[34] After the Civil War, Wilson's daughter Annie married Thomas S. Boston, a talented musician who was deeply invested in the arts and theater and who also practiced daguerreotyping for a time. In short, Wilson was living and writing in a world of photographers. Photography was especially important to midcentury Afropolitans like Wilson who saw themselves as progressive, forward-looking, and committed to an emerging industrial modernity.

I've noted that the "Afric-American Picture Gallery" is a work of several paradoxes, including the fact that it reproduces no actual pictures. It's also the case that the Picture Gallery suppresses photography as a signifier at the same time as it feels deeply shaped by the rise of this technology and its transformation of the visual field. Ethiop's ekphrastic descriptions often work like freeze-frames, akin to the camera capturing a still image taken from life, or to a moving panorama paused on its scroll. Indeed, the panoramic optics of Wilson's sketches contain many such moments, where the observer's optic scanning pauses and lands on an object worthy of sustained description, a word picture isolated from the milieux of life.

Throughout the Picture Gallery, Ethiop also describes not only the content of various objects but also the quality of light that illuminates them. Of course, lighting was a major concern in the exhibition of works of fine art in the nineteenth century, especially before the invention of electric lighting. But photography was literally "light writing," and as such, questions of light and lighting became a major site of theories and craft debates among early photographers. Photography journals and manuals often offered lighting techniques and workarounds that were especially important before the invention of flash photography. The most famous photographer of Wilson's era, Mathew Brady, touted natural skylights in his Broadway studio for the most ideal light. Ethiop regularly mentions how art objects in the picture gallery are lit. From a positionality that moves between the role of curator and the art critic, he is also sure to mention when certain pieces could benefit from being hung in better light.

In short, even though Wilson does not mention a single daguerreotype in his gallery, photography's presence is apparent. In the 1850s, Daguerreian studios also doubled as informal gallery spaces where patrons could view portraits, landscapes, and other works while they waited for their portraits to develop. In other words, picture galleries were crucial and rare places where the public could view fine art in the antebellum period. For example, an advertisement for Mathew Brady's famous Daguerreian Gallery on Broadway (figure 1.3) shows how the photography studio could also function as an art museum in the period.

There were also Black (or Afric-American) picture galleries in antebellum America, including those owned and operated by the early and prolific African American photographer James Presley (J. P.) Ball. In an 1855 illustration of J. P. Ball's studio in Cincinnati, landscape paintings and sculptural busts are visible alongside daguerreotypes lining the walls (figure 1.4). This illustration of Ball's studio appeared as a foldout in a pamphlet titled *Splendid Mammoth Pictorial Tour of the United States Comprising Views of the African Slave Trade; of Northern and Southern Cities; of Cotton and Sugar Plantations; of the Mississippi, Ohio and Susquehanna Rivers, Niagara Falls, &c.* The pamphlet was a textual tour of the scenes represented on the panorama exhibited in Ball's studio, which focused on the horrors of slavery from the Middle Passage to enslavement in the Americas. A six-hundred-yard canvas that was moved along two poles, the panorama likely included paintings by the African American landscape artist Robert Seldon Duncanson, who worked for a time in Ball's studio (plate 7).

The connections between J. P. Ball and William J. Wilson are tantalizing. For one, it's significant that Ball's text, like the Picture Gallery, operates as an ekphrastic, "pictorial tour," with entries describing each image on the panorama. It's also possible that Wilson visited Ball's *Splendid Mammoth Pictorial Tour* when Ball toured with it in the Northeast. The medium of the moving panorama clearly shaped the form of the Picture Gallery: Patrons would listen to a narrator describing scenes on the panorama as they passed

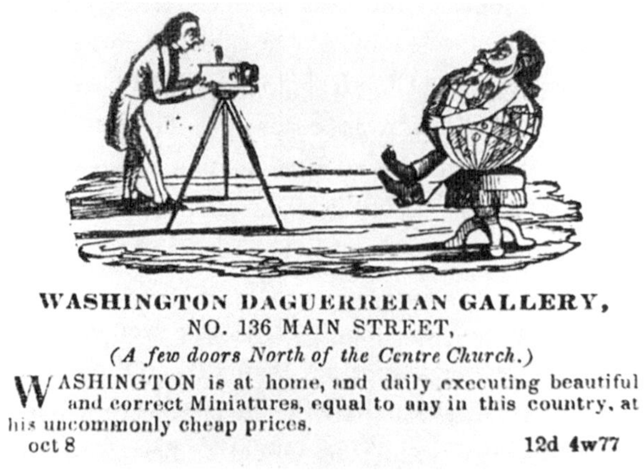

1.2 Advertisement for Augustus Washington's Daguerreian Gallery in Hartford, Connecticut.

by, just as Ethiop provides a narrative tour of the picture gallery's scenes and portraits.[35] We might, then, place Ball's *Splendid Mammoth Pictorial Tour* alongside a series of other likely source texts for the Picture Gallery, including McCune Smith's "Heads of the Colored People" and Frederick Douglass's speeches on photography.

Furthermore, the networks of dialogical exchange that characterized Black intellectual production in the 1850s included photographers like Ball, as well as Patrick Reason, Augustus Washington, and other Black visual producers and creatives in New York. Born free in Virginia in 1825, Ball trained with an African American daguerreotypist from Boston named John B. Bailey, and subsequently opened a small studio in Cincinnati in 1845. Like many early studios, Ball's first business venture failed. He subsequently turned to working as an itinerant photographer, settling eventually in Pittsburgh and then in Richmond, Virginia. Later, he would return to Cincinnati to open another studio. He practiced daguerreotyping there for many years before moving to Minnesota and then to Montana in his later years. Willis says that Ball's Great Daguerreian Gallery of the West was the most successful studio in Cincinnati in its time. It was also touted as an example of a great gallery operating in the West, "far from the Eastern centers of daguerreotyping."[36] Ball's patrons came from many different backgrounds and social stations; they included prominent and ordinary Black citizens who were keen to have their likeness taken and preserved as an image. Enslaved people were among those who flocked to Ball's rented room in Richmond. In border states like

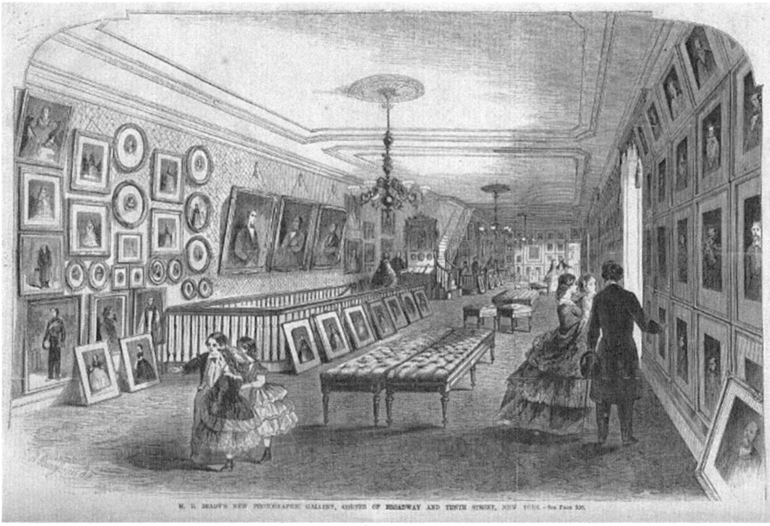

1.3 "M. R. Brady's New Photographic Gallery," *Frank Leslie's Newspaper*, January 5, 1861.

Ohio and Montana, Ball must have photographed a number of people who had fled from or were otherwise manumitted from slavery. It's thus striking that in the printed illustration of Ball's studio shown in figure 1.4, we see only white viewers in his gallery. This fact helps to draw out one of the most important gestures of Wilson's Picture Gallery: It intentionally centers Black viewers within the gallery space.

A Gallery of Illustrious Americans

When readers saw the "Afric-American Picture Gallery" in the *Anglo-African Magazine*, they most certainly thought of the photographic picture galleries that were sprouting up in urban centers across the nation. Wilson's gallery also reflected the ideas of a growing movement in the 1850s that sought to use photographic technologies to produce portraits that were aesthetically pleasing and could rival portraits done in oil. In these images, sitters were posed as if they were going to appear in a painting. The era's most fervent proponent of photographic portraiture was Mathew Brady, the "Brady of Broadway" who was also the most famous American photographer of his era and was well known to Wilson and his cohort. Brady believed that it was the photographer's role to record and "preserve" the "faces of [the nation's] historic men and mothers"; in so doing, he, according to Alan Trachtenberg, "defined the first significant

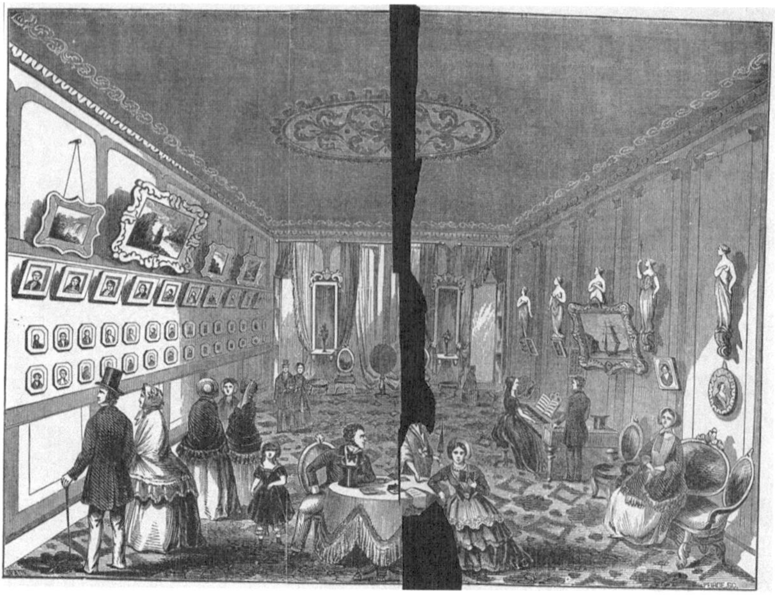

1.4 J. P. Ball's studio in Cincinnati, Ohio. From J. P. Ball, *Ball's Splendid Mammoth Pictorial Tour of the United States Comprising Views of the African Slave Trade; of Northern and Southern Cities; of Cotton and Sugar Plantations; of the Mississippi, Ohio and Susquehanna Rivers, Niagara Falls, &c.* (Cincinnati: Achilles Pugh, 1855), torn page. Houghton Library, Harvard University.

public role for American photography."[37] Brady was also interested in defining the role of the photographer as a kind of historian: "More than any other American, Brady shaped the role of the photographer as a natural historian, one who keeps records of the famous and the eminent, as well as the run-of-the-mill citizen."[38] Brady's Daguerreian Studio on Broadway sought to fulfill these lofty aspirations for the new photographic technology: The walls of the gallery were lined with daguerreotypes of American celebrities, statesmen, and leaders. While waiting for their own photographs to develop, patrons could view Brady's gallery of illustrious Americans with an eye to meditating on the qualities and virtues of the nation's "great and good."[39]

In 1850, Brady published *The Gallery of Illustrious Americans*, a book of daguerreotyped lithographs of notable Americans. Modeled after the encyclopedias of biographies that were popular in the antebellum book market, each photographic portrait appeared in Brady's *Gallery* with a biographical entry. Trachtenberg says that Brady's studio gallery and book gallery were both "an enshrinement of national icons analogous to that of Roman household gods, the gallery performed a quasi-religious function in a republican culture which had overthrown a system of deference based on social station and birth."[40]

My suggestion here is that as an ekphrastic, textual gallery of prominent figures in Afro-diasporic history, the "Afric-American Picture Gallery" is itself a kind of book of photographic portraits. Its connection to Brady's *Gallery of Illustrious Americans* is perhaps most clear in Ethiop's description of picture VII, when the Picture Gallery widens its lens beyond the United States to survey the story of slave rebellion and revolution in the Caribbean. This portrait, hanging in the "southeast" corner of the gallery, depicts Toussaint Louverture, famed leader of a revolution that began as a slave rebellion, overthrew the French colonial government, and led in 1804 to the founding of Haiti, the first independent Black state in the Western Hemisphere. A former slave turned celebrated military hero and political leader, Louverture was exactly the kind of "distinguished black" figure Wilson sought to venerate in his gallery. Indeed, much of the Picture Gallery operates as a who's who of Black military and political leadership in the Atlantic world. Like Crispus Attucks, Toussaint was another figure of the Revolutionary era who became a key symbol of militancy and heroism for Black abolitionists in the 1850s.

Ethiop calls this picture "a most beautiful portrait of one of the greatest men the world ever saw," and says that it is aptly hung in "a favourable position and in good light as it ought; as it portrays the features of one of God's and Earth's noblemen long since retired."[41] But just when we think Ethiop will go on to describe the portrait itself, he tells us that he's not up to the task: "Far be it from me to venture to a description of either the picture or the man. I have no pencil and no pen with which I can do it. Some future historian in other times, will yet write the name of Touissant L[ou]verture higher and in purer light than that of any man that has lived up to to-day."[42] Blurring the line between sketching a portrait and writing a sketch, Ethiop says he will not attempt an ekphrastic description because of insufficient tools of the craft ("I have no pencil and no pen with which I can do it"). He also suggests that his skills are not developed enough to capture Toussaint in all his sublime greatness. Here as elsewhere in the text, he depicts Toussaint surrounded by an aura too powerful to be captured by words.

This is another moment in the text where Wilson connects his picture gallery to the work of history writing, suggesting to his readers that "some future historian" should take up Toussaint as their subject. Indeed, history was itself emerging as a discipline in Wilson's time, and as John Ernest has shown, African Americans in the period understood that correcting the historical record was central to their struggle.[43] Ethiop embraces that idea, and at the beginning of his description of picture VII, he presents his own theory on how picture-viewing relates to the work of reconceiving the past. Pictures, Ethiop notes, are "teachings by example," but they also have the power to conjure up an entire historic epoch as well as its lessons: "A picture of a great man with whose acts we are familiar, calls up the whole history of his times. Our minds thus become reimpressed with the events and we arrive at the philosophy of them."[44] Operating as a memory tool, pictures reimpress historical events onto the viewer's consciousness. They also have the capacity to present a historical narrative far beyond what might be represented within any one frame: "A picture of Washington recalls to mind the American Revolution, and the early history of the Republic. A picture of Thomas Jefferson brings before the mind in all its scope and strength that inimitable document, the Declaration of Independence."[45] Wilson goes on to say that his own theory of images as history was formulated not while looking at the faces of Washington or Jefferson but while contemplating the portrait of Toussaint. Here as elsewhere, Wilson suggests that Black images are the best fodder for Black thought.

Wilson does not seem to be drawing on any one existing rendering of Toussaint. Instead, he asks us to imagine the image of Toussaint alongside images of founding fathers like Washington and Jefferson, but also next to more humble, everyday images, including "a once beloved mother, an almost forgotten grandfather whose image perhaps we bear, or a long lost child, once the centre of our affections."[46] Ethiop concludes his description by noting that this portrait brings to mind the whole history of Haiti, "that gem of the sea," shifting from a focus on Toussaint's individual deeds to his embodiment of the collective will and actions of a whole people.

The next stop of Ethiop's gallery tour, "Picture VIII.—So[u]louque and His Court," is framed as an extension of picture VII, a piece that represents a divine fulfillment of what Toussaint began. The Toussaint and Soulouque images might be read as a diptych. This portrait also completes the history lesson that Ethiop had begun in his description of the previous picture: "If any thing else was needed to carry the mind over the field of Haytian events, and complete our history, this additional picture ought to be sufficient."[47] Picture VIII depicts Faustin Soulouque, the Haitian military leader who led the postrevolution nation as president from 1847 to 1849, then appointed himself emperor and ruled as Faustus I for another decade. A constellation of portraits surround the Picture Gallery's portrait of Soulouque, depicting the "magnates that move[d] round his Imperial person" and served him. "So[u]-louque and His Court" emphasizes the emperor's grandiose imperial power, the domain of his rule, and his absolute authority over Haiti and its people. An image of democratic rule this is not: Indeed, one of Soulouque's first acts was to establish a Haitian nobility on the island. Waging war on the island's mulatto class and white Europeans, he invaded the Dominican Republic three times during his reign. Soulouque presented Wilson with a seductive model of Black power and military rule, one that also trafficked in a fantasy about wealth, power, and regality for a people who had been held in chains for centuries. Soulouque's reign would come to a disastrous end just a few months before Wilson installed his portrait in the Picture Gallery; in 1858, another rebellion broke out on the island. In January 1859, Soulouque was driven into exile and the Republic of Haiti was restored. Writing in March of that year, Wilson nonetheless represents Soulouque as if he still sits securely on the throne.

Toussaint is not far from this imperial portrait of the emperor, which hangs "beside that of L[ou]verture." This picture of Soulouque seems to dwarf that of the previous pieces in the gallery, both in its regality and in its size, which Ethiop says "is of largest." Ethiop concludes by noting that he believes these likenesses to be genuine and "up to the originals," based on the "descriptions given me of these persons." Here the ekphrastic referents—the "originals"—are not paintings or engraved portraits, but the very faces of those represented. And those faces, in their individuality and nuance, depart significantly from the kinds of gross caricatures and stereotyped representations of Black people that filled what Ethiop aptly refers to as the "*American prejudice Market.*"[48]

Visual representations of Soulouque in the 1850s included several illustrated portraits and scenes from the transatlantic print sphere, all of which reflected both global curiosity and anxiety about a Black monarchy rising in the Caribbean Sea. It's not clear whether Wilson references a real image here, though the regality of the sketch certainly resonates with a widely circulated image of Faustus I, dressed in his coronation garb, that appeared in the *Illustrated London News* in 1856 (figure 1.5). The presentation of Soulouque surrounded by his "magnates" also lends an aura to the image, while investing Wilson's gallery of representative Black leaders with regal majesty and symbolic wealth. French Catholic signifiers matter here, as does Soulouque's legalization of voodoo during his reign. In this way, Wilson's portrait bears a charge that also feels connected to the powers of Black divination and Afro-diasporic spirituality.

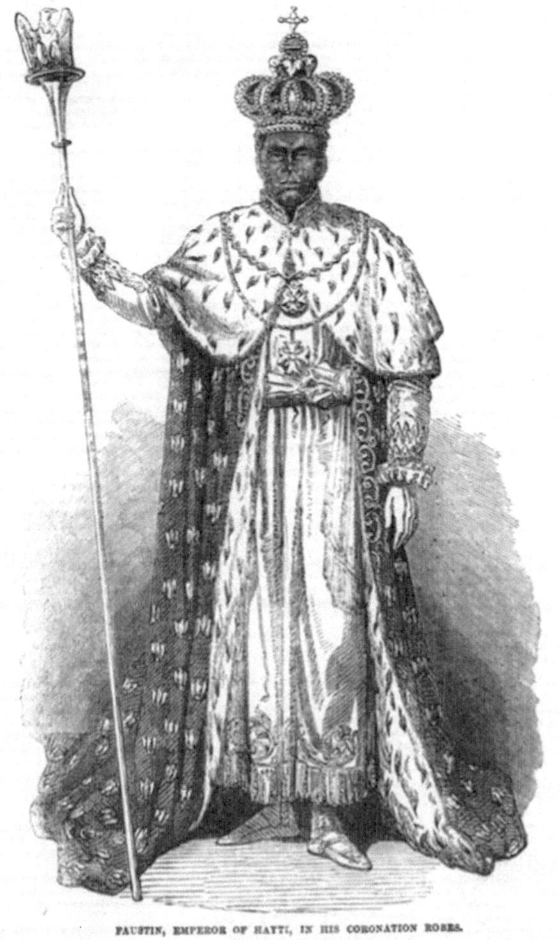

1.5 "Faustin, Emperor of Hayti, in His Coronation Robes," *Illustrated London News*, February 16, 1856.

Benjamin theorized that technologies of mechanical reproduction work to devalue the aura of the work of art. Increasingly detached from the authenticity of an "original," art produced under a regime of reproducibility and commodification also bears a diminishing relationship to both ritual and religion. This, Benjamin says, creates the conditions for the politicization of art.[49] My suggestion here is that Wilson takes that transforming aura under (racial) capital and reinvests it into the regal representation of Afro-diasporic figures of modernity. This attempt to hold on to the aura of the work of art to ennoble a regal Blackness is a signature characteristic of Wilson's theory of Black art in modernity.

The Picture Gallery's Photographic Unconscious

In opposition to private family photographs, objects of remembrance and sentimental value, the public portrait was intended to "stimulate a desire to identify with the qualities represented by the sitter."[50] The figures represented in Wilson's gallery were also intended to serve as objects of emulation for Black readers. At the same time, the status of the public and the private is fuzzy in these print galleries. Trachtenberg notes that in Brady's volume, "public gallery space is reconstructed in a bound volume that can be experienced in private."[51] Wilson's Picture Gallery serves a similar function as a gallery-book that can be consumed in the privacy of the reader's home. Picture galleries were places in the city where the public gathered to "gaze at pictures of the great and good . . . to see and to be seen."[52] But the "Afric-American Picture Gallery" also rejects this imperative—increasingly dominant in a society of mass spectacle—to be wholly seen and visible. In this and in other ways, the Picture Gallery contains an ambivalence about the politics of visibility.

The Picture Gallery also reflects broader cultural anxieties raised by the invention of photography. At the same time as Wilson constructs an illustrious gallery of notable peoples of African descent in the style of photographic portraiture as it was developing in the 1850s, the photographic image was not a stable or coherent vehicle of truth in its moment of historical emergence. In addition to destabilizing ideas about individuality and personhood, communities also worried about the spiritual ramifications of this new technology: Was the camera's fixing of an image a form of soul capture? How did the seemingly endless reproducibility of natural and human forms square with the idea of God's singular hand in creation? Was it a sacred or profane act to desire a memorial image of a departed loved one? Wilson and his cohort identified as forward-looking modern intellectuals, keeping pace with if not ahead of their peers, but they were also active members of their church communities, and for many of them, religious faith was a major part of their lives. Photography would continue to raise lingering spiritual questions—and fears—into the 1850s and 1860s, even for liberated, modern bohemians living in the heart of an industrializing city. Fears about this new medium of visualization also arose from laminations of photography and death. As Kimberly Juanita Brown has recently chronicled, that lamination has been structured by a profound anti-Blackness: "Since photography's invention, Black life has been presented as fraught, short, agonizingly filled with violence, and indifferent to intervention."[53] Indeed, despite the utopian views of advocates like Douglass, the history of photography is also, undeniably, "a catalog of othering, surveillance, and the violence of objectification."[54]

Thus, at the same time as Wilson insists on the political importance of Black visual representation, his Picture Gallery responds with ambivalence to photography's unprecedented documentary powers. But the text's repression of photography in response to that ambivalence does not just produce erasures; it is also a *productive* force, creating several fascinating effects in the text's field of signification. For example, the text essentially absorbs the photographic apparatus, hiding it from the reader's view. The portraits in Wilson's gallery were, as I discussed above, created in conversation with the rise of photographic portraiture in the 1850s, but these images occupied a liminal position between photography and painting. Benjamin notes that the reproducibility of art radically transformed its function and value in a consumer society. Photography was especially formative in this transitional period in the role of art under the influence of a variety of forms of mechanical reproduction. Wilson's text registers this moment of historical and economic transition by treating terms of art as fields of experimentation and play. The portrait is both a painting and a photograph. "Picture" has a similarly capacious meaning in the Picture Gallery, in a historical moment before the term *picture* became linguistically narrowed down to mean a photograph, or a child's drawing. In Wilson's text, a "picture" can signify many things and is a site of proliferating signification and open possibility. "Sketch" has a similarly capacious meaning and is a site of much play throughout the text. For example, Ethiop presents his own descriptions as "sketches," playing with the idea that a sketch can be a piece of writing or a work of art, both done quickly on paper.

While readers of the *Anglo-African Magazine* most certainly associated Wilson's title—the "Afric-American Picture Gallery"—with the photography studios that were becoming all the rage across the nation, no photographs appear within the imagined space of the gallery itself. We can work to understand this curiosity in several different ways: For one, as Benjamin notes, the true impact of new technologies cannot be understood until long after their initial dissemination. In their moment of emergence, new forms can be understood only through already existing forms. Trachtenberg notes that at the beginning of the Daguerreian period, many were convinced that daguerreotypes were drawings. It would take decades before it would become clear how profoundly photography would transform visual art. In its moment of emergence, commenters only addressed "the question of whether photography is an art," not realizing how it was poised to upend the entire field of art, especially its claims to originality, authenticity, and what Benjamin calls cult value.[55]

Photography's transformation of fine art was also obscured because it was initially practiced by technicians, tinkerers, and itinerant peddlers, rather than by those recognized as artists. At first competing with the market in miniature portraiture, the first American daguerreotypists were portrait peddlers, itinerant photographers, and sometimes former miniaturists themselves, or "city entrepreneur[s] with an established gallery and hired hands" who sought professional stature. Brady was among those in the first generation of practitioners who sought to elevate photography from a craft to a respected profession. The wrenching of photography from its "lowly" origins into a form of refined artistic practice would take time, effort, and advocacy by those with significant forms of social capital and economic power.[56]

The Picture Gallery's photographic unconscious—where photography is at once everywhere and under erasure—signals Wilson's participation in this labor of elevating photography into a field of fine art in the period, an act that paradoxically put the photograph itself under erasure. It also suggests a fundamental hesitance about the uses to which photography's documentary powers could be put. Indeed, in presenting portraits that are not quite photographs or paintings, the Picture Gallery suggests an ambivalence about the speed and efficiency with which the camera could "capture" its subject. Such a question was of special importance to a group of disenfranchised people who did not themselves own or control the means of (image) production. Photography's documentary powers could also be put to more sinister purposes. Celebrated as a uniquely democratic—if even American—form, photography was also from its very beginnings used to catalog and criminalize the poor, people of color, and people with disabilities, all those whose bodies did not conform to the idealized national body politic. By the 1850s, the New York Police Department was already compiling a "Rogues' Gallery" to identify criminals and "would-be" criminals by visual type. Before the publication of his *Gallery of Illustrious Americans*, Mathew Brady had himself, in 1846, contributed a group of images of inmates housed at the Blackwells Island Penitentiary to Marmaduke Sampson's *The Rationale of Crime*, a phrenology text that taught readers how to "read" a "criminal head." These and other midcentury works anticipated projects that linked photography to eugenics later in the nineteenth century.

Photography also emerged at the same time that American chattel slavery intensified. As Matthew Fox-Amato has documented, slaveholders were quick to use the new medium to exert new forms of control over their presumed property. By the 1840s some were already commissioning photographs of the people they held in bondage. Fox-Amato notes that too little attention has been paid to the intertwined developments in photography and chattel slavery and that "pressing questions remain unanswered about the historical collusion between a particular social structure and a new visual technology that took the United States by storm. How did photography shape the culture and the politics of American slavery? And how, in turn, did slavery shape the development of photography—as an aesthetic form and as a set of cultural practices?"[57]

Racial scientists, like slaveholders, were quick to mobilize photography and its claims to an uncomplicated "truth" to prop up tenuous arguments about the supposed biological differences between different racial and ethnic groups. Infamously, in 1850 the Columbia, South Carolina, physician and slaveholder Robert E. Gibbes arranged for seven enslaved men and women from area plantations to be photographed by local photographer J. T. Zealy. Stripped bare or half-bare and forced to pose in the parlor space of Zealy's Columbia studio, the resulting daguerreotypes were sent to the Harvard scientist Louis Agassiz, who wanted further "proof" of his theory of polygenesis: that human beings were created by God as distinct races, with no common ancestor. The Zealy daguerreotypes are a powerful example of how photography has been used to both taxonomize and terrorize subjugated populations. Held privately by Agassiz for his research, and likely only circulated among colleagues and friends, the images remained unknown to the public until they were rediscovered in the attic of Harvard's Peabody Museum in the 1970s.[58]

While Wilson may not have known about the Zealy daguerreotypes, especially given their private, even secretive conditions of production and circulation, their historical existence was part of a broader regime of forced visibility that yoked photography to the logics of white supremacy. Although Wilson celebrates the powers of visual representation for the uplifting of the race, the text itself does not uncritically celebrate the visual; instead, it displays an indirect, and at times even baroque, relationship between words and images, as well as between images and things.

It's also telling that except for the enslaved youth Phillis Wheatley, the Picture Gallery does not include a portrait of a still-enslaved person. Wilson's focus is on representing and celebrating former slaves turned heroic freemen and distinguished figures born free. Enslaved people appear more often within Wilson's ekphrases of landscapes, reflecting a historical reality in nineteenth-century American painting as well. Instead, the image of the slave—tortured, objectified, fraught—is a central part of the text's photographic unconscious. Wilson does give us one portrait of a nonelite member of the race: a working-class Black youth named Tom Onward, who works as the gallery's assistant. But Tom's portrait is mentioned only briefly and does not become the site of study like the other portraits in the gallery. It's also significant that Tom has to bring his own "likeness" into the gallery, saying that he "desires that it may be hung up."[59] The provisional hanging of Tom's portrait in the picture gallery is a significant departure from the rest of Wilson's "illustrious portraits." While it's easy to dismiss or critique Wilson's class politics given his inattention to working people, this fascinating moment in the text suggests a recognition of how photography could be used as a tool of surveillance, criminalization, and capture, especially for people who lacked resources, capital, and privilege. The transformation of Tom into a portrait is marked by a sense of melancholy, of what might be lost in the very moment when a subject gains access to perceptibility by being fixed to and by the portrait. The genius of Tom and other city boys like him is connected to how they otherwise evaded the camera, the police, and the state. Wilson celebrates such fugitive tactics in many other places in his writings and, indeed, partakes in them through his own wayward strollings and wanderings.

Images of enslaved and nominally free Black workers are thus present in the gallery, but often on the margins and only visible in quick glimpses. Black women have a similarly marginal, almost spectral position. They, like photography, occupy a central place within the text's unconscious: mostly invisible yet everywhere exerting influence on the field of representation. Wilson does give us a portrait of the enslaved poet Phillis Wheatley, but she is framed as a poetess and youth, not as a political actor. In another moment, he offers a quick sketch of "a colored lady" who turns her nose up at the gallery's collection and calls it "nonsense." Ethiop treats this woman with disdain, describing her as an "old maid, a little dimmed in sight; somewhat faded."[60] The Picture Gallery does not give us portraits of Frances Harper, Harriet Tubman, Sojourner Truth, or any other women freedom fighters or notable race women of the moment. As I've noted, the Picture Gallery is exceptionally metatextual, referencing and using issues of the *Anglo-African Magazine* as a source text for its own imaginings. But the text largely ignores Black women, even intellectuals like Harper, Sarah Mapps Douglass, and Mary Shadd Cary who themselves contributed pieces to the magazine. Black women artists are also excluded, from fine artists like the sculptor Edmonia Lewis to the many women arts educators and students who surrounded

Wilson in his capacity as a school principal and member of Brooklyn's Black elite. Ultimately, imagining free, fearless Black women in Wilson's gallery of Black excellence is beyond the scope of the "Afric-American Picture Gallery." This absence points to a significant limit to Wilson's speculative imagination.

This elision of Black women as figures of political and artistic agency coexists, paradoxically, with the text's reliance on domestic constructions of space and sentimental cultures of photography and art-making. Indeed, the photographic gallery was itself a kind of parlor space, a richly decorated interior that was meant to warmly receive patrons. Jasmine Nichole Cobb has written about the parlor as a crucial site of Black women's intellectual and artistic production in the nineteenth century.[61] Wilson's picture gallery is ostensibly a public institution, but Ethiop repeatedly expresses frustration at the intrusion of visitors from the street. One of the fantasies of the Black Forest tale is that it gives Ethiop access to a picture gallery located deep within a mountain cave and thus far away from the loud, distracting crowds of the city. The cave gallery is ultimately a fantasy about having access to a deeply private space that enables the flourishing of contemplation and interiority.[62]

Wilson's gallery bears additional connections to the parlor, and to the private rather than public sphere. As a periodical text, the gallery was meant to be read and consumed by an individual. One gets the sense that Wilson imagines readers reading silently and privately, rather than out loud and collectively as David Walker encouraged in his *Appeal to the Coloured Citizens of the World* (1829). Many readers must have read the *Anglo-African* in the parlor. Similarly, the text itself bears resemblance to women's albums and friendship albums of Wilson's moment, which were circulated among free Black women in the North and displayed in their parlors. Wilson himself contributed a short essay to the second edition of Julia Griffiths's abolitionist gift book, *Autographs for Freedom*, which I discuss further in the next chapter. As a work literally compiled from clippings from the antebellum print sphere, the Picture Gallery is in many ways closer to a scrapbook than a public gallery.[63]

Photography and Black Bohemia

Wilson's ambivalence about the status of Black art in the age of mechanical reproduction becomes even clearer when we place his writings next to the responses of other bohemian creatives to the invention of photography in the 1840s and 1850s. Most notably, Walt Whitman was an early advocate who believed the daguerreotype was an exhilarating new form of representation that could produce a vibrant, vibrating presence of the real. Like many of his comrades, Whitman enthusiastically embraced photography and saw it as a radical, American form, filled with democratic possibilities.

It's worth repeating that there are many similarities to trace between William J. Wilson and Walt Whitman. Brooklyn was beloved to them both; they both wrote bold, experimental texts that celebrated the movement of desire and the modern city's support of new forms of pleasure; they were both newspaper correspondents and commentators on Brooklyn's rise as a center of industry and culture. Trachtenberg notes that "in the 1840s Whitman wrote frequently for a number of Brooklyn newspapers, and in his accounts of rambles in the metropolis across the river he often commented on new, interesting sights, on art exhibitions and buildings under construction, on streetcars and the colorful, zestful crowds—and on the new portrait galleries."[64] One could easily think Trachtenberg was writing about Wilson's contributions to *Frederick Douglass' Paper* in the 1850s.

Both Wilson and Whitman also composed their own picture galleries. In the mid-1840s, Whitman wrote lines of poetry in his notebook that he titled "Pictures" and that he would finally publish under the title "My Picture-Gallery" in 1880:

> In a little house keep I pictures suspended, it is not a fix'd house,
> It is round, it is only a few inches from one side to the other;
> Yet behold, it has room for all the shows of the world, all memories!
> Here the tableaus of life, and here the groupings of death;
> Here, do you know this? this is cicerone himself,
> With finger rais'd he points to the prodigal pictures.[65]

Ethiop, too, "points to the prodigal pictures" "with finger rais'd."

Whitman's interest in photography as an avenue of self-expression and communion with others extended beyond the philosophical. The famous frontispiece illustration of the author appended to the 1855 edition of *Leaves of Grass* was likely modeled after a photograph (figure 1.6). Through his direct gaze and casual, loafing stance, Whitman seeks to make a direct, even sensual connection between himself and the viewer, despite the mediations of photography, lithography, and the book itself. Whitman had his portrait taken many times in New York studios in the 1850s, including at Plumbe's Gallery. His "A Visit to Plumbe's Gallery" in 1846 recounts his visits to this and other photographic studios on Broadway.

We have no corresponding photographic portrait of Wilson, but we do know that he too visited Plumbe's famous studio. In a March 11, 1853, column

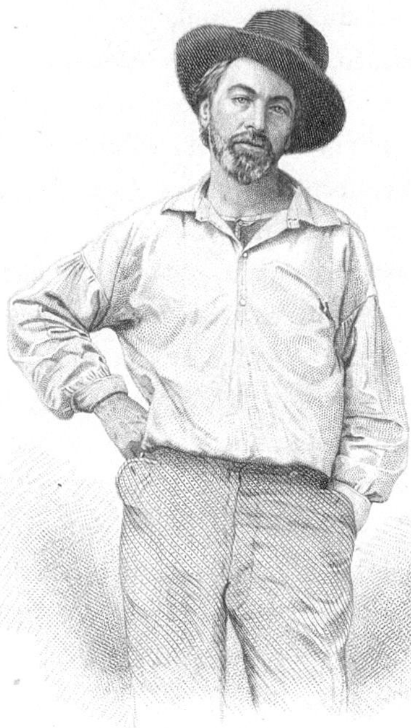

1.6 Walt Whitman, *Leaves of Grass* (Brooklyn: Rome Brothers, 1855), frontispiece.

in *Frederick Douglass' Paper*, he talks about stumbling into that establishment after being "strongly attracted by some fine specimens of daguerreotypes in oil, hanging in a Broadway stair passage":

> In my minute examination of them without heeding, found I had wound my way up the ample and tastefully hung stairs, where I was confronted by a very polite gentleman, inviting me within a splendid chamber, artistically hung with the finest specimens of daugerrean [*sic*] likenesses in oil, and otherwise perhaps in the country. Likenesses thus taken in oil are so accurate, so life-like, that they seem to be life itself. The individual is before you. There is no mistaking it. The Gallery, let me say, was no other than the distinguished PLUMB[E]'s and Ethiop was strongly solicited by that gentlemanly proprietor to sit for a miniature. The next time he goes to Gotham, he thinks he will submit.

Here Wilson recounts an actual visit to one of the Daguerreian galleries that helped to inspire his own Picture Gallery. His reference to "daguerreotypes in oil" and their unbelievable lifelikeness again points to the fact that Wilson was living through a period of profound transition, a moment in which there was still a categorial fuzziness around painting and photography, as well as between the photographer and the painter.

Whereas Whitman viewed photography as an ideal medium of self-representation, in which the sitter was imagined as a kind of collaborator, cocreating with the operator, Wilson approached the camera with more caution. After being "strongly solicited" to sit for his portrait by the "gentlemanly proprietor," he says that the next time he goes to Gotham, "he thinks he will submit." Here, then, we have William J. Wilson not exactly embracing photography as a premier venue for Black representation, but *deferring* his own capture by the photographer-painter. Wilson says he "thinks" he will sit for his picture, but not now. Such deferral tracks with the evasions and repressions of the photographic apparatus in the Picture Gallery. Framing sitting as a kind of submitting further suggests that photography was not an inherently egalitarian medium, but one suffused by power dynamics that structured the rest of society. And of course, by framing sitting as a form of submission Wilson presents the photograph as a potential tool of domination. This moment quickly conjures the figure of the captive/slave; it also slyly suggests that the invention of photography was tightly bound to other regimes of industrial production in an economy driven by enslaved labor. And of course, given his self-stylization as a bohemian, Wilson's language of submission is also meant to be playful, suggesting that there might be a pleasure to submitting, a pleasure not disconnected from the economy or the positions of racialized power produced by it. Moreover, by saying that he *thinks* he will submit, Wilson expresses a productive ambivalence around the will to visualization for Black subjects in the period, illuminating the visual field as one that is structured by the very same power relations that structure a white supremacist, slaveholding state.

Ethiop goes on in the March 11, 1853, column to offer a striking word portrait that brings the world of New York's fashionable Black dandies into the orbit of Broadway's Daguerrean studio scene. It's a portrait that also polices the rabble-rousing noncompliance of the city's Black youth:

> A little incident occurred while in this establishment worth mentioning: Two well-dressed colored *lads*, about fifteen years of age, came swaggering in, and, though with a strong flavor of Black Broadway (*alias*

> Church Street) about them—sporting large box coats, tight pants and patent boots, and a Havanah each, coupled with their swaggering air—yet I soon detected that one was employed in the establishment. What struck me most, was the careless indifference, and insolence of manner with which he received some special directions of the proprietor, and I could but conclude that it was one of the reasons why, with our young men, it was situation today, and evacuation tomorrow.

Ethiop describes these two youth as classic dandies—exuding decadence, rushing for no one, and smoking Cuban cigars while "sporting large box coats, tight pants and patent boots." In naming a "black Broadway" on Church Street, Ethiop suggests a whole world of fashion, style, and "swagger" that operates adjacent to Broadway and largely under the radar of white people in the city. He offers a glimpse of a place where pleasure reigns supreme, but he quickly suppresses that world, and its riotous, unruly forms of freedom and self-expression. Realizing that one of these lads was an employee in Plumbe's studio, Ethiop decries his "careless indifference" to the directions of the proprietor and says that such insolence helps to explain the problem with unemployment among young African Americans in the city ("it was one of the reasons why, with our young men, it was situation today, and evacuation tomorrow"). At the same time, the entrance of these two lads into the studio disrupts the logics of whiteness that structured both the Daguerreian studios of Broadway and the use of photography to capture, taxonomize, and objectify human subjects. The lad's "insolence of manner"—his noncompliance—is a refusal of work at the same time as it is a refusal to legitimate the photographer and the photographic enterprise, similar to Ethiop's own deferral of his "submission" to the camera. It's quite possible that this noncompliant young man even served as a model for the gallery boy Tom in the Picture Gallery.[66] As "rowdy youth" who roam the city and refuse to take their labors seriously, they evade their capture and "framing" by both photography and the racial state.

Ultimately, new regimes of visibility ushered in by technologies of mechanical reproduction—including lithography and photography—presented both exciting possibilities and real perils for African Americans seeking self-determination and the means for self-representation in a white supremacist society. Ethiop's note about "submitting" to the camera articulates the work of Black art in the age of mechanical production to the machinations of slavery and racial capitalism. Other early theorizers of photography, from Paul Nadar to Walter Benjamin, did not address how regimes of image-making were directly connected to an industrializing world system motored by slavery and other forms of racialized, coerced labor. The rise of a technology able to capture the trace of a real "thing" happened at the same time the world was being transformed into a world of commodities. William J. Wilson contributes to nineteenth-century philosophies of the image by reminding us of those regimes of objectification that haunted both photography and a capitalism that was inseparable from racial domination and exploitation.

2

"Our Essentially Aesthetic or Art-Nature"

LATE ANTEBELLUM BLACK AESTHETICS

> At any moment the reader is ready to turn into a writer.
>
> **Walter Benjamin**, "The Work of Art in the Age of Mechanical Reproduction"

The "Afric-American Picture Gallery" was not the only ekphrastic Black portrait gallery published in the 1850s. In 1854, James McCune Smith's "Heads of the Colored People" offered readers of *Frederick Douglass' Paper* lively "word portraits" of the Black working class in New York City. That same year, Frederick Douglass installed a virtual gallery in the middle of a graduation speech he delivered at Western Reserve College in Ohio.

Titled "Claims of the Negro, Ethnologically Considered," Douglass's speech set out to discredit the pseudoscientific theories that were increasingly being used to uphold the institution of slavery as abolition threatened to topple it. Douglass understood that these theories were deeply connected to both a scopic regime of race and a growing sphere of visual culture rooted in anti-Blackness. Recognizing that proslavery ethnologists and naturalists will always elevate and idealize whiteness while debasing and distorting Blackness, Douglass noted, "If, for instance, a phrenologist or naturalist undertakes to represent in portraits, the differences between the two races—the negro and the European—he will invariably present the *highest* type of the European, and the *lowest* type of the negro." In response, Douglass asks his listeners to replace the biased racial typologies propped up by American race science with what Sarah Blackwood has called a "wonderfully alternative picture gallery."[1] Douglass's picture gallery, as rhetorically erected within his speech, is composed of the "heads" of prominent Black masculine intellectuals including "A. CRUMMEL, HENRY H. GARNET, SAM'L R. WARD, CHAS. LENOX REMOND, W. J. WILSON, J. W. PEN[N]INGTON, J. I. GAINES, M. R. DELANY, J. W. LOGUIN, J. M. WHITFIELD, J. C. HOLLY" and "hundreds of others I could mention, [that] are all better formed, and indicate the presence of intellect more than any pictures I have seen in such works [of ethnology]." This particular iteration of ekphrasis has a number of fascinating effects, one of which is that Douglass brings portraiture into the orbit of American racial science, a significant gesture given how racial science depended on visual types and illustrations to "prove" hierarchies of racialization. This moment also recalibrates the speech so that it can proceed on aesthetic rather than scientific grounds.

Douglass's fleeting evocation of a Black portrait gallery is so arresting that it immediately slows down the speech. Like the Picture Gallery that Wilson would construct a few years later, it has a decelerating effect within the accelerating tempo of the late 1850s. Like the imaginative tableaux of intellectuals it offers, it freezes listeners in time. In so doing, it also transforms the speech's relationship to the urgencies of Douglass's political moment. In turning listeners from the grossly instrumental arguments of racial science to a speculative gallery of art, Douglass disrupts the speed of both anti-Blackness and abolitionism. This moment of Black ekphrasis asks listeners to consider a different political tempo: It is a pause marked by a Black aestheticism that prioritizes the temporalities produced by the Black radical imagination over and above the instrumentalist temporalities of dominant political grammars. It is a moment that refuses to play the game of mainstream debates while simultaneously admitting the inevitability of being hailed by them.

While scholars, including myself, have elucidated how "Claims" speaks to scientific and religious contexts of the 1850s, the speech also keys into questions and debates about Black aesthetics in the 1850s that were playing out in literary works and in periodical discourses throughout the period.[2] Most obviously, "Claims of the Negro" sought to oppose and challenge the ascendancy of racial science as an ideological cudgel amid intensifying anti-abolitionism, anti-Blackness, and sectionalist discord in the 1850s. Even more immediately, it was crafted as a response to Josiah Nott and George Gliddon's 1854 tome of racist diatribe and pseudo-history, *Types of Mankind*. Douglass further refers back to Samuel George Morton's 1837 *Crania Americana* to extract moments in that text that reflect the depth and consistency of the author's prejudice.

Douglass's speech also came on the heels of a lively correspondence between two prominent Black intellectuals—William J. Wilson and James McCune Smith—that had been taking shape in the pages of his own newspaper since 1851. Thus, behind the manifest content of Douglass's speech against racial science, there lies a rich citational structure and engagement with Black aesthetic theory as it was taking shape among Black intellectuals in the 1850s. It seems likely, for example, that Douglass's portrait gallery, itself a kind of provisional, experimental gesture of counter-archiving in and against American racial science, was influenced by Wilson's own theories of Black art in *Frederick Douglass' Paper*. Douglass must have also had McCune Smith's "Heads of the Colored People" in mind. Curiously, Douglass does not include James McCune Smith among the heads of prominent Black intellectuals in his imaginary gallery, though Douglass does reference him as an authority at the end of the speech. This is a serious omission, and possibly a slight, since McCune Smith was the most prominent African American physician in the country, a noted intellectual, and a committed abolitionist. Douglass was, in fact, vocal in his critique of "The Heads of the Colored People," critiquing it for fetishizing a folksy and at times overly sensual account of the Black working class rather than putting before the public eye a pantheon of upright, respectable representatives of the race. Perhaps this is why McCune Smith is himself excluded from Douglass's virtual pantheon of Black masculine excellence: It was either a jab or a joke. Or perhaps it was both.

While McCune Smith was excluded from Douglass's speculative picture gallery, Douglass does install McCune Smith's rhetorical sparring partner—William J. Wilson—in his gallery of illustrious "heads." Wilson would himself extend Douglass's provisional portrait gallery with his own ekphrastic experiment in Black portraiture a few years later. It's possible that Douglass's speech directly inspired Wilson to do so. Either way, Wilson clearly created his Picture Gallery as part of the creative conversations and collaborations that were happening among coteries of African American writers and artists in the 1850s.

As much as Wilson and his cohort were invested in the powers of visual representation to elevate the race, rhetorical authority was of paramount importance to them. Indeed, the flexing of artful rhetorical styles and forms of address constituted a major part of the exchanges between correspondents, and between correspondents and editors, in the Black periodical sphere, as in the broader world of antebellum newspapers and magazines. From 1851 to 1855, McCune Smith, as "Communipaw," and Wilson, as "Ethiop," produced a stunningly varied and voluminous correspondence within the pages of *Frederick Douglass' Paper*. As, respectively, the newspaper's New York and Brooklyn correspondents, Communipaw and Ethiop debated political issues, discussed current events, and argued about the most effective ways to organize their communities. Writing to—and often against—each other, their columns record a moment when, as Communipaw observed, the "colored people" were "awaking to the necessity of struggling for their rights."[3] But Douglass's newspaper also provided a space where the two could meditate on the role of aesthetics in the elevation of the race. Their exchanges reveal how African American writing in the 1850s was deeply shaped by the format of the newspaper, as well as by lively debates about the role of Black art in a society defined by racial domination and exploitation.

This chapter contextualizes the Picture Gallery by placing it within the dynamic landscape of African American intellectual and writerly community in the late antebellum period. At the end of Nafissa Thompson-Spires's short story collection *The Heads of the Colored People* (2018), the author notes that she took inspiration from the nineteenth-century Black sketch tradition, in which writers like Wilson (writing as Ethiop), James McCune Smith (writing as Communipaw), and Frances Harper (writing as Jane Rustic) "narrate[d] black life from the mundane to the obscure" in stories that "span[ned] the didactic to the macabre."[4] Much of this sketch work appeared in periodicals serially, and, as Derrick Spires argues, serialization played a fundamental role in African American literary history before the twentieth century.[5] The fetishization of the novel as a coherent and hegemonic form in the American nineteenth century has tended to overemphasize the place of the African American novel in that period (of which there were only a few) at the expense of the myriad forms of writing and genres of print with which writers engaged. A focus on what Spires calls "serial blackness" also helps to illuminate how Black periodical writers were theorizing alternative relationships to both the temporalities of racial modernity and the temporal demands of abolition itself, refusing to remain in lockstep with an increasingly institutional movement that did not always center the actual needs of Black Americans, even as it continued to speak in their name.[6]

Moving beyond book history, Spires also explores the philosophical dimensions of serialization. For my part, I'm interested in the way seriality sheds light on how Black writing in the 1850s always registers abolitionist history with a difference. Serial Blackness, to my mind, gives us a way to understand the specificities—and even eccentricities—of late antebellum periodical works that, like the Picture Gallery, stood somewhat apart from abolitionist propaganda. Indeed, suspicion of Garrisonianism can be found in multiple columns by both Communipaw and Ethiop. At one point, Communipaw even says that Garrison and his party "have left us poor, and blind, and bleeding."[7] Serial fictions like the Picture Gallery and McCune Smith's "Heads of the Colored People" expressed a hesitant and at times suspicious relationship to the dominant grammars of abolition. In so doing, they produced new forms and theories of Black aesthetics, forged in relation to—but often at a critical distance from—the norms and rhetoric of white abolitionists. Indeed, the meandering and philosophical nature of Ethiop's and Communipaw's columns couldn't be further away from the dogmatism and immediacy of abolitionist propaganda in the years immediately preceding the Civil War.

This chapter also takes up Ethiop's correspondence with Communipaw to further explore the forms of experimentalism, playfulness, and dialogic exchange that characterized Black writing in the late antebellum period. This sparring correspondence in *Frederick Douglass' Paper* most certainly influenced Wilson's entrée into fiction writing with his publication of "Terance Ludlam" in *Frederick Douglass' Paper* in 1854 and the "Afric-American Picture Gallery" in the *Anglo-African Magazine* in 1859. We can be sure Wilson had McCune Smith's "Heads of the Colored People" in mind when he penned the "Afric-American Picture Gallery," since that series was published *within* McCune Smith's correspondence to *Frederick Douglass' Paper*. As in McCune Smith's "Heads," the Picture Gallery presents readers with various "heads" of African Americans in his gallery. Wilson also writes Tom, the picture gallery's "boy," as an allusion to McCune Smith's gallery of New York's working folk in his own series. In other words, Black writing in the late antebellum period was characterized by a deep dialogism. It's impossible to fully understand these works without their various intertexts and the webs of intellectual exchange that shaped them.

I begin by situating the Picture Gallery within a broader landscape of experiments in Black fiction writing in the 1850s, all of which were shaped by the rise of commodity capitalism and the formalization of an American literary marketplace. While tracing the networks of African American men's writing in the period, I suggest that Wilson's writing was also deeply shaped by both the sketchbooks of famed New York writer Washington Irving and the scrapbook cultures of African American women. Throughout, I develop a framework for understanding both the theory and practice of Black aesthetics in the 1850s. I'm especially interested in the idea of intuitive construction as a way of capturing the dialogic method of writers like Wilson and McCune Smith; I also consider how Douglass contributed to ideas of Black ekphrasis and aesthetics, and how he was interpellated into exchanges with Wilson and McCune Smith.

My ideas here are inspired by the improvisational and open-ended quality of the texts and periodical correspondence that are the focus of this book. They should themselves be taken as experimental and open to further revision by future interlocutors and constructivists. I'm also inspired by McCune and Smith's consistent interest in "sketching" and composing "outline portraits," as well as the sheer, unfiltered eccentricity and flights of fancy that characterize their prose. In this way, the concepts outlined below are intended as a provisional scaffolding on which future scholarship, curating, and creative production around the Picture Gallery and its various intertexts might take shape.

Black Fiction and the Rise of Commodity Capitalism

Carla Peterson's account of the beginnings of the African American novel tradition in the 1850s frames that history through the rise of consumer capitalism in the United States, arguing that this was a critical decade in which Black writers began experimenting with fiction writing as way to gain a foothold in an emerging literary marketplace. At the same time that these writers were increasingly approaching their writing as "a commodity to be sold for a profit," their works spoke back to a broader capitalist system predicated on the exploitation and dispossession of Black life and labor.[8] She shows that for writers whose own lives were constantly shadowed by the threat of commodification under both slavery and the "free" market, fiction could provide a cloak of protection, within which authors were able to widen the space between the "I" of their own person and the "I" of the slave.

Peterson's essay provides a rich framework for understanding the landscape of Black fiction writing in the 1850s, from Martin Delany's novel *Blake; or, the Huts of America* (1859–62)—which was serialized in the *Anglo-African Magazine* and *Weekly Anglo-African*—to Harriet Jacobs's fictionalized autobiography, *Incidents in the Life of a Slave Girl* (1861). Peterson's meticulous study of the narrative structures, plots, and characters of the earliest African American novels did for the study of Black fiction what John Sekora's "Black Message/White Envelope" did for legitimating the study of slave narratives as literature in the 1980s.[9] This essay also remains important because of the attention it pays to the material realities of the lives of Peterson's authors, including the difficulties that dogged African Americans seeking any kind of stability in the labor market in this period. For Black writers in the decade preceding the Civil War, the goals for publication were often highly practical, writing not primarily to establish themselves as professional authors but to raise funds for a social cause or for their own survival. Peterson writes, "[Harriet] Wilson hoped to make enough money to care for her sick son, [William Wells] Brown to finance his stay in Britain without having to 'beg' his living from white abolitionists. Both Jacobs and Delany were eager to use the proceeds to further their espoused social causes—Jacobs, the antislavery movement; Delany, African-American emigration to the Niger Valley."[10]

Thus, for African Americans in the 1850s fiction writing was one of many strategies for making money in a world that increasingly demanded it. What, we might wonder, was William J. Wilson's place within the economic landscape of fiction writing in the 1850s? Peterson says that Black writers of the period "expressed varying attitudes toward commodity capitalism and suggested different solutions to Black underdevelopment," the strategic withdrawal of capital investment from communities paired with the superexploitation of Black labor in the marketplace.[11] Wilson did not ever publish a novel or a "begging book," in which an author sought much-needed financial support through the sale of their writing. As an educator and school principal, he had more economic security than most members of his community. We know that Wilson was a fierce advocate for the building of economic power and the accumulation of wealth in his community. Those positions would only strengthen over time, culminating in his appointment as the cashier of the Freedman's Savings Bank in Washington, DC, after the Civil War. And yet Wilson's financial situation was still precarious. His obituary notes that the failure of the Freedman's Bank bankrupted him and caused him to lose his "handsome" property; Wilson left the bank somewhat disgraced. An appended note to the obituary suggests that a group of Wilson's friends might publish a book of Ethiop's writings as a fundraiser for his widow and daughter.[12]

Harriet Wilson's *Our Nig: or, Sketches from the Life of a Free Black*—published in 1859, the same year as the Picture Gallery—was, unlike the Picture Gallery, explicitly written and sold to raise funds for its author. Wilson's autobiographical novel opens with this striking note, saying that her narrative was produced out of conditions of deprivation and necessity: "Deserted by kindred, disabled by failing health, I am forced to some experiment which shall aid me in maintaining myself and child without extinguishing this feeble life."[13] Wilson's fictionalized account of her own childhood experiences of captivity and abuse within a white household in New England showed how "slavery's shadows" loomed large even in the "free" North. *Our Nig* is especially keyed into the isomorphy between indentured servitude and enslavement under racial capitalism for Black girls and young women, who occupied a particularly vulnerable place within the nation's socioeconomic hierarchy.

Writing under the threat of indigency and death, Wilson says her circumstances forced her to this narrative "experiment." While *Our Nig* may appear to be a simple story because of how it draws on tropes and narrative structures from children's literature, it is a deeply innovative and modern work, like other Black textual experiments from the 1850s. For example, the novel is unapologetically pessimistic about the prospect of abolition, since both slavery and anti-Blackness are so deeply entrenched in American society, including in the Northern states. Chapter 12's epigraph, taken from Ecclesiastes, captures this sentiment clearly, noting that there's "nothing new under the sun." *Our Nig*'s nihilism is a world away from the forward-looking nature of mainstream abolition in 1859. Instead, the text shares an affective comportment with other late antebellum Black texts that approached politics with hesitance, ambivalence, pessimism, and, at times, with a separatist militance. It's also significant that Harriet Wilson's appeal, like David Walker's *Appeal* (1829) three decades earlier, hails Black readers rather than white liberals: "I sincerely appeal to my colored brethren universally for patronage, hoping they will not condemn this attempt of their sister to be erudite, but rally around me a faithful band of supporters and defenders."[14] Writing in relative isolation in rural New Hampshire, Harriet Wilson sought the kind of community and solidarity William J. Wilson benefited from in his beloved Brooklyn.

Harriet Wilson also participated in the pseudonymous Black writing cultures of her moment. Just like William J. Wilson dropped a fictional avatar of himself into the Picture Gallery, Harriet Wilson would protect her identity and story through the avatar of Frado, the mischievous girl protagonist of *Our Nig* who is beautifully noncompliant and resistant to the white family's attempts to "domesticate" and control her. Just two years later, in 1861, Harriet Jacobs would use "Linda Brent" as a cover to hide her identity as a fugitive and to protect her own vulnerability as a woman who had experienced relentless forms of sexual harassment and abuse as an enslaved girl and young woman. While the drama of *Incidents in the Life of a Slave Girl* centers on Jacobs's enslavement and seven years hiding in an attic in Edenton, North Carolina, Jacobs composed the narrative while living in New York City and upstate after her escape from slavery. In other words, Jacobs was one of the fugitives sheltering in place in Wilson's New York. Did New York's scene of free Afropolitans and bohemians shape her novelistic technique? Or did the surrealness of fugitive testimony shape theirs? While *Incidents* has long been characterized by scholars as a novelistic slave narrative, more contemporary Black feminist art and criticism has gone further in illuminating its experimentalism and nuanced theorization of racial modernity, especially in the deeply symbolic and existentially rich "Loophole of Retreat" chapter.[15] We know that Jacobs and Wilson traveled in overlapping social circles. Jacobs also joined Wilson in the exodus of Black educators and activists from New York State to the South during the Civil War. Indeed, Jacobs's and Wilson's overlapping trajectories point to how Black writing in the late antebellum period was taking shape through very specific sociopolitical—and geographical—matrices.

Those same matrices of space, movement, and writing were also shared by the emigrationist and Black nationalist Martin Delany. Delany was a frequent visitor to New York City in the 1850s. He also contributed to the emigration plans of the African Civilization Society in Brooklyn. Indeed, the Picture Gallery's closest fictional intertext may be Delany's *Blake; or, The Huts of America* (1859–62), since the two works were published serially in some of the same issues of the *Anglo-African Magazine*. I have talked elsewhere about the experimentalism of Delany's *Blake*, focusing on how the speculative narrative of the novel emerged alongside Delany's engagements with natural science and commitments to empirical methods.[16] Delany's text shares with the Picture Gallery a fantastical representation of both space and time, as well as a roaming, fugitive protagonist. Delany's own speculations on astronomy appeared in the *Anglo-African* alongside installments of both *Blake* and the Picture Gallery. Here again we see that the *Anglo-African* showcased the writings of an African American vanguard as it was consolidating in the late 1850s. From Harriet Wilson's and Harriet Jacob's fictional autobiographies to William J. Wilson's and Martin Delany's speculative fictions, the years from 1859 to the outbreak of the Civil War witnessed the emergence of an ambitiously experimental and modern genealogy of African American writing.

Wilson's Sketchbook and Scrapbook

Even though Wilson did not publish a novel to make money during his lifetime, his writing clearly registers an aesthetics being shaped by the market, the transformation of the world into one of commodities, and the commodification of creativity itself. The Picture Gallery was very much a part of this experimental turn in Black letters in the late 1850s: one that was shaped by the rise of the American novel, the temporalities and format of the newspaper (as well as its temporal demands on contributors to produce according to set deadlines), and material conditions on the ground. In addition to being part of the flowering of African American fiction writing in the years leading up to the Civil War, Wilson's and McCune Smith's writing was deeply connected to—and made important contributions to—the New York sketch tradition, which originated with Washington Irving's *Sketch Book of Geoffrey Crayon, Gent*, a collection of stories that were first published serially in 1819 and 1830 under the pseudonym Geoffrey Crayon. Irving was central to the development of New York's vibrant periodical culture, founding the literary magazine *Salmagundi* in 1807. There he also coined "Gotham"—which Wilson frequently used—as a name for New York City and developed a satirical style that would profoundly shape the tenor and content of antebellum newspapers.

Propelled by new editions of his writings, illustrated editions, and a developing national literary culture that rallied around Irving as a founder of American literature, Irving's influence on US culture in the 1850s was significant. Irving was also a major if underrecognized influence on African American writers in the period. For example, William Wells Brown brought Irving into the orbit of his own method of textual collage and appropriation by plagiarizing, audaciously, "from the famous chapter on plagiarism" in Irving's *The Sketch Book of Geoffrey Crayon*."[17] For his part, Wilson claimed his position as a literary descendant of Irving—and of New York's tradition of letters, more broadly—by continually pointing readers back to his own sketchbook, both in the Picture Gallery and in his other writings. Irving continued to be widely read and influenced periodicals and book-length publications throughout the 1850s, including George S. Foster's urban periodical sketches, which were collated and published as *New York by Gas-Light and Other Urban Sketches* (1850) and *New York in Slices* (1856). Wilson and McCune Smith had certainly read Foster's wildly popular urban sketches. Both writers also allude to Irving across their own writings. Their dipping into the gothic bears a clear inheritance from Irving's ghost stories, such as "The Legend of Sleepy Hollow." Their satirical accounts of New York's people and happenings were also deeply shaped by Irving's own newspaper columns.

McCune Smith directly placed himself in a literary genealogy descending from Irving when he claimed the pen name Communipaw, the name Dutch settlers gave to the land they confiscated in the 1610s along the Hudson River in present-day Jersey City. Communipaw was one of the Dutch West India Company's first settlements in the area that would become New York and New Jersey. Deeply concerned with the history, culture, and mores of Dutch settlers in the region, Irving published his "Guests from Gibbet-Island: A Legend of Communipaw" in the *Knickerbocker* magazine in 1839, a story that includes a tale about a wayward "cross-grained curmudgeon of a negro, named Pluto, who was a kind of enigma in Communipaw."[18] McCune Smith's reference to Communipaw is a direct reference to Irving's story and, by extension, to the mixed-race "enigma" of Pluto. John Stauffer notes that McCune Smith called himself a descendant of Communipaw.[19] He certainly knew that the area later named Communipaw had been an important crossroads for the Hackensack people and was a place with a rich history of resistance to imperialism. Its history as an "interracial community of blacks, Indians, and Dutch settlers who resisted British invaders" also connected to McCune Smith's investment in the politics and possibilities of interracialism for racial reconciliation in the union.[20]

Irving passed away in 1859, on the eve of the nation's hurtling into civil war and the same year the "Afric-American Picture Gallery" was published in the *Anglo-African Magazine*. Wilson's much-referenced sketchbook was an homage to Irving and to New York's mostly masculine sketch culture. But as chapter 1 detailed, through its practices of textual collaging and juxtaposition of image and narrative, the Picture Gallery also shows the influence of scrapbooking culture in the period, an activity primarily associated with women and the domestic sphere. Wilson himself registered the influence of domestic practices of making and creativity on his writing by occasionally referring to his sketchbook as a scrapbook.

Wilson's own "A Leaf from My Scrap Book" appeared in the second volume of Julia Griffiths's *Autographs for Freedom* (1854), an abolitionist gift book created by the Rochester Ladies' Anti-Slavery Society to raise funds for the movement. Wilson's essay takes up the oratory of Frederick Douglass and Samuel Ward but says not a single word about the content of their speeches. Written after "Frederick Douglass and Samuel R. Ward debated the 'question' whether the Constitution was or not a pro-slavery document" in 1849, Wilson does not take a position on the Constitution issue that was at the center of abolitionist debate, nor does he even remind readers of Ward and Douglass's respective positions.[21] Instead, his sketchbook-scrapbook impressions spin out an idiosyncratic theory of the respective rhetorical styles of Ward and Douglass and their effects on listeners, cast through a series of striking visual metaphors and ekphrastic description.

Like Douglass's own inscription in Amy Matilda Cassey's friendship album, Wilson's contribution to abolitionist women's gift book culture emphasizes his relationships not with Black women writers in the domestic sphere but with other Black masculine intellectuals in the public sphere.[22] This kind of defensive distancing from women and the domestic sphere happens in the Picture Gallery as well. "A Leaf from My Scrap Book" takes shape as a study of masculine contrasts. Where Douglass's power derives from his transcendent ability to alight the imagination, Ward's straightforward "appeals are directed rather to the understanding than the imagination"; "Mr. Douglass deals in generals; Mr. Ward reduces everything to a point"; "Douglass is a *lecturer*; Ward the *debater*; Douglass powerful in invective; Ward in argument. What advantage Douglass gains in mimicry Ward recovers in wit. Douglass has sarcasm, Ward point."[23] Wilson says that Douglass's rhetoric depends on the powers of seduction and the speaker's "irresistible charm": Captivated by Douglass's "genuine, earnest eloquence," listeners find themselves following him down "some fearful steep," an imaginative descent that, in transfixing readers, also produces a kind of reality-altering vertigo. In some ways, the journey mirrors Ethiop's journey to the Black Forest in the Picture Gallery. Wilson writes that to listen to Douglass is to be led downward, into a sublime terrain that captivates the senses. I cite at length because Wilson's argument is complex and multistepped:

> In his very look—his gesture—in his whole manner, there is so much of genuine, earnest eloquence, that they leave no time for reflection. Now you are reminded of one rushing down some fearful steep, bidding you follow; now on some delightful stream, still beckoning you onward. In either case, no matter what your prepossessions or oppositions, you for the moment, at least, forget the justness or unjustness of his cause and obey the summons, and loath, if at all, you return to your former post.
>
> Not always, however, is he successful in retaining you. Giddy as you may be with the descent you have made, delighted as you are with the pleasure afforded, with the elysium to which he has wafted you, you return too often dissatisfied with his and your own impetuosity and want of firmness. You feel that you had had only a dream, a pastime, not a reality.
>
> This great power of momentary captivation consists in his eloquence of manner—his just appreciation of words. In listening to him, your whole soul is fired—every nerve strung—every passion inflated—every faculty you possess ready to perform at a moment's bidding. You stop not to ask why or wherefore.
>
> 'Tis a union of mighty yet harmonious sounds that play upon your imagination; and you give yourself up, for a time, to their irresistible charm. At last, the *cataract* which roared around you is hushed, the

tornado is passed, and you find yourself sitting upon a bank (at whose base roll but tranquil waters), quietly meditating that why, amid such a display of power, no greater effect had really been produced.[24]

Douglass's oratory is cast as a kind of spellbinding weather event, one that has the capacity to captivate and even hypnotize listeners. One might think here about Christina Sharpe's claim that slavery was so mundane, so ambient, so totalizing, it was the weather.[25] Antislavery discourse thus had to wage its battles against an entire climate to denaturalize slavery's appearance as nature itself. Departing from the transcendentalist position, Wilson frames the aesthetic contemplation of nature as a distraction from thought, rather than as something that might enable it. Douglass's speeches, he argues, operate by taking readers out of the world of reason and reality and into the realm of the senses. But after it's all over—after the "cataract" that roared around you is hushed and the "tornado" has passed—listeners are left out in the cold. With no time for the listener to actually absorb and reflect on the speaker's positions, his ideas dissipate back into the air: "At last, the *cataract* which roared around you is hushed, the *tornado* is passed, and you find yourself sitting upon a bank (at whose base roll but tranquil waters), quietly." Wilson is most critical of Douglass for using language that is beautiful—and, crucially, beautifully arranged—but that ultimately lacks conceptual weight: "With copiousness of language, and finish of diction, when even ideas fail, words come to his aid—arranging themselves, as it were, so completely, that they not only captivate, but often deceive us for ideas; and hence the vacuum that would necessarily occur in the address of an ordinary speaker is filled up, presenting the same beautiful harmony as do the lights and shades of a picture."[26] Wilson seems most suspicious of the hypnotic effects of Douglass's words, not for a moral reason, but because they disallow the forms of contemplation that allow listeners to come to a place of true understanding. Even more condemning, he suggests that the "vacuum" of Douglass's ideas—the place where ideas should reside—is filled up with aesthetically pleasing words and images.

"A Leaf from My Scrap Book" shows Wilson deeply engaged with questions of aesthetics that concerned him and other members of his cohort, formulating an early kind of Black aesthetic theory that I discuss in more detail below. But he does not just forward an aesthete's position, valorizing the captivating powers of art above all else. Instead, he suggests that aesthetics without content—beauty without truth—can impede the process of judgment needed for listeners, viewers, or readers to come to their own positions, to reckon with alternative truths, and to possibly change their mind. This moment of an individual coming to a place of authentic understanding was of special urgency given the matter at hand: the violent oppression and torture of millions of people of African descent in the Union.

Wilson's own jangly rhetoric makes "A Leaf from My Scrap Book" an entertaining read, but it's also something of a scandal, for Wilson says that he prefers the speeches of Ward over Douglass, the most celebrated African American orator of the abolitionist movement. He does so in a publication sponsored by the Rochester Ladies' Anti-Slavery Society and edited by Julia Griffiths, Douglass's intimate collaborator, benefactor, and friend. It appears that even the conflict-loving Wilson thought twice about contributing this sketch for inclusion in the volume. He appends a note after his signature: "Note—It has been some years since the above sketch was drawn; and though my impressions, especially of Mr. Douglass, has [*sic*] undergone some slight change since,—seeing in him enlarged, strengthened, and more matured thought, still I think, on the whole, the careful observer will attest substantially to its correctness."[27] Wilson's note opens with an expression of hesitation but then concludes by reaffirming the validity of his original impressions. In such moments as when Wilson notes that "Douglass speaks right on; you acknowledge him to have been on the ground—nay, to have gone over the field," it seems important to recall that Douglass was born enslaved, while Wilson was not. Even Black intellectuals had difficulties squaring Douglass's avant-garde intellectualism and aesthetic commitments with his status as a former slave. One has to wonder about resentments that Wilson may have held against a figure like Douglass, who by 1854 had already attained status as a transatlantic celebrity.

As in the Picture Gallery, Wilson highlights writing-as-process and expresses a worry that publication—like public speech—can forestall the dialectics of thought and the movement of the imagination that characterizes the writing process. *Autographs for Freedom* was a book for holiday gift-giving that highlighted antislavery sentiments and statements of moral persuasion from prominent abolitionists, poets, and writers. Printed signatures were meant to add to the value of the gift book for buyers and recipients. In "A Leaf from My Scrap Book," Wilson draws out the material dimensions of both the gift book and abolitionist print cultures. In his asterisked note about Douglass, Wilson refers to his essay as an "outline portrait," like McCune Smith practiced in his "Heads of the Colored People" series and Wilson did in his own newspaper correspondence. Here Wilson again places himself in the genealogy of Washington Irving's *Sketch-book*, but he also stretches the genre of the "sketch" to frame Black writing as a deeply ekphrastic enterprise, always taking shape in conversation with visual art and its tools. As in the Picture Gallery's foregrounding of pencils, charcoal, and paper, Wilson's essay brings us back to materials and technologies that make print possible. His signaling of the "leaf" from his scrapbook draws readers' attention to the paper on which the gift book is printed, while also reminding them that before the contributions to *Autographs for Freedom* were typeset, they were composed by hand in sketchbooks or scrapbooks, or on loose paper. Wilson is always drawing us back to the basic craft and materials of writing, while asking us to imagine scenes of authorship and writing that precede publication.

In providing a metatextual analysis that points to the material infrastructures of abolitionist print, "A Leaf from My Scrap Book" makes a singular contribution to *Autographs for Freedom*. I mean this not to exceptionalize Wilson but to key us into a little-studied genealogy of aesthetic theory that was being developed by Black writers in the late antebellum period. In a fascinating way, Wilson becomes a kind of aesthetic mediator in the essay, shuttling between Ward and Douglass. His own theories of Douglass's imaginative visual field are expressed ekphrastically: Wilson asks readers to visualize Douglass's speeches by moving through a scene described in lush detail, even making this reader wonder whether his own writing falls victim to the aesthetic trap and conceptual void he attributes to Douglass's rhetoric. Anticipating a move in the Picture Gallery, in which Ethiop journeys through a forest landscape he had previously viewed on the walls of the gallery, Wilson conjures the world of Douglass's speeches by taking readers into what feels like a landscape painting. The Black Forest fantasy-quest, a kind of trompe l'oeil cast in narrative, operates through the same trick: Wilson plants a set of visual images in the reader's mind and asks them to follow him into the wilderness. It makes his arguments vivid, colorful, and rich like an oil painting. But it also, more broadly, keys us into the material and aesthetic grounds on which political abolitionism is made possible.

The presentation of Douglass's speech as a kind of landscape painting also has the decelerating effect that I have talked about elsewhere. Late antebellum Black aesthetics played with narrative speed partly as a response to the political urgencies and contingencies that were building in the moment. In "A Leaf," Wilson expresses not exactly a criticism about Douglass's rhetorical style, but a hesitance, a refusal to rush headlong down into the crevasse. He will do something similar through the figure of Ethiop in the Picture Gallery. Ethiop falls into the portal of a landscape painting and into the Black Forest, but this journey also enables him to have a slower, more thoughtful relationship to what he sees in the cave gallery he tours, tucked away deep in the Black Forest. For Wilson, it is ultimately art, not nature, that serves as a trustworthy object of analysis and contemplation.

Other Black Picture Galleries

Douglass opened his remarks at Western Reserve College in Ohio by commenting on the sheer exceptionality of the occasion: A self-taught former bondsman was invited by the members of an undergraduate literary society to provide them with instruction, enlightenment, and guidance on the occasion of a moment marked by a profound transition from institutional constraint to personal freedom.[28] He further relies on the exceptionality of these circumstances to lend gravitas to his speech: Douglass cites himself as the first person born into chattel slavery asked to speak at graduation exercises in the United States. Figuratively returning to the Baltimore shipyard scenes of his own 1845 *Narrative*, where he uses apostrophe to address ships who have more freedom of movement than he does as a slave, Douglass figures the graduating students sitting before him as ships unencumbered by the crushing weight of bigotry and structural oppression. Outfitted with privilege and education, they are ready to cast off on the "voyage of life": "[you] not wholly unlike the gallant ship, newly launched, full rigged, and amply fitted, about to quit the placid waters of the harbor for the boisterous waves of the sea."[29] This is the first rhetorical pause in the speech, in which Douglass sets a scene before the readers that unfurls like a moving panorama; the second such pause comes later, in which Douglass—for just a moment—installs a temporary, improvised gallery of Black art in the mind's eye of his listeners and, after the publication of the speech, his readers.

Given the controversy that swirled around Douglass's invitation to speak at Western Reserve, as well as a national context of stifling racial paternalism and political suppression in the wake of the passage of the Fugitive Slave Act and the Kansas-Nebraska Act's authorization of the expansion of slavery into the very Midwest where Douglass was speaking that day, we might think about Douglass on the podium in terms of how Anna Mae Duane talks about the "examination days" that structured the academic schedules and existential experiences of free Black students in the antebellum era. Across the Northeast and indeed almost anywhere that the "experiment" of Black education was happening in this period, Black students were required to perform their knowledge oratorically in front of white instructors, administrators, philanthropists, and journalists, in both informal and highly formal and orchestrated environments. According to Duane, even Black teachers, principals, and adult orators could not escape these infantilizing rituals of interrogation.[30] The stakes for establishing rhetorical authority were extremely high for all Black public speech in the antebellum period, as they continue to be today; one's own status not only as an adult, but also as a human, was at stake.

As the speech continues to unfold, we see Douglass meticulously establishing his own rhetorical authority as a former slave speaking before a white, or mostly white, audience in an anti-Black society. But when it comes to the actual content of his speech, Douglass both expresses and performs hesitation about taking up a pressing topic of the times—the attempt to excise Black people from the "family of man" in natural history: "There are three ways to answer this denial. One is by ridicule; a second is by denunciation; and a third is by argument. I hardly know under which of these modes my answer to-day will fall. I feel myself somewhat on trial; and that this is just the point where there is hesitation, if not serious doubt." At the same time that Douglass describes and, indeed, provides a compulsory rhetorical performance of his humility at being asked to speak before an educated and elite audience, one also gets a sense of how anti-Blackness and the political tenor of the day narrowed the range of his expression, tone, and determined the contours of his speech acts. From the outset, Douglass tells his listeners that the question of Black humanity is easily settled; it is something recognized even by animals: "The horse bears him on his back—admits his mastery and dominion. The barn-yard fowl know his step, and flock around to receive their morning meal from his sable hand. The dog dances when he comes home, and whines piteously when he is absent. All these know that the negro is a MAN." In other words, Douglass knows this debate is below him. Early on, he says with what one senses as a kind of low-key exasperation, "Away, therefore, with all the scientific moonshine that would connect men with monkeys." Later, in another moment where he feels compelled to walk through the baseless arguments of yet another racist naturalist, he notes that "the man writes himself a blockhead."

Douglass's pedagogical argumentation in "Claims" proceeds through the working through of several excerpts from naturalists; his pedagogy also turns both performative and visual, as in one moment when he holds up a grammar written by Dr. M. B. Anderson of Rochester University. In this moment, Douglass (literally) points to a white text on stage to legitimize his own demonstration of the faulty linguistic arguments made by racist ethnologists. It's also difficult to ignore the clear religious symbolism conveyed in this moment, in which Douglass holds up a work of white ethnology as one would hold up a Bible during a sermon. Such moments of intensive citationality of both the Bible and antiracist science suggest that while Douglass knew that pseudoscientific arguments about Black inhumanity were both stupid and sacrilegious, he also knew that their existence in a white supremacist society made their dismantling an absolute necessity.

But this isn't, finally, where Douglass lands. Moving from a set of opening rhetorical gambits marked by hesitation and frustration to a set of disputations rooted in close readings of polygenetic arguments laid out in natural history texts and popular newspapers, Douglass ultimately settles into a more measured and more aesthetic mode, inviting listeners to conjure an image of a picture gallery of Black excellence.

Communipaw Versus Ethiop

Just as "A Leaf from My Scrap Book" provides a metatextual analysis of abolitionist rhetoric and print, the Picture Gallery is as much an experimental remediation of the antebellum print sphere as it is a work concerned with questions about Blackness and art in an industrializing society. The series is a dynamic space in which Wilson draws from the archive of the magazine to reflect on and remix the *Anglo-African Magazine* itself. For example, one visitor comes into the gallery wanting to talk to Ethiop about contributing to the *Anglo-African*. Another section draws heavily on an essay from the magazine devoted to the Colored Conventions movement. In other places, Wilson playfully addresses his editor, Thomas Hamilton. Wilson devotes one painting to the revered position of the Black newspaper editor in society, but at other points mildly ribs the *Anglo-African* and its editor. Wilson's virtual address to Hamilton resonates with Wilson's lively correspondence with McCune Smith. Wilson often explicitly hails other Black intellectuals, from Wheatley and Hamilton to McCune Smith and Martin Delany. Among other things, these interpellations point us to the dialogical exchanges that marked Black intellectual and creative production in the late antebellum period. They suggest how Wilson's own thinking, writing, and writing about thinking was deeply shaped by conversations with his interlocutors. Wilson and McCune Smith's correspondence also traffics in the homosociality of the bourgeois public sphere: Often directly addressing the newspaper's editor as "My Dear Douglass," they do not hesitate to triangulate him in their exchanges (Ethiop dares to say this; Communipaw dares to say that).

McCune Smith and Wilson's correspondence is itself worthy of a monograph, so here I'll only be able to characterize it in "broad strokes," to use a Wilsonian phrase. A practicing physician and pharmacist with a medical degree from the University of Glasgow, McCune Smith's columns as Communipaw show off his scholasticism and his cosmopolitanism. They also register his alignment with a growing internationalism and global solidarity movement that was building in the wake of the 1848 revolutions in Europe. While squarely situated within New York's Black elite, McCune Smith was on the side of labor, always reminding readers—as well as Wilson and Douglass—that the movement must center the needs and interests of the most marginalized: nominally free Black workers and enslaved people. McCune Smith's columns flex his own intellectual and cultural capital, but at the same time they insist that it will be the organization of the proletariat that will bring freedom to the masses.

Ethiop's columns are more "provincial" than McCune Smith's, and deliberately so. For example, in a column that discusses recent fads in fashion and music, he complains about the American fetishism of all things European, especially its culture and luxury commodities. Wilson's columns are also more American insofar as they center the workings and expansion of the national economy. Since in the United States, Ethiop argues, money rules everything, the struggle for liberation and elevation must be undertaken on economic grounds. Throughout the multiyear correspondence, he is unwavering in his focus on the importance of Black entrepreneurship, arguing that the elevation of the race is dependent on both the accumulation of wealth and the adoption of bourgeois values. Taken together, these columns are marked by a recurring confrontation between McCune Smith's idealism and Wilson's realism. McCune Smith was guilty of sometimes romanticizing the Black working class and fetishizing their supposed "sensuousness" and "primitiveness." Where McCune Smith valorizes a Black folksiness, Wilson often judges the folk, charging them with both laziness and profligacy. Ethiop also refuses to admit how anti-Black racism and discrimination impeded upward mobility at every turn.

Ethiop and Communipaw also try, at different points, to undermine the other's rhetorical authority. For example, Ethiop says he writes from a superior vantage point, observing New York from Brooklyn Heights, while McCune Smith writes "far away" in his "wigwam" in the "boggs of the Jerseys": "His wigwam is located far away among the boggs of the Jerseys—my hut is on Brooklyn heights. While he, with the great orb of day peering in his face, is compelled to strain his vision in taking a morning survey of Gotham, I, with that *bright Eye of the morning* in the back-ground, gilding beautifully all before me and around, have but to look down from my pleasant height upon that goodly city; witness its first day-break revel[l]ings; news boys croak out the merits of their respective papers."[31] Writing for a periodical sphere that increasingly privileged first-person, frontline accounts, Ethiop notes that he is closer to the action. His perspective of the city is also superior because it is an elevated one, looking down from above, while Communipaw is lambasted as an "Indian" writing from his lowly "wigwam." This jab also bears an interesting relationship to McCune Smith and Wilson's class politics. Ethiop subtly critiques Communipaw for being "distant" from the working people he claims to love and represent: It is Ethiop, not Communipaw, who can hear the "news boys croak[ing] out the merits of their respective papers." His mention of Communipaw's "wigwam" points to Indigenous presence in the Communipaw settlement, as well as to McCune Smith's own commitments to interracialism, but it's also a way of wielding anti-Native sentiments to mock his interlocutor.

In addition to covering current events from strikingly different perspectives, Wilson and McCune Smith theorize African Americans' relationship to both the economy and the broader cultural sphere. In one particularly rich column, Communipaw defines Blackness itself in aesthetic terms, saying African Americans are "an aesthetic people" with an "inborn love of art": "There is another element in our general character, little understood by those who would doctor us. We are, as a writer in *Putnam* states, an aesthetic people: we have an inborn love of art: how much this explains! Poor black humanity, too poor to have marbled halls and picture galleries of its own, cleaving to the walls and the ceilings and the halls where these things be, would rather be a door keeper in the temples of art, than a rawboned angular struggle with wiry independence!" Ethiop was not the only one developing a theory of art in a developing commercial sphere structured by inequality and racism. According to Communipaw, African Americans "cleave" to the walls and halls of arts institutions because they are "too poor to have marbled halls and picture galleries" of their own. As a people with a fervent "art-nature" but little access to the means of image production and exhibition, they will do anything to be in art's presence—even opting to be a lowly "door keeper" in the "temples of art" rather than working freely and independently. Communipaw's theorization of an almost essentialist "art-nature" is a fascinating moment that anticipates theories of the Black aesthetic as they would emerge during both the New Negro Renaissance and, later, the Black Arts Movement.[32] Communipaw goes on to suggest that Black refusals of industrial labor are directly connected to an inborn love of art: "Our industrial difficulty is accounted for. It was Athens, not Sparta, Italy, not Holland, which gave birth to the children of art: and today, if a stray artist be born in England or America, he must forsake the looms, the work shop dust, and the railroads, and go and eat Italian dirt. The reason why our youth do not learn trades, why our people are not mechanics, lies not in the difficulty of learning trades, or of pursuing them—no! It is in our essentially aesthetic or art-nature." Here the race's "art-nature" is associated with a guiltless refusal of capitalist labor. According to Communipaw, African Americans should not be blamed for their "industrial difficulty"; it is just that they have an inborn love of the beautiful, rather than the merely useful. Communipaw concludes not by trying to solve this conundrum—of Black people's love of art and lack of will to become industrial drudges—but by passing the baton to Ethiop. He asks, "But what are we to do with this natural, spiritual aesthetic being, the free black? I don't know, Mr. Editor: all I can hope to do is to describe this case: tell you what you have to deal with. *Ethiop*, living on Long Island, is *'rooty,'* and before the convention, perhaps he can *resuscitate* something which will be of service." Communipaw refers here to Ethiop's election as a delegate to the 1855 Colored Convention in Philadelphia, from where Ethiop reported on the conference proceedings for Douglass's paper. Communipaw and Ethiop would often leave these kinds of breadcrumb trails for each other. Sometimes they would decide to follow the trail; other times, they would choose to follow their own line of flight, working to steer the conversation in an entirely different direction. Perhaps unsurprisingly, Ethiop chooses not to respond to Communipaw's heady theories on art and Blackness in a work-obsessed society striated by racial discrimination and class division.

Late Antebellum Black Aesthetics and Intuitive Construction

As McCune Smith's treatise on Black "art-nature" shows, African American writers in the 1850s were not just experimenting with received literary forms; they were also developing their own aesthetic theories. Geoffrey Sanborn has written about William Wells Brown's preference for aesthetic forms drawn from the world of popular spectacle and mass attractions.[33] Michael Kelly says that a few years later, during the Civil War, Frederick Douglass was developing his own aesthetic theory in his lectures on photography.[34] Wilson was doing the same in "A Leaf from My Scrap Book" in *Autographs for Freedom*.

Communipaw and Ethiop also used the dialogic space of the newspaper to debate the role of art—and aesthetics more broadly—in the elevation and liberation of the race. I want to further suggest that a mode of intuitive construction was a central part of Black writing in this period, especially in periodical contexts. This way of working bears a fascinating comparison to what the Diotima School of Italian feminism called *affidamento*, or "entrustment," the idea that thought can only happen through the support and encouragement of another, or, in the terms of Cesare Casarino and Andrea Righi, "the practice of relying on another feminine figure in order to support the expression of one's desire."[35]

The argument I want to pursue here in relation to the dialogism of late antebellum Black writing is that the *expression* of intuition can only flourish through the support and affirmation of another, or others. Such affirmation is especially crucial in the contexts of a society built on heteropatriarchy, white supremacy, and the pernicious combination of anti-Black racism and sexism directed at Black women that Moya Bailey has labeled "misogynoir."[36] It can be difficult to trust oneself in a world that doesn't trust you. Or as the Milan's Women Bookstore Collective, one of the key spaces of Diotima's flourishing in the 1970s and 1980s, argued, "Authority is received originally from another human being who is in a position to give it, who has the authority to give. But she cannot have it if the person who needs to receive it does not acknowledge it in her."[37] This is a form of intuition that is deeply intersubjective and that, in fact, requires the support and encouragement of another to be made manifest in the world beyond one's individual mind.

Entrustment, then, is the process through which the subject comes to trust their own intuition in a society structured by dominance and subjugation. Entrustment further resonates with how Kevin Quashie has talked about girlfriends in Black feminist art, literature, and sociality, in which a singular and individual sense of self is replaced by a more fluid and communal understanding of identity, always developing and changing in relation to others.[38] It is also connected to how Audre Lorde theorizes the erotic, as a deep reservoir of intuitive knowledge and source of power that women have been trained to ignore and suppress.[39]

The perhaps unlikely leap I want to make here is from feminist theories of intuition and entrustment to the intertextual intimacies of McCune Smith, Wilson, and other writers in the period, which included Black women writing under pseudonyms. Women were more likely to publish writing cloaked in the protections of anonymity because of the dangers of exposure and violence in the public sphere. Intuitive construction is a framework particularly attuned to the material conditions under which Black authors composed writing for newspapers and magazines in the period. Produced in response to editorial deadlines, other forms of labor and demands on one's time, and conditions of social urgency, writing for periodicals had to be completed quickly and was thus guided by intuition. Periodical publications also depended on practices of entrustment, those forms of support and counsel from fellow correspondents and editors.

Elizabeth McHenry asks scholars to pay closer attention to what she calls the "workspaces" of African American literary production as a way of bringing into view the infrastructures of authorship and neglected genres that provided the scaffolding on which Jim Crow–era literary production was built.[40] I similarly want to suggest that we refocus around the material conditions of authorship for Black antebellum writers in order to better understand how the conditions of writing—the where, when, and how of composition—shaped the actual form of these works. Thinking about work conditions as the conditions of possibility for authorship in the period helps to illuminate, for example, why Delany's *Blake* takes such a radical turn in its second half. Swept up in the fervor of 1859, Delany traveled to the Niger Valley to explore and lay the groundwork for a Black settler colony organized under the auspices of the African Civilization Society in Wilson's Brooklyn. When texts are written under conditions of dislocation, precarity, and movement, we are more likely to find fissures, gaps, and breaks in narrative and plot.[41]

Black writing in the late antebellum period was defined not so much by the form of call and response as by the line of flight, in which a literary experiment or call is made and then picked up and further extended by another writer.[42] In other words, African American writing in the 1850s took shape through dynamic and collaborative chains of entrustment. For example, McCune Smith's "Heads of the Colored People" sketch series appeared in installments in *Frederick Douglass' Paper* from 1852 to 1854; Douglass extended "Heads" with his installation of an alternative picture gallery in his "Claims of the Negro" speech in 1854; and William J. Wilson expanded Douglass's gallery with his own speculative gallery in 1859. The Black sketch tradition emphasized provisional texts and "outline portraits" in the hopes that other writers-turned-collaborators would provide further shading and detail in their own writings. These writers regularly sparred with one another but also goaded each other on. They theorized Black art and politics in ways that are often fragmentary and open-ended. They encouraged each other to take the baton and run with it.

Feminist theories of intuition and entrustment offer one way into the method of construction in Black writing in the late antebellum period. Walter Benjamin's writings on creativity provides another. For Benjamin, children's creativity lies in their "capacity for inventive reception based on mimetic improvisation."[43] Not yet interpellated into the sedimented habitus of capitalist modernity and bourgeois culture, children translate perception and contemplation into "active transformation." They have not yet been taught to distrust their intuition (though much of parenting, even today, remains aimed at disciplining the child's intuitive connection to the world and natural ability to translate that connection into gestures, play, art, and other forms of construction). Commenting on the lack of scholarly commentary on the place of the child in Benjamin's philosophy, Buck-Morss writes, "Imagery of the child's world appears so persistently throughout Benjamin's opus that the omission of a serious discussion of its theoretical significance in practically all commentaries on Benjamin is remarkable—a symptom, perhaps, of precisely the repression of childhood and its cognitive modes which he considered a problem of the utmost political significance."[44] Benjamin is particularly drawn to the capacity of children to act fearlessly on the world ("children are absolute *monsters* of activity"). But most pressingly for my theorization of intuitive construction, Benjamin was fascinated by what Gershom Scholem described as the "yet undistorted world of the child and its creative imagination."[45] Indifferent to the "preformed world that adults have created" (the world of commodities and bourgeois respectability), children "do not so much imitate the works of adults as bring together, in the artifacts produced in play, materials of widely differing kinds in a new *intuitive relationship*."[46] Benjamin's interest in intuitive construction among children is particularly helpful for understanding the picture gallery's use of the fairy-tale tradition to build a whole world within the text, as well as the way it draws readers back again and again to the primary tools of artistic expression shared by both children and adults alike: pencil and paper. Especially in the speculative flights that make up the Black Forest fairy tale, we see Wilson experimenting with the principles of intuitive construction and their illumination of a world that is always being actively constructed and potentially transformed through play.

Wilson and McCune Smith made the most of the periodical format: The everydayness of the newspaper and the need for constant content opened a space in which they felt free to play with topic, style, and tone. The importance of satire and wit to these exchanges further lends them a kind of expansiveness and a casual jocularity. At the same time, the intuitive and dialogic compositions of Black masculine epistolatory cultures in the period were also connected to the exclusion and surveillance of Black women's writing and publication. Editorial control plagued Black women throughout the antebellum era: Eric Gardner, for example, has written about how newspapers like the *Christian Recorder* surveilled Black women's contributions through draconian editing, neglect, and exclusion.[47] Douglass and many other editors deliberately constructed Black newspapers as spaces of Black homosocial exchange. Contributions of women writers to periodicals were heavily edited, disciplined into sentimental forms, or rejected for publication. This is all to say that while masculine intuition was given relatively free range within the space of the newspaper, femme intuition was suppressed and surveilled. Black femme intuition can rarely be detected in these sources because it was not trusted.

At some level, writers like Douglass and Wilson knew that Black women's knowledge and materiality made their own expression possible. Remember that Wilson wrote as Ethiop as an allusion to the poetic genius Phillis Wheatley. In "Claims of the Negro, Ethnologically Considered," Douglass acknowledged his own indebtedness to the maternal line of reason: "Intellect is uniformly derived from the maternal side."[48] The sacred memory and impression of Douglass's mother also frames his 1845 and 1855 narratives. It is much more difficult to locate dialogic networks of Black women's published writing in the late antebellum period, although they were the bedrock on which men's homosocial exchanges were built. Black women's entrustment and cocreation must be located in other sites of exchange, including literary societies, schools, and the parlor room. In opposition to the intimacies registered in places like Black women's friendship albums, the comradery of Black men's writing is more appropriately defined by a kind of distant flirtation and, at times, with the performance of critical detachment. This is a space where writers inspire each other to experiment with form, satire, and wit, but rarely change each other's minds. The exchanges of Wilson and McCune Smith, in this way, might be understood as being closer to how biographers Howard Eiland and Michael W. Jennings describe Benjamin's relationship to his interlocutors as a Kantian "unsocial sociability" rooted in a "dialectic of solitude and community."[49] This is a "friendship of friends who maintain distance in their relations."[50] This is all to say that Black women's contributions and thought thrummed underneath the Black masculine print sphere and made it possible, even when their labor wasn't visible on the page.

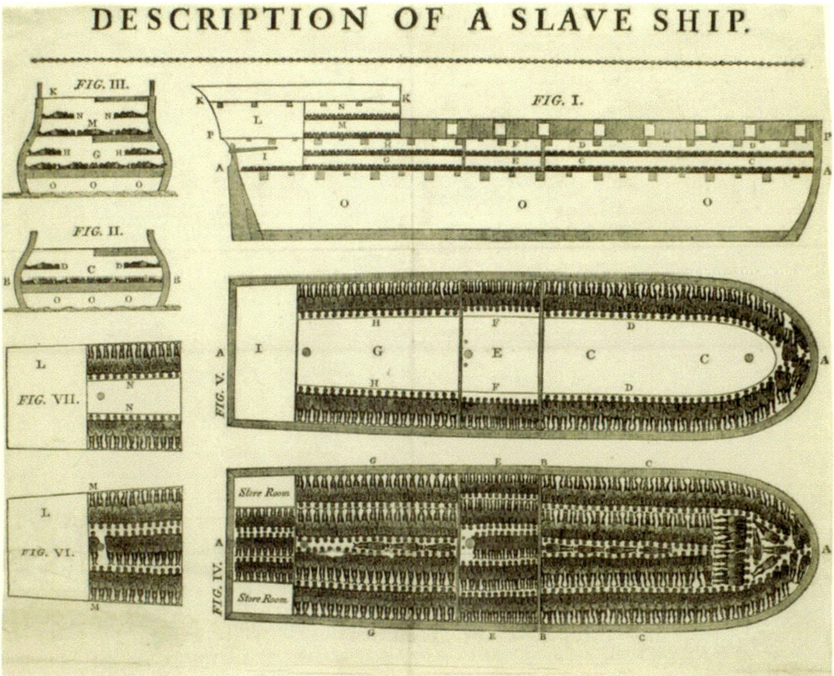

1 *Description of a Slave Ship* (London: James Phillips, for the London Committee of the Society for Effecting the Abolition of the Slave Trade, 1789).

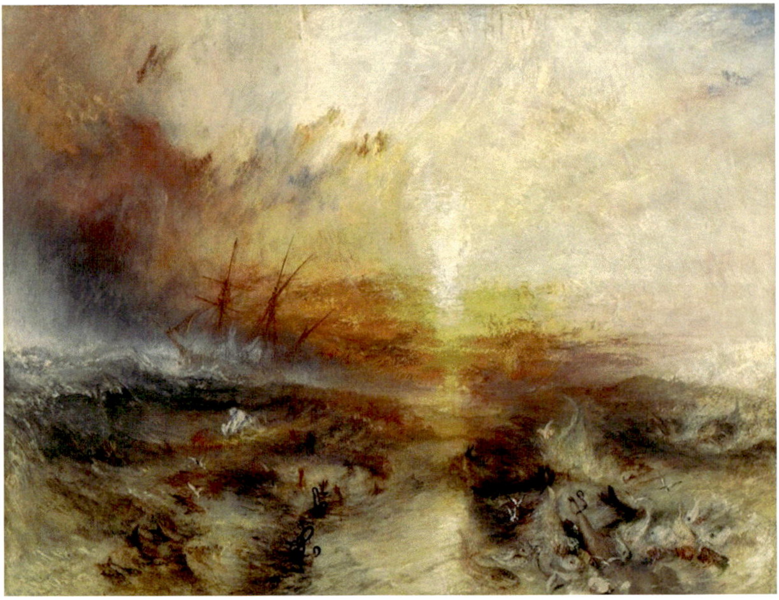

2 J. M. W. Turner, *Slave Ship (Slavers Throwing Overboard the Dead and Dying, Typhoon Coming On)*, 1840. Oil on canvas, 35¾ × 48¼ in. Museum of Fine Arts, Boston, Henry Lilly Pierce Fund.

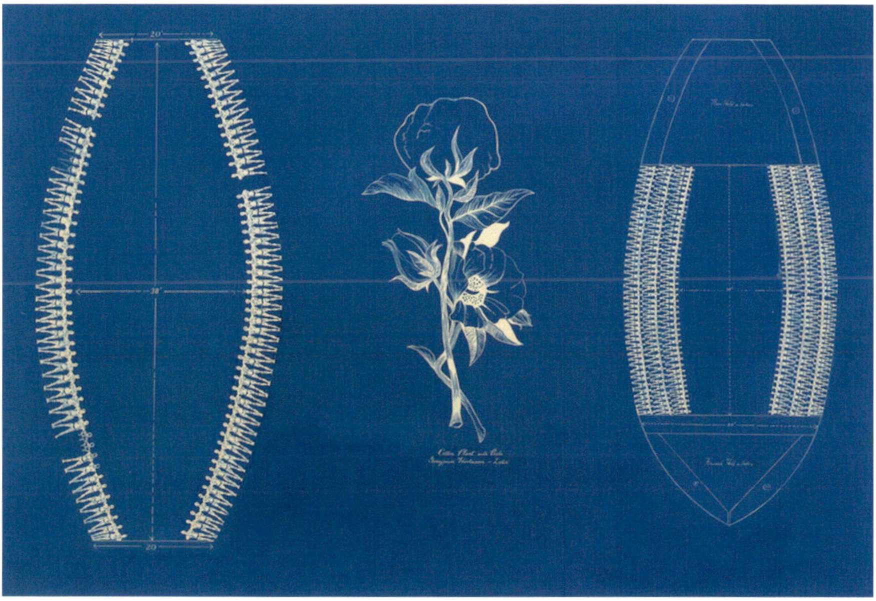

3 Malcolm Bailey, *Untitled, 1969*, 1969. Acrylic on composition board, 48 × 72 in. Whitney Museum of American Art, New York; purchase, with funds from the Larry Aldrich Foundation Fund.

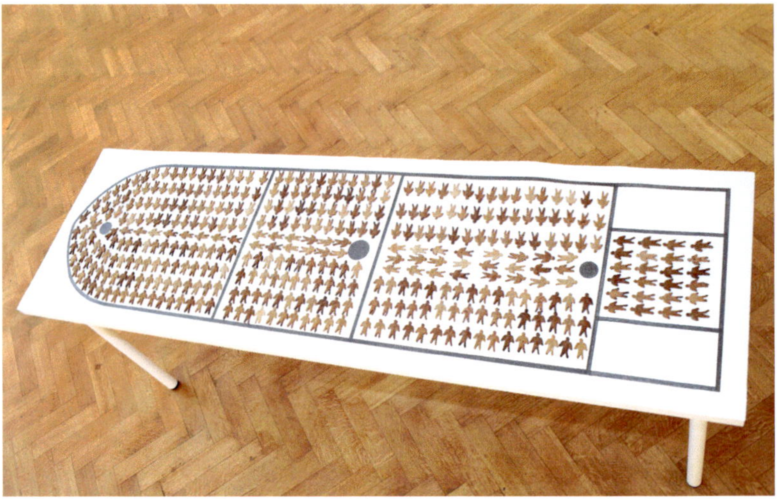

4 Mary Evans, *Gingerbread*, 2012. Mixed media. Tiwani Contemporary, London.

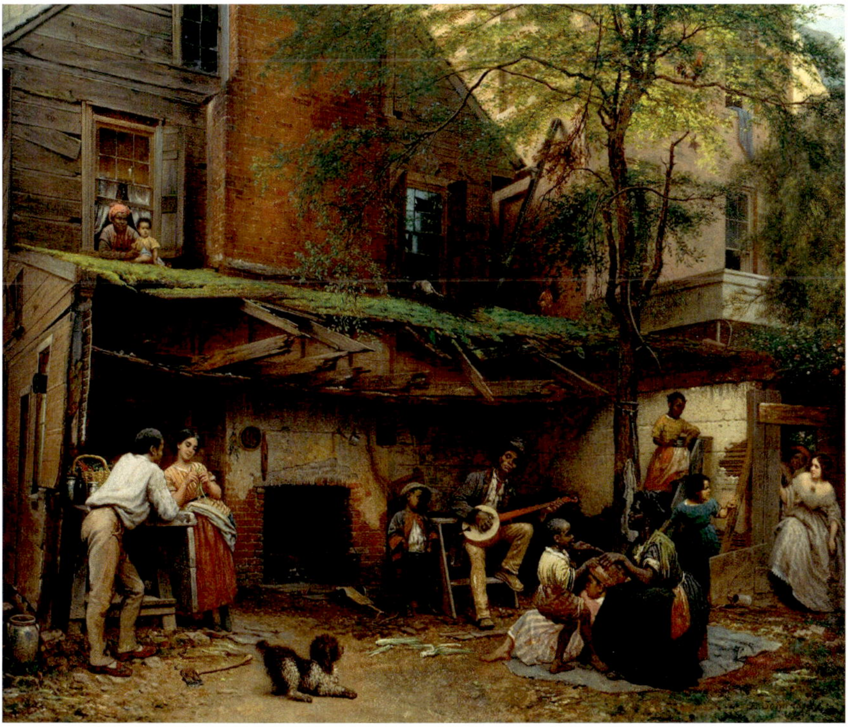

5 Eastman Johnson, *Negro Life at the South*, 1859. Oil on canvas, 18¼ × 24⅛ in. Johnson's painting appeared the same year as the "Afric-American Picture Gallery." High Museum of Art, Atlanta, purchase with funds from the Fine Art Collectors with leadership gifts from Mr. and Mrs. Henry Schwob, Mr. and Mrs. Terry Stent, Mr. and Mrs. Austin P. Kelley, Mr. and Mrs. John L. Huber, Dr. and Mrs. Gerald M. Stapleton, Mr. and Mrs. Noel Wadsworth, and the Collections Council Acquisition Fund, and funds from the Winter Family Foundation, and through prior acquisitions.

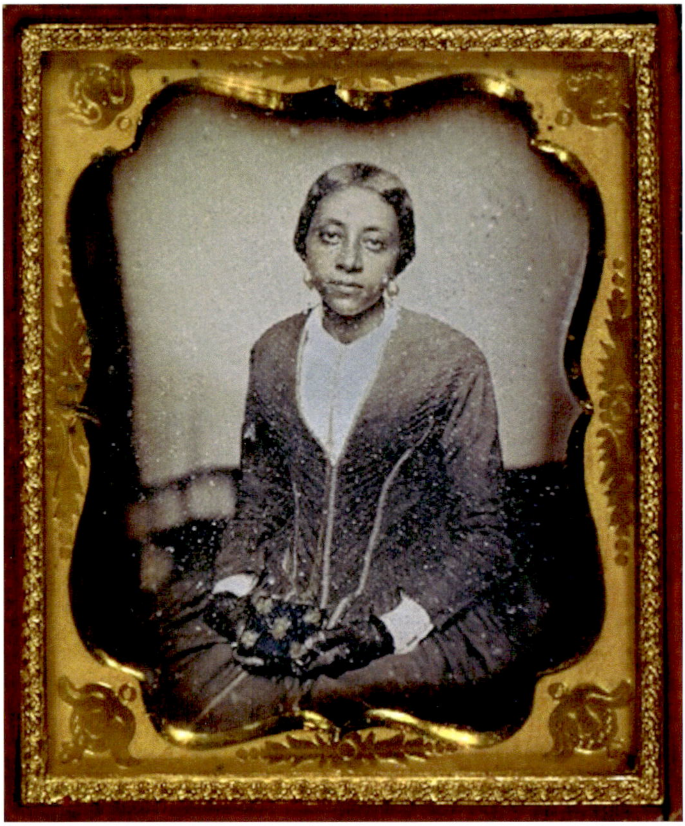

6 Augustus Washington, Unidentified sitter, 1855. Daguerreotype. American Colonization Society Records, Library of Congress, Washington, DC.

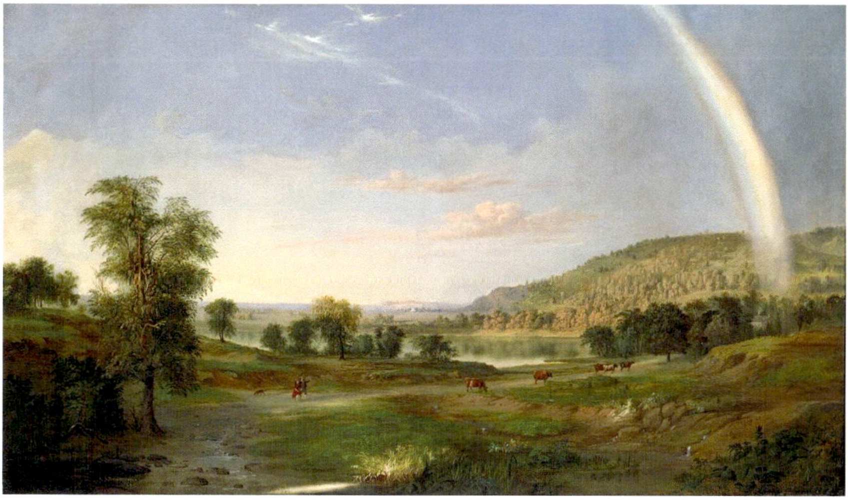

7 Robert Duncanson, *Landscape with Rainbow*, 1859. Oil on canvas, 30 × 52¼ in. Painted by Duncanson the same year the "Afric-American Picture Gallery" was published. Smithsonian American Art Museum, Washington, DC.

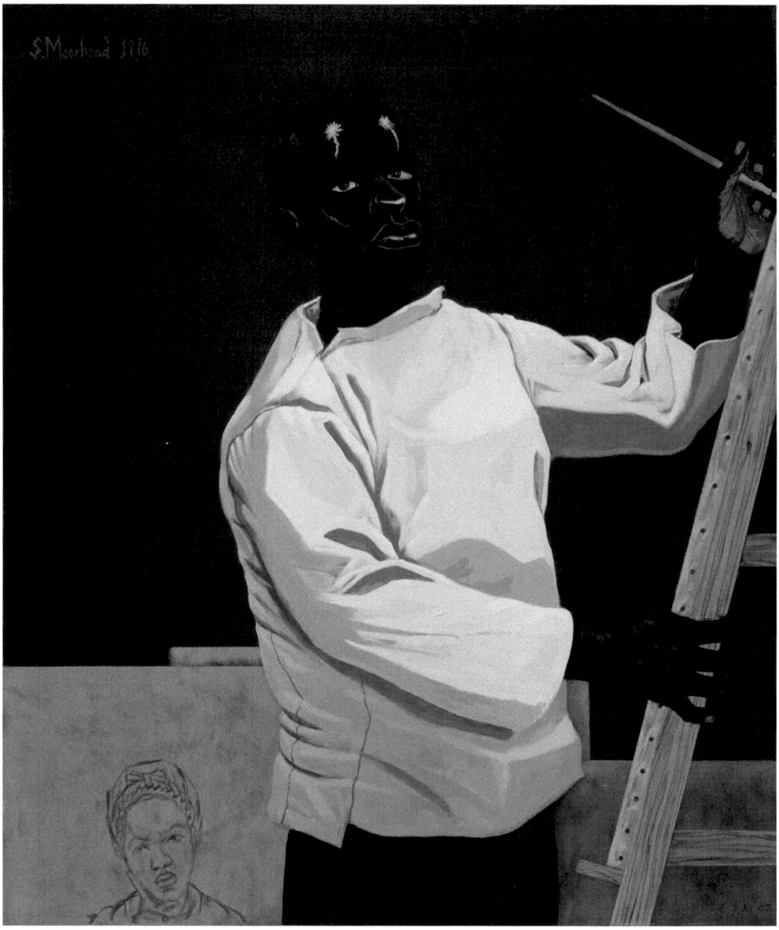

8 Kerry James Marshall, *Scipio Moorhead, Portrait of Himself, 1776*, 2007. Acrylic on PVC panel, 28 × 22 in. Private Collection.

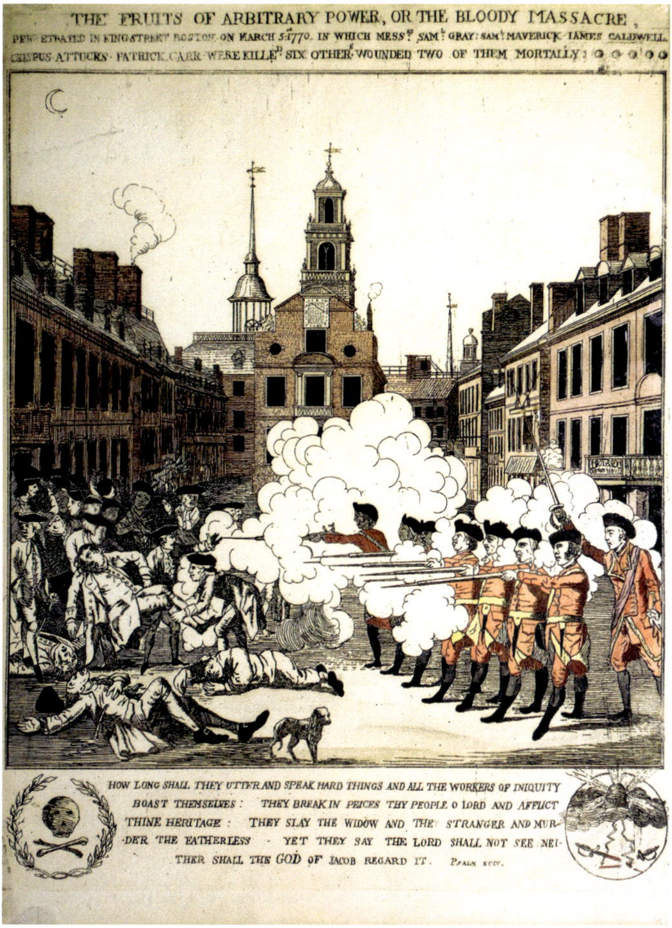

9 Henry Pelham, *Fruits of Arbitrary Power, or the Bloody Massacre*, 1770. Hand-colored engraving. American Antiquarian Society, Worcester, Massachusetts.

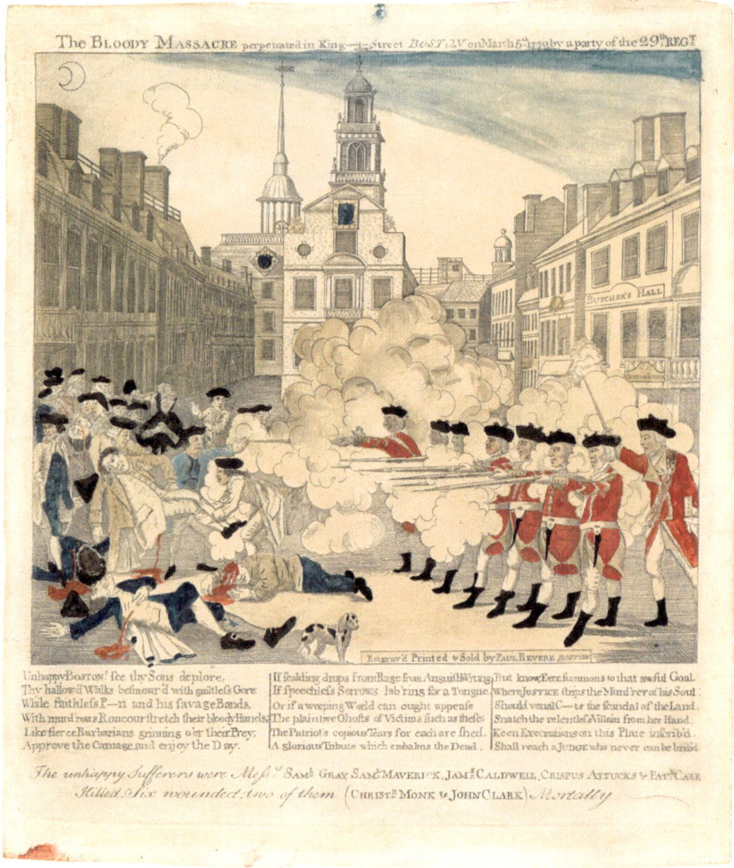

10 Paul Revere, *The Boston Massacre*, 1770. Hand-colored engraving, after Pelham's engraving. Metropolitan Museum of Art, New York, Gift of Mrs. Russell Sage, 1910.

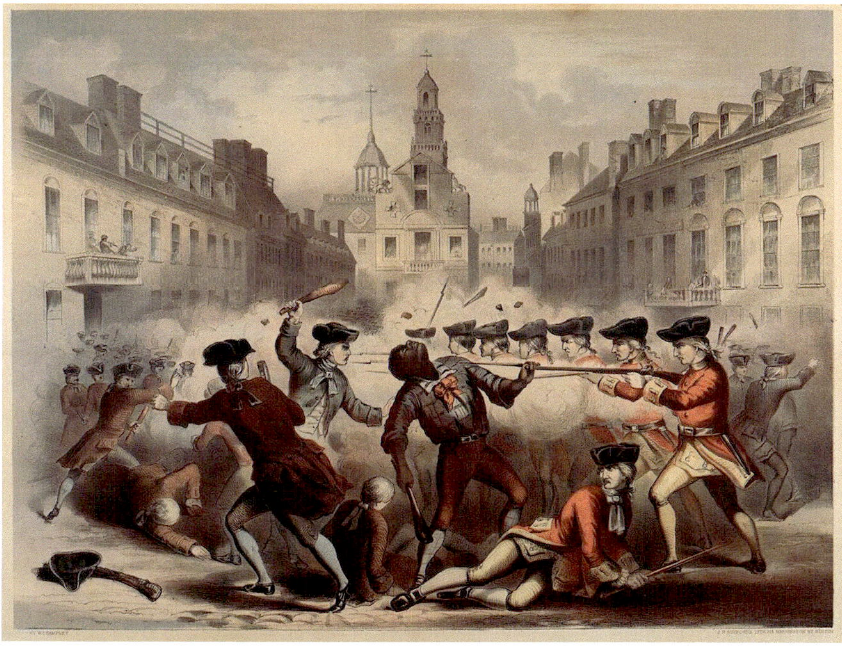

11 J. H. Bufford, after a drawing by W. L. Champney, *Boston Massacre, March 5th, 1770* (Boston: Henry Q. Smith, 1856). Chromolithograph, 17¾ × 24 in. Boston Athenaeum, Boston.

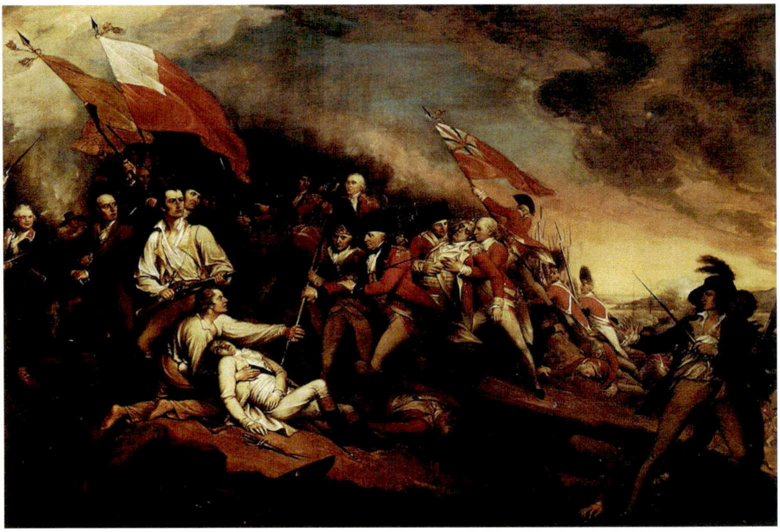

12 John Trumbull, *The Death of General Warren at the Battle of Bunker's Hill, June 17, 1775*, 1834. Oil on canvas, 72½ × 108 in. Wadsworth Atheneum, Hartford; purchased by Daniel Wadsworth and members of the Atheneum Committee.

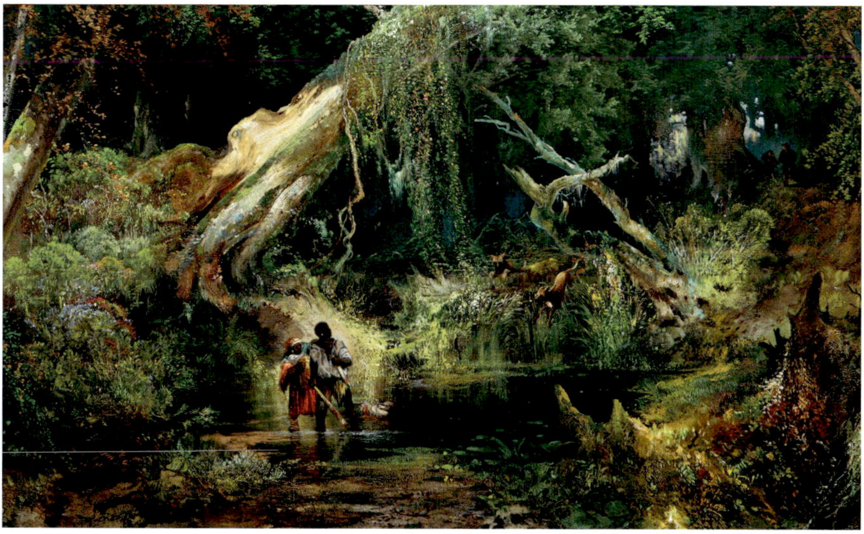

13 Thomas Moran, *Slave Hunt, Dismal Swamp, Virginia*, 1861–62. Oil on canvas, 34 × 44 in. Philbrook Museum of Art, Tulsa, Gift of Laura A. Clubb.

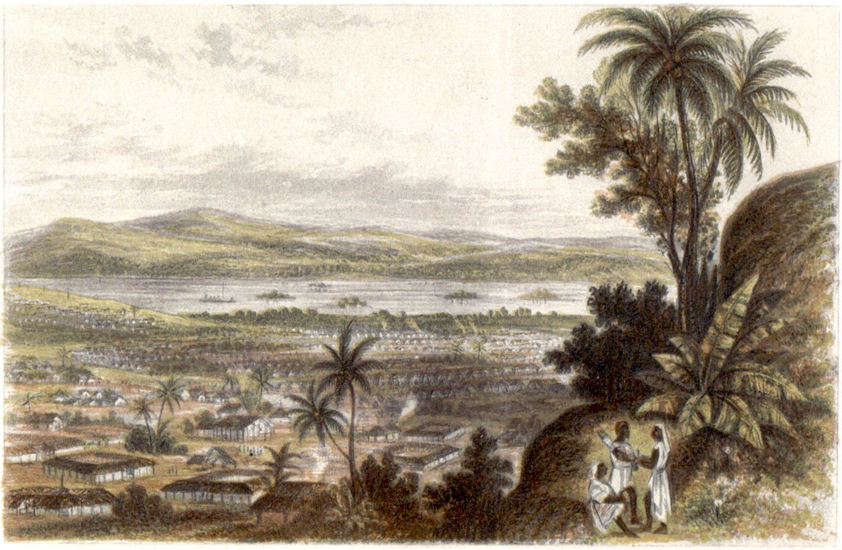

14 Sarah Parker, *Abbeokuta; or, Sunrise Within the Tropics: An Outline of the Origin and Progress of the Yoruba Mission* (New York: Robert Carter and Brothers, 1854), frontispiece.

3

"Sung Their Praise to Listening Worlds"

TWO ETHIOPS COMMUNING ACROSS TIME AND SPACE

> I had just finished the last sketch, and wrapped myself up in the happy consciousness of its justness, my old mood stealing over me, my mind traversing back to the days when Banneker lived and told of the stars and of the rising suns, and Wheatl[e]y sung their praise to listening worlds, when a loud rap at the door brought me to a sense of the present moment and to my feet.
>
> **Ethiop**, "Afric-American Picture Gallery," *Anglo-African Magazine*, July 1859

> The distracted person, too, can form habits.
>
> **Walter Benjamin**, "The Work of Art in the Age of Mechanical Reproduction"

One thing the "Afric-American Picture Gallery" does, beyond plot and theme, is to register the transformation of the experience of viewing fine art under the conditions of industrialization, urbanization, and the beginnings of mass culture and consumption in the mid-nineteenth century. Ethiop wants to become absorbed in the works before him, but he is constantly being distracted by life beyond the frame: by the pull of the city, by interrupting visitors, by the technologies of a new industrial age, and by the disorientation produced by daily acts of racial terror, intimidation, and kidnapping in his beloved Gotham.[1] The series is peppered with moments of distraction and of attention being led astray from works of art that are, according to Romantic models, supposed to absorb the viewer and provide the grounds for an immersive aesthetic experience.[2] Aesthetic absorption does finally occur in the series, but it happens, tellingly, outside the Picture Gallery itself, when Ethiop journeys through a mythic Black Forest to visit the cave gallery of a Black artist and hermit, living and producing art off the grid. As I explore more fully in chapter 4, the Black Forest quest represents a significant detour in the series itself, breaking with the form of a gallery tour that structures earlier installments of the series. But interestingly, the narrative detour happens through a moment not of distraction but of intense absorption in a work of art: Prior to his journey to the Black Forest, Ethiop had been looking at a landscape painting of the Black Forest that had been brought into the picture gallery by the gallery's "boy," Tom. Ethiop looked so deeply and so carefully at the work that the next installment finds him sucked into the painting, traversing the very landscape he had been viewing in the previous installment. This is, among other things, a fascinating moment that suggests that distraction and absorption are two sides of the same coin. My own writing on the Picture Gallery finds itself similarly traversing the Möbius strip of absorption and distraction: The gallery at times opens onto a dizzying array of social contexts, intertexts, and histories; at other points, it feels so idiosyncratic and so hermetically sealed (as when readers are locked up in the cave gallery) that there's nothing to do but focus.

Let's hope that what Benjamin says is true: "The distracted person, too, can form habits."[3] Inspired by the flights of imagination and the dialectic of attention and distraction that animate Wilson's text, in this chapter I take a detour of my own, turning to a sustained consideration of the poetry of Phillis Wheatley, as cast through her arresting representation in the Picture Gallery. I follow Wilson's description of Wheatley's famous frontispiece portrait, a crucial ekphrastic freeze-frame moment that slows down the kinetic pace of the narrative and asks readers to meditate on the precious life and sacred art of an enslaved teenager poet from eighteenth-century Boston. I use this chapter to flesh out the textual relationship Wilson builds with Wheatley, a sacred communion with another Black artist forged across time and space. I begin not with Wilson but with Wheatley's ideas about the intermedial and communal nature of Black art as they were being registered in her poetry, a poetry written in the contexts of intense surveillance and isolation that nonetheless sought precious—if often fleeting—connection to Black community through the multisensory dimensions of poetic verse itself. Wheatley's poems bring Black art and Black artists into relation through play with the senses and through an experimental mixing and melding of different genres and forms. In this way Wheatley's poems resonate with what Tina Campt identifies as the particular *hapticity* of contemporary Black art and life.[4] This mode of solidifying community through haptic connection would also show up in the dialogic and intermedial experiments of Wilson and his intellectual cohort in the 1850s; they are also on full display in Wilson's own ekphrastic treatment of Wheatley in the Picture Gallery.

Wilson's inclusion of a "Head of Phillis Wheatley" in his speculative gallery was part of a broader memorialization of the poet in antebellum culture. Margaretta Matilda Odell, a Wheatley family descendant, in 1834 published *Memoir of Poems of Phillis Wheatley*, a highly biased work reflecting family interest and white supremacy that nonetheless did much to recirculate Wheatley and her verse into the 1840s and 1850s.[5] A series of lithographs and visual reproductions of Wheatley's portrait also appeared in literary biographies and other print formats in the 1850s. And of course, she was a consistent reference point in the Black press, appearing in the *Freedom's Journal* as early as the 1820s. When William Wells Brown published his collective biography of the race, *The Black Man*, in 1863, his portrayal of Wheatley relied on Wilson's ekphrastic description of the poet in the Picture Gallery. *The Black Man* was published by none other than the *Anglo-African Magazine*'s editor and printer Thomas Hamilton, on "48 Beekman Street" in New York. Wells Brown devotes almost the entirety of the entry not to laying out Wilson's life history and accomplishments, but to reproducing Wilson's account of Wheatley's portrait in the Picture Gallery, including its physiognomy-inspired description of Wheatley's face and profile. Just as Wilson does in the Picture Gallery, Wells Brown uses the *Anglo-African* itself as a kind of archive and as fodder for inspiration, pointing to the deep citationality of Black writing at this time, as well as the ways that Hamilton may have himself mediated and been involved with the text's production, drawing from his own beloved *Anglo-African* as source text. The entry also exemplifies the fascinating entangling of Wheatley with Wilson himself, within and beyond the frame of the Picture Gallery, a historical and aesthetic entanglement I explore throughout this chapter. This chapter concludes with the Picture Gallery's revision of visual representations of Crispus Attucks to explore Wilson's broader participation in the memorialization of Black heroes from the Revolutionary era to animate a new era of Black militancy in the years preceding the Civil War.

Ethiop in Drag

In a tantalizing moment in *The Practice of Citizenship: Black Politics and Print Culture in the Early United States*, Derrick Spires suggests that Wilson's Ethiop persona is an allusion not only to Ethiopia but also to the colonial poet of diaspora and revolution, Phillis Wheatley.[6] As Ivy Wilson has noted, African Americans in the late eighteenth and nineteenth century invoked Ethiopia to signal the profound contributions made by Africans to human civilization, the arts, and sciences. He further notes that Wheatley placed herself in that regal tradition of citation by way of Ethiopia even though she was from West rather than East Africa.[7] Indeed, in "To the University of Cambridge, in New-England," a poem that circulated widely in print and manuscript and was strategically placed near the beginning of her 1773 book, *Poems on Various Subjects, Religious and Moral*, Wheatley emphasizes her status as "An *Ethiop*" while warning readers about the mortal danger of sin:

> Ye blooming plants of human race divine,
> An *Ethiop* tells you 'tis your greatest foe;
> Its transient sweetness turns to endless pain,
> And in immense perdition sinks the soul. (Lines 27–30)[8]

In moments like this one, Wheatley plays on white readers' racist assumptions about the inferiority and wickedness of Africans, ideas that were deeply entrenched in both Enlightenment and Christian discourse in the eighteenth century. Here in "To the University of Cambridge, in New-England," as in so much of her verse, Wheatley's religious lesson doubles as a moral condemnation of the community in which she was forced to live and write: If a lowly "*Ethiop*" knows and understands the importance of avoiding a life of sin, then clearly Anglo elites should too.[9] Because the poem explicitly addresses incoming students at Harvard, the politics of age are also at play here: Readers knew that the poet was an enslaved teenager (stolen from her family in "Afric's happy seat" around the age of seven, forced across the Atlantic Ocean, kept in captivity by a merchant family in Boston, and denied a formal education), and her authoritative tone and admonishment of white boys at Harvard remains a kind of historical scandal that has the capacity to jolt twenty-first-century readers.[10] It delights this one. These young men were, after all, essentially her peers, and they included young enslavers and soon-to-be enslavers, the kind of people, like the people in her household and in her neighborhood, who kept her in "silken fetters."[11] Among the sins she counts are their careless inattention to their studies and their reckless refusal to treasure the educational privileges their station, class, and color affords them. The poem opens with a reminder of the poet's own life circumstances, which necessitate the presence of muses to "assist" her "pen." But these lines also include a savvy reminder of the link between Africa and the birth of Western civilization in Egypt, as well as a reminder of her background as a child stolen into slavery:

> While an intrinsic ardor prompts to write,
> The muses promise to assist my pen;
> 'Twas not long ago since I left my native shore
> The land of errors, and *Egyptian* gloom. (Lines 1–4)

In one particularly biting moment, she warns these students, finger wagging, to "Improve your privileges while they stay," pointing to the immense amount of privilege that has enabled their acceptance at such an institution (privileges not shared by Wheatley), while reminding them that their "stay" at Harvard, like their "stay" in life, will be fleeting. In other words, an admonishing Wheatley recommends that students get right with God. Life is temporary, and death, like Christ, is the great equalizer of privilege and opportunity.[12]

Wheatley also brings Harvard itself within the purview of her critique: After all, the title of this powerfully didactic poem addresses not the students of the University of Cambridge but the institution itself ("To the University of Cambridge, in New-England"). Wheatley was thus already in 1773 writing about the politics of diversity, inclusion, and exclusion in America's university system, an institution she knew was filled with enslavers and was endowed by blood money from the slave trade. The poem doubles as a statement about her exclusion from the university because of her race and gender even though she was locally known as a genius. In addressing the school directly, and in being commissioned to write a poem addressed to students, we see Wheatley not fully excluded, but temporarily included long enough for her to directly address incoming students. As Joanna Brooks has so compellingly shown, white elites, especially white women, relentlessly interpellated Wheatley into the networks of bourgeois feeling and performance of sentiment that were central to the cementing of social connection and polite society in the period, compelling her to perform emotional labor for them: to mourn for them, to instruct them, and, in this case, to scold their children.[13]

Drawing on an Enlightenment association between Blackness and melancholia, white women were especially keen to have Wheatley grieve for them, soliciting elegies when children or family members passed.[14] When Wheatley uses the term *sable*, she is drawing on a tangle of associations, as the term refers at once to the color black, to darkness, and to "black clothing, especially as a symbol of mourning."[15] Looking forward to Du Bois's veil and Paul Laurence Dunbar's mask, Wheatley shrouds herself in mourning garments again and again in her poems, an ambivalent gesture that at times seems to be foisted on her by white society and at other times feels like a garment she pulls over herself, shrouding herself in black/Blackness to put a barrier between herself and prying eyes. When Wilson installs Wheatley in his gallery, he also draws on this history of Wheatley and veiling. In describing her portrait he says, "The whole make-up of this face is an index of healthy intellectual powers, combined with an active temperament, over which has fallen a slight tinge of religious pensiveness."[16]

Wheatley uses the first poems in her book to name herself as an "Ethiop," a moniker that sits at odds with and even challenges her appellation as a "Negro-Servant" in the front matter and frontispiece of the collection. More than a simple surrogate for a racial nomenclature, Wheatley takes on Ethiop as a poetic persona. Her self-naming in these opening poems is also a significant act of renaming, given that her name of origin was stripped from her when she was stolen and sold into slavery: Her master and mistress named her "Phillis" after the slave ship that "brought" her to the Americas. Wilson's Ethiop was also no mere nom de plume: Not only did Wilson write under the pen name Ethiop in Black periodicals in the 1850s and 1860s; in the Picture Gallery, he also transforms his writerly persona into a literary character.[17] Mirroring his own interests in aesthetics and the illumination of writing-as-process, always forged in relation to other artistic mediums and genres, Ethiop doubles as a literary avatar for Wilson. Like the proliferating simulacra of images across the Picture Gallery, Ethiop circulates as an uncanny double of the author himself. Furthermore, by taking on and breathing new life into Wheatley's own poetic avatar of "Ethiop," Wilson destabilizes the authority of the author (anticipating poststructuralist announcements of the death of the author and asking us to think instead about what Foucault described as the author-function) while challenging androcentric literary authorization in the period. Rather than imbuing himself with authority through the rhetorical hallmarks of self-possessed Black manhood (Douglass) or the tropes and conventions of an American literature that was increasingly consolidating itself as a coherent national tradition (the American Renaissance), Ethiop instead reroutes literary influence through a network of Black writing and experimentation that begins with a young African woman.

Importantly, though, that young woman is never quite herself—never gives us her whole, real self—even in her most confessional verse. In other words, both Wheatley and Wilson experiment with language and forge critique from the protective cover of their Ethiop avatars.

Wilson does not position Wheatley as a kind of literary beginning, or even as a literary foremother (as W. E. B. Du Bois would several years later), but as a site of becoming, from which his own writing takes inspiration.[18] That inspiration includes a snippet of his own verse that he composes about Wheatley and places after his description of her portrait in his gallery. Black experimental aesthetics in the 1850s routinely jettisoned literary models of singular genius in favor of a model that understood Black writing to be something forged sometimes in collaborative community, sometimes in contentious dissensus, but always in relation. Even in the Black masculine epistolatory cultures in which Wilson participated and about which Radiclani Clytus has brilliantly elaborated, writers did not adhere to conventions of originality, genius, and pure origins.[19] Black writing instead takes shape and theorizes itself as a site of recursive and dialogic production, endlessly growing not in linear models but in rhizomatic structures that diverge from normative forms of literary influence, inheritance, and genealogy.

Writing in the context of a growing proto-Black nationalist ethos that deployed Ethiopia as a broad, imaginative frame for political desire and even longing, Wilson's use of "Ethiop" also riffs on the writer's participation in Black emigration debates in the 1850s.[20] Somewhat paradoxically, Wilson forwarded his positions *against* African emigration while writing as Ethiop. I also want to signal Wilson's use of "Afric" in the "Afric-American Picture Gallery" here, since "Afric" appears in several of Wheatley's poems. The "Afric-American Picture Gallery," like the *Anglo-African* itself, was experimenting with racial nomenclature as a way to forge new relations and new horizons for Blackness—in the midst of, and possibly as a challenge to—the consolidation of a politically legible model of racial identity as it was being mobilized and circulated by white abolitionists in the years leading up to the Civil War.[21] Here Wilson looks to Wheatley and the nimble ways she experiments with a multifaceted range of descriptors for Blackness, creating, in the process, new affective and political registers for Black art.

Wilson's donning of his Ethiop persona is also a form of cross-gendered literary drag and performance, linking to both the bohemian dimensions of Wilson's writing and to the Black antebellum epistolatory cultures in which Wilson participated. Taking Ethiop as his pen name, Wilson participated in American newspaper cultures that trafficked in irony, wit, and sparring between columnists that echoed back to Wheatley's Revolutionary period and continued to be an object of interest for Black militants like Wilson, McCune Smith, and William Nell (author of the 1855 book *The Colored Patriots of the American Revolution*). By writing in drag as Wheatley's poetic persona, Ethiop, he was also reminding readers of the dangers of the public sphere—and the dangers of publishing—for Black subjects across gendered identity and expression. Wilson writing in drag *as* Wheatley, moreover, is an invitation to further explore the queer dimensions of the picture gallery itself, including the text's interest in "reading," dragging, and other forms of playful, extravagant banter.

Throughout the Picture Gallery, Wilson also draws Wheatley into the orbit of a vibrant culture of memorialization, in which African Americans in the antebellum period venerated Black heroes from the Revolutionary era to inspire their own struggles. Indeed, Wilson includes Wheatley in a pantheon of Black war heroes alongside figures like Crispus Attucks and Toussaint; in so doing, it draws out the militancy of Wheatley's poetry, as well as its attunements to the politics of war, race, and slavery. Indeed, Wheatley's neoclassical evangelical verse was no poetry of polite decorum and genuflection. It is strikingly—almost shockingly—direct, shaped by a didacticism that was characteristic of Calvinist verse in the late eighteenth century, but that took on more radical dimensions when wielded by an enslaved African teenager. Wheatley's poetry has no interest in the art of persuasion; instead it is characterized by a militantly direct mode of address. Her stunning rhetorical authority was authorized by an evangelical culture that was deeply didactic and, while barring women from the clergy, sometimes endowed them with the power to informally serve as spiritual guides and pedagogues. Wheatley's stern didacticism and the rhetorical power she wields over white people was thus, in part, made allowable because she placed herself within a tradition of female "poet-minister[s]" who acted as arms of evangelical instruction and didacticism.[22]

Ultimately, Wheatley uses the authority of the evangelical "poet-minister" and turns it into a strategy of Black feminist insurgency. Indeed, Wheatley's poetry took no prisoners. I want to think seriously about Wheatley writing on the cusp of war and mass death in the colonies. Poems like "To His Excellency General Washington" explicitly place her within a tradition of Revolutionary War writing, but, more broadly, she took up themes of war and revolution to forge a Black militant poetics that sought ground, territory, and tactics on a different, often ethereal, plane, and that used the language of national independence to imagine a Black freedom unfettered from the nation itself.[23]

Here again is an important connection to William J. Wilson, whose writing was also shaped by the accelerating tempos and intensification of the political atmosphere amid the coming of the Civil War, even though those themes are not always registered at the level of plot. In other words, both Wilson and Wheatley are linked through their engagement with a poetics of Black militancy and war, even when their work seems more focused on questions of aesthetic representation and the powers of imagination. By including Wheatley in his gallery of Black excellence, Wilson commemorates Wheatley as a hero of the Revolutionary era, and as a lodestar for Black activists living through another historical moment of social upheaval and political transformation.

Wheatl(e)y Communing

Writing amid enslavement, surveillance, and war, Wheatley also sought connection and communion with other Black artists. Through her poetry, she engaged in the crucial imaginative terrain of liberation that Robin D. G. Kelley calls freedom dreaming.[24] Like Wilson and his correspondents, Wheatley was invested in how Black people could inspire and amplify each other's work in a colony and then nation that denied them humanity, education, and access to one other. As Wendy Warren has discussed, slavery in New England was for many a profoundly isolating experience, especially for enslaved people living in rural areas apart from any sense of family or community.[25] That experience of service in the context of excruciating isolation would continue to appear in Black writing in New England right up until the beginning of the Civil War, especially in Harriet Wilson's 1859 narrative *Our Nig*, a searing portrait of Black indentured servitude as slavery by another name. Forced isolation is a powerful tool of political suppression, as we know from the history of prisons and solitary confinement. It was also a primary way that the "liberal" North maintained social control over African Americans; Northerners were particularly anxious about communication between enslaved and free people. Given this culture of isolation, surveillance, and silencing, it's incredibly significant when we find glimpses of Wheatley talking directly about her kidnapping, dreaming about the significance of freedom of the mind, soaring through the sky, and, in some moments, hoping for and writing to possible Black readers and fellow artists.[26]

And Black artists, in turn, sought connection with Wheatley. In 1778 the enslaved poet Jupiter Hammon, writing from Hartford, Connecticut, penned a poetic hymn addressed to the young poet, although it's unclear whether Wheatley ever knew of its existence. In this poem of evangelical instruction and direct address, Hammon encourages Wheatley in her efforts to become closer to God through adoration, devotion, and the perfection of her craft: "Come you, Phillis, now aspire / And seek the living God / So step by step thou mayst go higher / Till perfect in the word" (9.1–4).[27] Hammon also positions *himself* as a devoted follower of Christ through verses that simultaneously cite biblical passages and Wheatley's poems. A fascinating work authorized simultaneously by the divinity of God and the divinity of Wheatley herself (that "pious youth"), Hammon's poem is thus an exegetical exercise that sanctifies Black art and artists in communion through Christ's sacrifice and blessing. By echoing lines from Wheatley's own poems like "On Being Brought from Africa to America," Hammon also identifies himself as a living Black reader of Wheatley's poetry. This is a singular moment in American poetics where an enslaved poet speaks to another enslaved poet. Hammon, like Wilson, also sought connection through the poet's stylization of herself as an "Ethiop," referring to her as an "Ethiopian poetess."

Hammon communes with Wheatley through an elaborate structure of poetic citation, but he also hopes they will meet in heaven: "Dear Phillis, seek for heaven's joys / Where we do hope to meet" (17.3–4). We see something similar in Wheatley's correspondence with Obour Tanner, an enslaved woman and Christian living in Newport, Rhode Island. Separated by geographic distance and the innumerable constraints placed on Black mobility in the period, Wheatley and Tanner talk extensively about their meeting in heaven. Yet in her correspondence with Tanner, we can feel Wheatley using both artistic expression and the language of Christian piety as modes that might join her in communion with other Africans in *this* life. Tara Bynum's exquisite analysis of the Tanner-Wheatley letters emphasizes the forms of friendship that were articulated between these two women through the language of religious devotion and blessed fellowship.[28]

Wheatley, Hammon, and Tanner all used writing to establish sacred communion with one another, but those connections were often precarious, contingent on white mediation, and virtual. Hammon's "Address to Miss Phillis Wheatly" sanctifies and honors Wheatley's poetry, but it also hints at the fragility of connection in this moment of profound social isolation for Africans in New England. The poet's name is misspelled on the published broadside: Hammon's poem is addressed not to "Wheatley" but to "Wheatly."

Moments like this one register the fragility of Black artistic connection in an enslaving and surveilling society. It's also significant that Hammon can imagine meeting only in the afterlife, a theme that resonates with the evangelical preoccupations of the period but that also says something about how slavery worked not only through natal disconnection but also through the ongoing disruption and severing of kinship and community.[29] In a crucial and beautifully evocative meditation on Wheatley in a world of Black friendship—a world in which she wouldn't have had to always be thinking about her enslavement—Tara Bynum notes, "Wheatley's letters document a collective worship and reveal a friendship that asks us to consider what pleasure and friendship might look like to two enslaved women in New England. . . . Here are two women who understand that their mutual friendship is a friendship between one another and with God."[30] Wilson, too, would seek to make intimate connection with Wheatley, while at the same time signifying his distance from her, addressing her as "Oh! Wheatly" in his ode addressed to her in the Picture Gallery.

Like Hammon, Wheatley would use her poetry and access to a publication platform to hail and connect with another living Black artist in New England. Her *Poems on Various Subjects, Religious and Moral* includes a poem addressed to a young "*African* Painter," Scipio Moorhead, an enslaved teenager and visual artist who, like Wheatley, was the object of interest and educational investment by the woman who presumed to own him. Given the blessed friendship between Wheatley and Tanner, it is tempting to think about the friendship that may have existed between Scipio and Wheatley, both enslaved teenagers, aspiring artists, and neighbors in colonial Boston. But it's also difficult to imagine their relationship to one another unmediated by the surveillance of Scipio's mistress, Sarah Moorhead, who commissioned Wheatley to compose the poem. Indeed, Wheatley's relationship to Moorhead appears as a heavily mediated thing in the poem itself. "To S. M., a young *African* Painter, on seeing his Works" positions the poet as knowing Scipio solely through his "Works." And as in Hammon's poem to Wheatley, Wheatley seems able to imagine real relation only on "th' ethereal train" ("Thoughts on the Work of Providence," line 16), through a divine meeting in the afterlife: "There shall thy tongue in heav'nly murmers flow / And there my muse with heav'nly transport glow" ("To S. M.," lines 27–28).

"To S. M." is the poet's only known poem that directly addresses another person of African descent. It is also, Eric Slauter notes, her only known poem about visual art.[31] It takes shape as an exercise in ekphrasis that, like much of Wilson's picture gallery, has a fascinatingly opaque relationship to the works of art being described. Instead of a direct ekphrastic representation, in this poem Moorhead's "works" are a site of inspiration that spark Wheatley's imagination, allowing her mind to take flight and traverse an "ethereal plain" of meditation and contemplation.[32] In thirty-four melodious lines that meditate on the practice of visual art as a pious prayer and act of faith, Wheatley directly encourages the artistic and religious education of Moorhead: "Still, wond'rous youth! Each noble path pursue / On deathless glories fix thine ardent view" (7–8). But it is also a poem in which we see Wheatley being inspired by Black visual art and meditating on how Black art takes shape always in dialogue and through the mixing and melding of different forms. The poem opens with an account of the exhilaration Wheatley felt when viewing Moorhead's sublime work, giving her "soul delight," and "rushing on my sight" as if a completely "new creation." But of course, for Wheatley, any seemingly new creation is really an inspiration from God. Creative work is always inspired by God's muses but also, importantly, by other pious artists:

> Still may the painter's and the poet's fire
> To aid thy pencil, and thy verse conspire!
> And may the charms of each seraphic theme
> Conduct thy footsteps to immortal fame! (Lines 9–12)

Wheatley's is thus an articulation of a sacred Black aesthetics that takes place in the interstices between different forms (here, between poetry and painting) and through forms of lateral inspiration and creativity. The poet inspires the painter and the painter inspires the poet, but both the poet and the painter are enslaved teenagers isolated in white bourgeois homes and trying to survive and make art in a society structured by white supremacy, confinement, and greedy white desire. In this way, it makes sense that the horizon of Black art for Wheatley is heaven itself, a place where earthly depictions of classical (pagan) themes and topics will be replaced by "nobler themes" and "purer language": "No more to tell of *Damon's* tender sighs / Or rising radiance of *Aurora's* eyes" (lines 29–30). Given how both Black art and Black people were asked to serve as the objects of enjoyment for white people, it's significant, even revolutionary, that Wheatley turns from the secular and carnal pleasures of art to an art marked by goodness and purity produced in heaven. In a very material way, it is a way of imagining Black artists in pure relation to one another, outside the grip of white supremacy and possessiveness.

John Shields notes that Wheatley's theories of art draw inspiration from Horace's theory in *Ars Poetica*, "as in painting, so in the poem (*Ut pictura poesis*)."[33] Throughout "To S. M.," Wheatley draws poetic practice and visual art practice into an intimate proximity; by poem's end she pulls Moorhead even closer to her by turning him into a poet: "On what seraphic pinions shall we move / And view the landscapes in the realms above? / There shall thy tongue in heav'nly murmers flow" (lines 25–27). This was a period before literature—and even text—held the epistemological authority that it would by the twentieth century.[34] Well into the nineteenth century, poems were often thought of as *adornments* to visual illustration.[35] Throughout "To S. M." and in other poems, Wheatley plays with the direction of influence among different forms of artistic production, opening up a field of creative experimentation and intermedial play. The question of the hierarchy of the arts is something that will also concern Wilson throughout his writing, especially insofar as African Americans often lacked access to the materials and tools of the fine arts.

Harnessing the multisensory dimensions of poetry to connect to Black artists working in a visual medium, Wheatley's poems resonate deeply with what Tina Campt identifies as the *hapticity* of contemporary Black art and life. She defines the term this way: "Deriving from the root word 'haptic' (of or relating to touch), it's a term I use to describe some of the many forms of contact we experience as sensate beings in the world. They are forms of contact we are all too familiar with: physical contact (touching), visual contact (seeing), psychic contact (feeling), as well as sonic encounters with different frequencies and vibrations. . . . Hapticity is an effortful practice of exertion and an active form of struggle. It is the struggle to remain in relation to, contact or connection with another."[36] Campt further talks about hapticity as "the work of feeling implicated or affected in ways that create restorative intimacy."[37] Already in the 1770s, Wheatley sought such forms of restorative intimacy through the haptic orientations of her verse. She instantiates a theory of art that will be taken up and extended by Black aesthetes and cosmopolites in the late antebellum period, one that is dialogic and intimate and that plays with the multisensory dimensions of poetic form in order to connect to other Black artists and genres. But Wheatley is also interested in the limits of poetry as a way of connecting to her kin and fellow artists in an enslaving society that surveilled every line of her published writing. Many of her poems end with a silencing, a kind of muffling that must certainly be read in terms of the constraints placed on her own poetic and actual freedom. For example, "To. S. M." ends not with a return to Moorhead's "new creation" rushing over her senses, but with the work of art being sealed from her view: "Cease, gentle muse! the solemn gloom of night / Now seals the fair creation from my sight" (lines 33–34). Here the reader is asked to visualize the work of art being shrouded by the "gloom" of night, an image of darkness that echoes with the funereal veil ("sable") to which Wheatley refers in "On Being Brought" and in other poems, that melancholy mantle of Blackness that covers all in a world ruled by enslavement.

Yet despite this closing gesture of Moorhead's painting being sealed from view, it is ultimately Wheatley's ekphrastic poem itself that allows readers to "see" his works. Today we know about his art only *because* of Wheatley. "To S. M." thus also stands as an ekphrastic surrogate for visual works that were lost to the violences of theft, enslavement, and racial dispossession. Kerry James Marshall's 2007 portrait of Moorhead—in which Moorhead paints a self-portrait with a portrait of Wheatley on the floor behind him—further extends this genealogy of ekphrastic surrogacy and artistic communion across time and space (plate 8). Scholars have sometimes talked about Moorhead as if he was a practicing artisan in Boston. In reality, his artistic vision and aspirations remained tightly under the control of the Moorhead family. Sarah Moorhead wanted to encourage his studies and motivate his artistic vision, but she didn't care to free him. Shortly after Wheatley addressed this poem to Scipio, he was sold at auction. At this point, he disappears from the historical record. Thus, as with Wheatley, Moorhead's historical personhood is laminated to his artistic identity. Once Wheatley's art was no longer under the tutelage of the Wheatleys, it too flickers from view. While their works were archived in publication—Wheatley in poetry, Moorhead's art in Wheatley's poetry—their actual lives were squeezed and determined by illness, sale, and separation. This raises a broader question about how literary studies' investment in the death of the author can have catastrophic consequences for the study of early writers of color; it's usually the case that once their literary production ceases, scholars cease to care about them. A reminder of the premature deaths of so many Black writers in this period might encourage us to attend to their lives in different ways, even after their biographies disappear from the historical record.

Ethiops in the Picture Gallery

Wilson and his coterie would pick up on and theorize the ironies of the ephemeral for Black antebellum writers, publishing as they did in mostly nondurable formats while working under the constant pressure of anti-Black violence and threat of early death. Editors and contributors also turned to the ephemeral format of the newspaper and magazine to keep Wheatley's legacy and memory alive into the nineteenth century. The horizon here was both utopian and cumulative: Acts of archiving in popular print contributed to an ongoing project of memory-making through readers; subsequent acts of publication in such formats also extended the memory of Wheatley and the reach of her poetry through a chain of ephemerality made more durable through republication and further circuits of circulation.[38] These forms of memorialization in print also worked to claim Wheatley for the Black community, a sacred act of communion that was also a radical one given how intensely the Wheatley family surveilled and coveted her and her verse.

Wilson contributed to such efforts to claim and memorialize Wheatley in the decades following her passing. Like Wheatley's interest in using ekphrastic verse to connect to a fellow Black artist and to sanctify his art, Wilson would draw Wheatley into his own haptic, ekphrastic experiment, enshrining her portrait and a brief sketch of her life in the Picture Gallery. Ethiop's description of picture XXI, "A Head of Phillis Wheatley," appears in the "Fifth Paper" of the Picture Gallery, just after Ethiop's return from his journey to the Black Forest, which he calls "among the most remarkable of my meandering life."[39] This is one of the moments in the text where Ethiop describes coming back to the picture gallery as a return home that is also a return to focus, a place to study and contemplate after an energizing period of "rambling," adventure, and distraction.[40] To express this feeling, Ethiop turns to poetry, a fitting way to begin an installment that will ultimately turn to Wheatley:

> —Home again, and in fine spirits.
> Sound, sound the clarion, fill the fife [pipe];
> To all the sensual world proclaim,
> One crowded hour of glorious life
> Is worth an age without a name.[41]

Through our own "meandering" path, we too finally arrive and pause at Wheatley's portrait in the picture gallery, a work that, Ethiop says, is "both a constant charm and study for me."[42]

Ethiop's description of Wheatley's portrait may be the most directly ekphrastic representation to appear in the series: It clearly describes the famous frontispiece portrait of Wheatley that appeared at the beginning of the original publication of her book of poems in England and that would be reproduced in subsequent editions of the volume (figure 3.1). Wilson could have had this "original" engraving in mind (which was itself a copy, likely engraved from a painting of Wheatley that some scholars have attributed to Scipio Moorhead), or his source could have been one of the many reproductions of the portrait that appeared in literary biographies and other print sources in the antebellum period.[43] In fact, three separate publications reproduced Wheatley's portrait in 1855, just four years before the Picture Gallery appeared in the *Anglo-African*.[44] Or Wilson's source text may have been Margaretta Matilda Odell's 1834 volume, which included a portrait styled after the 1773 frontispiece, a brief "memoir" of the poet by Odell, and a selection of Wheatley's poems (figure 3.2). Odell's memoir is shot through with the biases of family interest and the possessiveness of a Wheatley descendant. It thus reproduces a fundamental violence of Wheatley's life, in which she circulated as a coveted token of status for the Wheatleys and as a symbol of their evangelical benevolence. Odell's family memoir was nonetheless an important text for Black antebellum writers and readers seeking access to Wheatley's poems and information about her life. It seems quite likely that Wilson was using Odell's memoir as a reference when composing his "Head of Phillis Wheatley" sketch, especially since Ethiop's narrative follows the format of Odell's memoir: a description of the portrait, followed by a biographical sketch, followed by a snippet of verse.

Acts of Black reading and revision of Odell's memoir challenged a long history of white people both within and beyond the Wheatley family laying claim to Wheatley and her verse, a greedy possessiveness that was often, ironically, authorized by liberal views and antislavery sympathies. Odell herself positions her (unauthorized) memoir as an abolitionist one, "dedicated to the Friends of the Africans." Opposing the attempt to keep Wheatley's legacy under the thumb of her enslavers long after her passing and into the next century, William J. Wilson wrests the poet from the grasp of the Wheatley family and other white elites, instead placing her portrait and verse in intimate relation to other Black subjects in his picture gallery. The entry also highlights and honors Wheatley's own kinship connections in her life through an evocation of the loving imprint of Wheatley's mother, which, Ethiop says, forever remained with Wheatley, "stolen at the tender age of seven years from the fond embraces of a mother whose image never once faded from her memory."[45]

I want to suggest that intimacies forged among Wheatley, Hammon, and Moorhead anticipate the dialogic and haptic forms of Black aesthetics that interested late antebellum aesthetes like William J. Wilson and James McCune

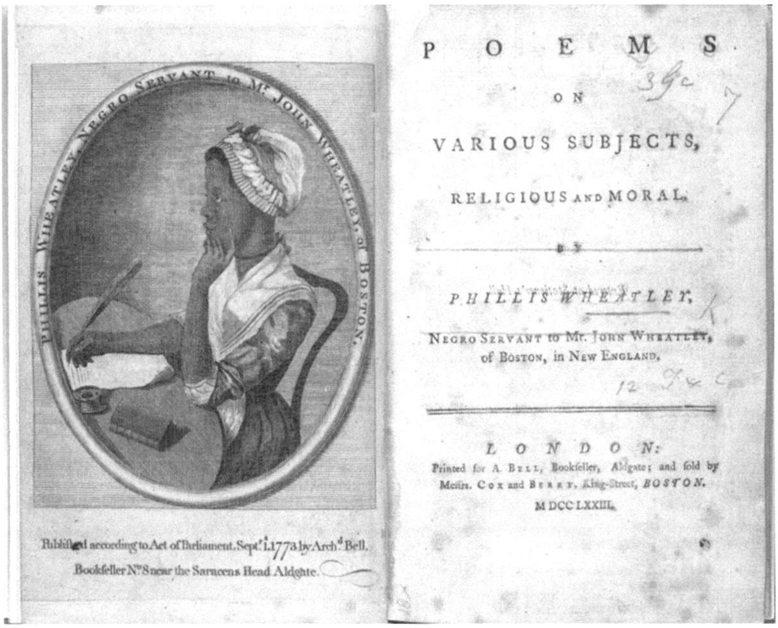

3.1 Phillis Wheatley, *Poems on Various Subjects, Religious and Moral* (London: A. Bell, 1773), frontispiece and title page.

Smith. As with Wheatley's ode to Moorhead, Wilson used the ekphrastic terrain of his Picture Gallery to connect with Wheatley across space and time. Ethiop emphasizes Wheatley's superior physiognomy in his description of her portrait ("The facial angle contains full ninety degrees; the forehead is finely formed, and the brain large"), a reflection of her intellectual capacity and her adherence to traditional standards of beauty and femininity ("To this may be added a small mouth, with lips prettily turned, and a chin—that perfection of beauty in the female face—delicately tapered from a throat and neck that are of themselves perfection").[46] Ethiop honors and sanctifies the poet by elevating her frontispiece portrait, an object from the print sphere, into a work of fine art. Of course, this is an ekphrastic exercise marked by ambiguity and irony, since the "Afric-American Picture Gallery" is not an actual gallery of fine art but another text embedded in the print sphere, like Wheatley's portrait in her book of poems.

Wheatley's sketch thus provides Wilson with another opportunity for more haptic play and multisensory connection, a way of thinking of Black aesthetics in communion, across time, space, and form. Ethiop's use of the

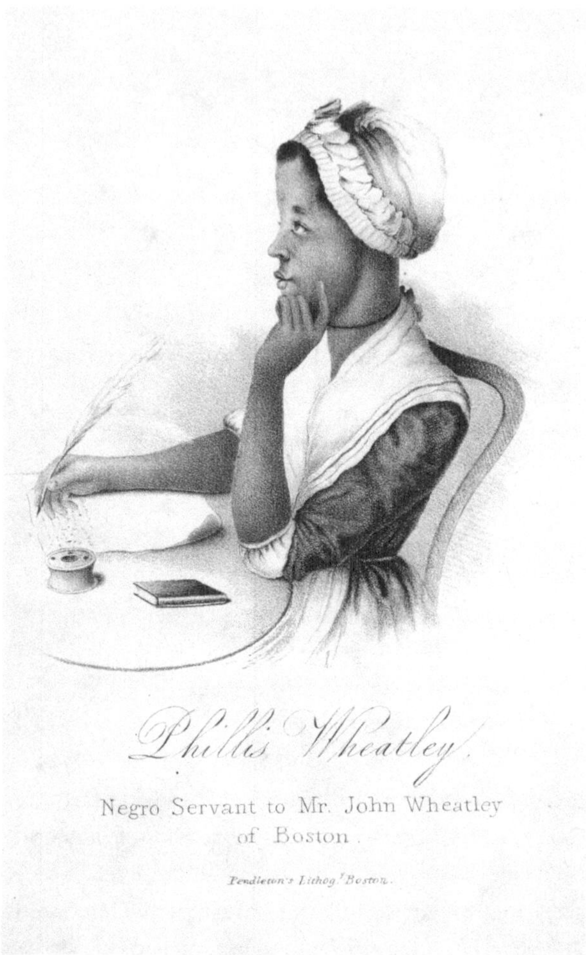

3.2 Phillis Wheatley, *Memoir and Poems of Phillis Wheatley, a Native African and a Slave*, with memoir by Margaretta Matilda Odell (Boston: Geo. W. Light, 1834), frontispiece.

language of "head," as in McCune Smith's "Heads of the Colored People," is another deliberately ambiguous ekphrastic exercise, spanning writing, portraiture, and sculpture. Fittingly, before closing, Wilson will move on to another genre: poetry. Like Hammon's "Address to Miss Phillis Wheatl[e]y," Wilson's sketch of Wheatley doubles as a document of his own reading of Wheatley's poetry. And like we saw in Hammon's hymn, Wheatley inspires Wilson to turn to the resources of verse, writing this original seven-line ode:

Oh! Wheatl[e]y!
What degrading hand, what slavish chain,
What earthly power could link thy nobler soul
To baser things, and check its eagle flight?
Angel of purity, child of beauteous song,
Thy harp still hangs within our sight
To cheer though thou art gone.

Here Wilson picks up on the many moments where Wheatley figures herself in flight, bemoaning the "slavish chain" that sought to "check" her soul's "eagle flight." As Wheatley encouraged Moorhead to join her in heaven, on that more "noble plain," Wilson similarly frames Wheatley as an "angel of purity," and as a muse for his own writings as well as for all who toured the picture gallery: "Thy harp still hangs within our sight / To cheer though thou art gone."[47] No mere honorific ("Oh! Wheatl[e]y!"), an apostrophe by a nominally free Black writer addressed to a poet who had herself been "[a] sold thing, a bought chattel" illuminates the great stakes and political import of apostrophe's powers of animation and the lyricization of agency that Virginia Jackson has recently theorized. Whereas antebellum apostrophe was often anti-Black, through forms of address that made "poems into racialized people," Wilson instead uses apostrophe to directly address Wheatley and bring her into a vivifying world of beloved community.[48]

At the very end of this sketch, Ethiop turns suddenly didactic, suggesting that "the lady visitors to the Gallery would do well to make the head of Phillis Wheatley a study."[49] Again, Ethiop's language here is playfully and ambiguously haptic: Is such a "study" an invitation for "lady visitors" to observe and contemplate Wheatley's portrait as they look at it? Is it an invitation to write about it, to produce a pencil sketch or other artistic work in their notebook? Or is it a suggestion to "study" the portrait with an eye to emulating the poetess? Throughout the text, Ethiop plays on the multiple meanings of the term *sketch* to open a multisensory field of creativity and connection for readers. He does something similar here with the language of "study." In this way, the picture gallery asks readers to imagine themselves occupying many intersecting roles: readers and critics, but also aspiring writers and visual artists, or amateurs who dabble in all these fields, as Ethiop does. More concretely, Wilson sought to encourage readers to submit their own creations to the *Anglo-African Magazine*, reminding readers that the series, like the magazine itself, is a provisional work, always open to further revision, extension, and collaboration.

Across his writings, and throughout the Picture Gallery, we see William J. Wilson seeking to inspire creative expression among his readers, encouraging them to use whatever tools they had at hand and in whatever formats piqued their interest. He was a staunch advocate for Black visual representation as a crucial avenue for self-determination in a crucial moment of Black institution building and the accruing of political power. But no known image of Wilson exists. This is a historical irony that speaks to the deep paradoxes and aporias of Black visual culture in the age of enslavement. And as we have already seen, the powers of ekphrasis were many: Text could at times serve as a surrogate for (withheld, destroyed, never created) Black images; as this chapter has shown, ekphrasis was also used by writers to connect to and visualize other Black artists.

Wilson understood the power of Wheatley's image. Wheatley did too. When she wrote to the Countess of Huntingdon five weeks after arriving in London to secure a publisher for her collection of poems, she reminded her of the portrait: "I should think my self very happy in Seeing your Ladyship, and if you was So desirous of the Image of the Author as to propose it for a Frontispiece I flatter myself that you would accept the Reality."[50] Wheatley plays with the relationships among art, image, Blackness, and authenticity just as Wilson does in his theorizing of the work of art under racial capitalism. Here Wheatley reminds the countess of her desire to see an image of Wheatley in her book of poems—indeed, "so desirous of the Image of the Author"—and playfully suggests that the countess might entertain the possibility of seeing "the Reality": that is, Wheatley in the flesh. In her first letter to the countess, in which she enclosed a manuscript of her elegy for George Whitefield, Wheatley also reminds her that all humans are made in the image of God, "the Divine Benefactor whose image you bear by filial imitation."[51] Wheatley's evangelical commitments lead her to remind the countess that all humans are made in the image of God, and thus all humans are copies, "filial imitation[s]" of the Divine Creator. Wheatley thus was already theorizing the simulacra ("filial imitation") in 1773: She understood the politics of fungibility under slavery, and she countered the degradations and disconnections of print through the affects and aesthetics of hapticity, connection, and faithful community. Through this scene of Wheatley composing her correspondence, we might glimpse a speculative image of Wilson as refracted through Wheatley herself: two "Ethiops" writing at their desks (see figure 3.1).

Another Martyr of the American Revolution

After concluding his portrait of Wheatley, Ethiop says that this sketch—and his "happy consciousness of its justness"—caused an "old mood" to steal over him, "my mind traversing back to the days when Banneker lived and told of the stars and of the rising suns, and Wheatl[e]y sung their praise to listening worlds."[52] Wheatley's inclusion in the Picture Gallery was part of Wilson's broader interest in commemorating Black revolutionaries from the late eighteenth century. The project of turning to the past for models of heroism became increasingly important to Black abolitionists in the 1850s as they moved toward a more militant stance, one that included the possibility of using revolutionary violence to topple the institution of slavery.[53] This work was also a way of articulating a patriotism rooted in the brave actions of those Richard Newman calls "black founders," rather than in the hagiography of enslaving Founding Fathers.[54] Indeed, Newman argues that this project of "conjuring a black classical era" was central to the mission of the *Anglo-African Magazine*: "As sectional battles over slavery intensified, a new magazine sought to inspire African American reformers by recounting the historic struggles of black activists during the early Republic. . . . 'We had giants in those days!' the editors exclaimed of the men (and we now know women) who built the black community's first autonomous organizations, launched black abolitionism, and redefined African Americans' place in both America and the Atlantic world."[55] Newman goes on to note that Hamilton and his cohort understood that without the freedom-fighting activities of Black Americans "during the Age of Jefferson . . . African Americans' struggle for justice would not have assumed so central a place during the Age of Lincoln."[56]

Wilson's investment in creating a pantheon of Black heroes for a new era of revolutionary struggle is most clear in picture 3, "The First Martyr of the Revolution." Here Wilson both engages and revises cultural myths about Crispus Attucks, the sailor and whaler of Black and Indigenous descent generally regarded as the first person killed in the Revolutionary War. Attucks was one of the sailors, stevedores, dockworkers, and other members of colonial Boston's multiracial working class who, on March 5, 1770, faced off with British soldiers in front of the Customs House in what would become known as the Boston Massacre. In the chaotic confrontation, British soldiers shot into a large crowd, killing Attucks and four other men. In his defense of the British soldiers put on trial for murder, John Adams referred to the assembled crowd that day as "a motley rabble of saucy boys, Negroes, and molattoes, Irish teagues and outlandish jack tars."[57] Attucks and his comrades were simultaneously maligned for their anarchic, disorderly actions—directly linked to their low social stations and ambiguous racial origins—and held up as brave, revolutionary heroes ushering in a righteous war in which the American colonies sought to shake off the chains of their oppressor.

Wilson's decision to install "a head of Attucks" in the picture gallery is deeply connected to his interest in the politics of race and American republicanism throughout the series. It is also connected to a complex and racially charged history of visual representation of the Boston Massacre. In 1770, Paul Revere made and distributed a print of the massacre scene after an image created by Boston artist Henry Pelham (plates 9 and 10). Revere's graphic took many creative liberties: For one, he split the American crowd and the British sentries into two sides, a projective fantasy of organized battle that obscured the actual chaos of the event. In reality, colonists hurled snowballs at the British guards, and they, in turn, shot their muskets into a crowd of hundreds. In the Revere engraving, the killing of Attucks is also ambiguously represented: Some copies of the print use brown ink to show a man of color with chest wounds; others do not. The figure who may represent Attucks is also decentered visually, appearing within the crowd rather than on the front lines of the confrontation. In sum, the Revere print does not prioritize Attucks as a leader or martyr of the American Revolution.

In the nineteenth century, visual depictions of the Boston Massacre shifted in ways that tracked alongside changing political cultures and the strengthening of the abolitionist movement. Most notably, an 1856 lithograph restored Attucks's prominent role and sacrifice in the bloody confrontation (plate 11). Working from the Revere print, this adaptation brings Attucks to the center of the scene. The lithograph emphasizes Attucks's Blackness as well as his militant agency: He holds a club in one hand and the barrel of a gun in the other, usurping control of a historical and visual narrative that had marginalized him. The darkening of his skin tone over time was part of efforts to align Attucks's story with Black activism and social protest in the age of slavery; initial accounts of Attucks referred to him as a mulatto and often emphasized his Native ancestry. Attucks's legal status at the time of the massacre was fuzzy: Born enslaved in Framingham, Massachusetts, he had run away from his master at least once; at the time of the massacre, he may have still been a runaway, or he may have since secured his freedom legally. Contemporaneous accounts note that he was likely only in Boston temporarily; just back from a sea voyage in the Bahamas, he was scheduled to leave on a ship headed to North Carolina's coast.

By the late 1850s, Attucks had become a crucial icon for the abolition movement. For Black abolitionists Attucks was a symbol of African American courage and sacrifice for the nation's war against tyranny. In 1855, William C. Nell published *The Colored Patriots of the American Revolution*, a sweeping history of Black patriots and their heroism during the American wars against the British in both 1776 and 1812. Nell was the son of a Revolutionary War soldier. He researched both the American Revolution and the War of 1812 for many years before publishing his book. Anticipating a later monument of revisionist history, Du Bois's *Black Reconstruction* (1935), *Colored Patriots* seeks to correct the historical record surrounding the Revolutionary era, making the efforts of Black soldiers central to the success of the American Revolution and, thus, to the nation's founding. Nell understood that the erasure of Black military service was deliberate and operated to bury Black claims to citizenship rights: "Of the services and sufferings of the Colored Soldiers of the Revolution, no attempt has, to our knowledge, been made to preserve a record. They have had no historian. With here and there an exception, they have all passed away, and only some faint traditions linger among their descendants. Yet enough is known to show that the free colored men of the United States bore their full proportion of the sacrifices and trials of the Revolutionary War."[58]

With his 1855 volume, Nell set out to be the historian to those resigned to the zone outside history and thus outside Being itself. The book opens with a rousing account of Attucks's sacrifice for the American cause and is paired with a powerful illustration depicting the event. Citing the long iconographic history of Attucks, this image shows Attucks lying on the ground in the center of the battle scene, rather than standing upright as in the 1856 lithograph (figure 3.3). Nell's image thus resonates, not quite with visual representations of Black rebellion and self-defense from the period, but with abolitionist propaganda of the time that centered Black suffering and anti-Black violence under the lash of slavery and racism.

Nell's work on the "colored patriots" would become increasingly relevant as the nation moved closer to civil war. In 1858, he and a committee of activists and reformers established a Crispus Attucks Day and began annual commemorations in Boston. These events in honor of Attucks's memory would be held annually through the end of the Civil War. The first commemoration doubled as a social protest of the *Dred Scott* decision. The night featured oratory, music, sketches, and other entertainments; "souvenirs of Attucks and other Revolutionary relics" were also exhibited for viewing. Some broadsides advertising these events also reproduce the lyrics of Charlotte Forten's "Red,

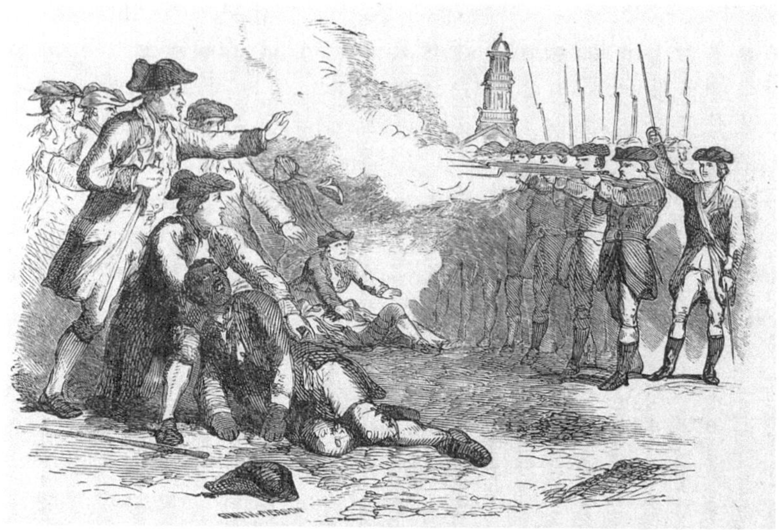

3.3 Crispus Attucks lying wounded by British gunfire during the Boston Massacre on March 5, 1770. From William C. Nell, *Colored Patriots of the American Revolution* (Boston: Robert F. Wallcut, 1855).

White and Blue" and note that Forten's song, written for the first Attucks Day in 1858, will be performed. Forten's lyrics emphasize loyalty to the Union but also suggest that the coming of the Civil War was a form of divine retribution: "Should War wage its wide desolation / And threaten the land to deform / We'd rally the men of the nation / And laugh at the threatening storm."[59] In 1863, members of the Fifty-Fourth Massachusetts Colored Regiment were present at that year's commemorative exercises; their presence made clear that the memorialization culture around Attucks was part of a broader effort to bring Black soldiers into the Union effort, and, more generally, to suggest that the time for passive resistance was over (figure 3.4).

Wilson's ekphrastic portrait of Attucks is thus part of the Black memory work and commemorations of him that were already happening in the 1850s. Wilson certainly read *The Colored Patriots of the American Revolution*, as did the rest of his cohort. At the same time that these hagiographic works sought to establish African Americans as deserved members of the nation's body politic, they also flirted with the ongoing possibility, not of Black incorporation through citizenship, but of a Black rebellion that overthrows the government. Ethiop says that this head of Attucks is a "fine likeness of a bold, vigorous man,—just such, as would be likely to head a revolution to throw off oppression."[60]

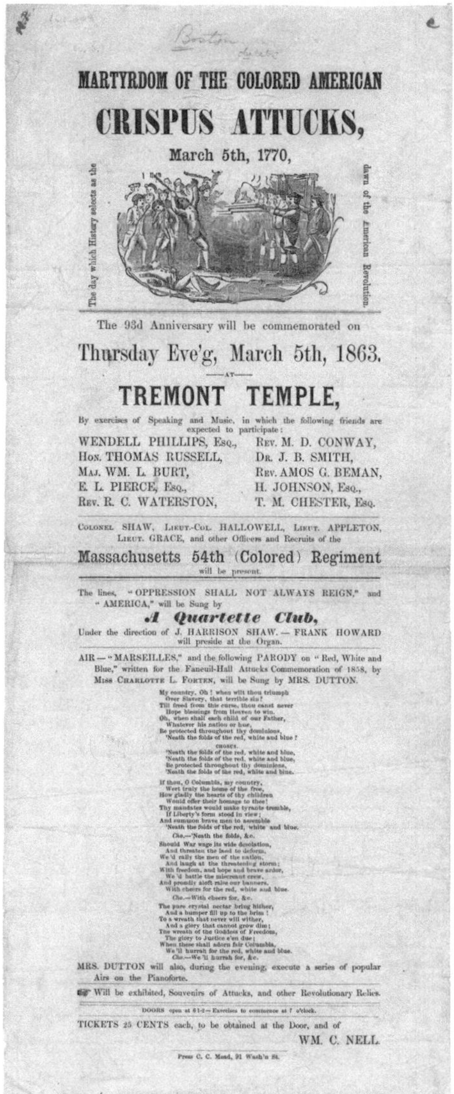

MARTYRDOM OF THE COLORED AMERICAN

CRISPUS ATTUCKS,

March 5th, 1770,

The day which History selects as the dawn of the American Revolution.

The 93d Anniversary will be commemorated on

Thursday Eve'g, March 5th, 1863.

—AT—

TREMONT TEMPLE,

By exercises of Speaking and Music, in which the following friends are expected to participate:

WENDELL PHILLIPS, Esq.,
Hon. THOMAS RUSSELL,
Maj. WM. L. BURT,
E. L. PIERCE, Esq.,
Rev. R. C. WATERSTON,
Rev. M. D. CONWAY,
Dr. J. B. SMITH,
Rev. AMOS G. BEMAN,
H. JOHNSON, Esq.,
T. M. CHESTER, Esq.

Colonel SHAW, Lieut.-Col. HALLOWELL, Lieut. APPLETON, Lieut. GRACE, and other Officers and Recruits of the

Massachusetts 54th (Colored) Regiment

will be present.

The lines, "OPPRESSION SHALL NOT ALWAYS REIGN," and "AMERICA," will be Sung by

A Quartette Club,

Under the direction of J. HARRISON SHAW.—FRANK HOWARD will preside at the Organ.

AIR—"MARSEILLES," and the following PARODY on "Red, White and Blue," written for the Faneuil-Hall Attucks Commemoration of 1858, by Miss Charlotte L. Forten, will be Sung by MRS. DUTTON.

My country, Oh! when wilt thou triumph
Over Slavery, that terrible sin?
Till freed from this curse, thou canst never
Hope blessings from Heaven to win.
Oh, when shall each child of our Father,
Whatever his nation or hue,
Be protected throughout thy dominions,
'Neath the folds of the red, white and blue?

CHORUS.

'Neath the folds of the red, white and blue,
'Neath the folds of the red, white and blue,
Be protected throughout thy dominions,
'Neath the folds of the red, white and blue.

If thou, O Columbia, my country,
Wert truly the home of the free,
How gladly the hearts of thy children
Would offer their homage to thee!
Thy mandates would make tyrants tremble,
If Liberty's form stood in view;
And summon brave men to assemble
'Neath the folds of the red, white and blue.
Cho.—'Neath the folds, &c.

Should War wage its wide desolation,
And threaten the land to deform,
We'd rally the men of the nation,
And laugh at the threatening storm;
With freedom, and hope and brave ardor,
We'd battle the miscreant crew,
And proudly aloft raise our banners,
With cheers for the red, white and blue.
Cho.—With cheers for, &c.

The pure crystal nectar bring hither,
And a bumper fill up to the brim!
To a wreath that never will wither,
And a glory that cannot grow dim;
The wreath of the Goddess of Freedom,
The glory to Justice e'en due;
When these shall adorn fair Columbia,
We'll hurrah for the red, white and blue.
Cho.—We'll hurrah for, &c.

MRS. DUTTON will also, during the evening, execute a series of popular Airs on the Pianoforte.

☞ Will be exhibited, Souvenirs of Attucks, and other Revolutionary Relics.

DOORS open at 6 1-2—Exercises to commence at 7 o'clock.

TICKETS 25 CENTS each, to be obtained at the Door, and of

WM. C. NELL.

Press C. C. Mead, 91 Wash'n St.

3.4 Broadside, *Martyrdom of the Colored American Crispus Attucks, March 5th, 1770*, announcing the ninety-third anniversary commemoration of the Boston Massacre at Tremont Temple, March 5, 1863 (Boston, 1863).

In this way, the Picture Gallery sought to intervene in the dominant grammars of American citizenship in the period, establishing Black humanity and rights through perpetual reminders of the role that enslaved and free African Americans have played in fighting against British tyranny and embodying the democratic ideals of the nation. At the beginning of his description of picture 2, Ethiop notes the willful and ideologically produced amnesia surrounding the role played by a man of color in the Revolutionary War: "It may not be generally known, and it may not be particularly desirable that the public should know, that the First Martyr of the American Revolution was a colored man; that the first bosom that was bared to the blast of the war was black." Readers may note here that the abolitionist claiming of Attucks simultaneously worked to erase his Indigenous heritage.

Further, it is significant that Wilson's portrait extracts Attucks from the chaotic scene of war and the "motley rabble" with which he is assembled in the original Revere print and in subsequent reproductions of the scene. Wilson's portrait represents Attucks as a major hero of the American Revolution by drawing out his individuality. The figuring of Attucks as a martyr further invests this ekphrastic portrait with a spiritual charge. William Nell's engraving of Attucks lying prone and held by his brethren was certainly a crucial visual source for Wilson. Nell's own illustration cites another work: a famous post-Revolutionary painting of the Battle of Bunker Hill by John Trumbull, where General Joseph Warren is represented as a Christlike pietà figure, meant to elicit pity and compassion from the viewer (plate 12).[61] Figuring Warren as a Christian martyr further frames his death on the battlefield as a form of divine sacrifice. In replacing Warren with Attucks, Nell and Wilson challenge this narrative: They construct a new visual iconography of the American Revolution, with Attucks anointed as its leader, while subtly reminding readers that it has always been enslaved people who have made the greatest sacrifices for the nation.

Ethiop explicitly places Attucks within a long tradition of Judeo-Christian imagery depicting the sacrifices of Christian martyrs and the sacrifices of Christ himself. For example, he emphasizes Attucks's blood flowing out of his veins: "The first blood that drenched the path-way which led up to American liberty, was from the veins of a colored man."[62] This image clearly riffs on Jefferson's famous statement that "the tree of liberty must be refreshed from time to time with the blood of patriots and tyrants." But with blood flowing from Attucks veins, it's also an image that recalls Christ's martyrdom, his sacrifice for humanity, and, perhaps most poignantly, his betrayal. Attucks was martyred for the American cause, but the Founders would ultimately betray his sacrifice by refusing to grant freedom to the very people who had fought for their freedom.

In turning back to the American Revolution, Ethiop vests Wheatley, Banneker, Attucks, and other Black founders with heroic status, honoring their contributions and anointing them as models for a new revolutionary age. He does something similar in his representation of both Toussaint Louverture and Soulouque, both of whom are depicted in an opulent regality, and through whom Ethiop maps a more global and diasporic history of revolution stretching from the late eighteenth century to Wilson's present. In being figured as saints, muses, angels, kings, and queens, these historical figures are depicted in the Picture Gallery surrounded by what can only be described as an aura. But that aura was not just rooted in Judeo-Christian discourses of martyrdom; it was also produced, as detailed in chapter 1, by transformations in new technologies of mechanical production under industrial capitalism in the mid-nineteenth century.

4

Ethiop in the Black Forest

CRUISING, FANTASY, AMBIVALENCE

> The pleasure of the undertaking lies in the absence of any arrangement how or where to go, time and liberty being the only requisites.
>
> **William J. Wilson**, "Terance Ludlam," *Frederick Douglass' Paper*, August 11–18, 1854

This book has explored how William J. Wilson's writing navigated art-making as industrial capitalism consolidated around him, a world in which people, their labor, and their creative output were being increasingly commodified and exchanged on the open market. The stakes of artistic commodification were especially high for a population forcibly commodified as slaves or nominally free workers and where Blackness itself circulated as a fungible object of cultural, political, and economic exchange.[1] Wilson, as we have seen, was a keen observer of economic developments in midcentury America, and his theorizations of capital almost always happened on the move, through Ethiop's movements as a flaneur strolling through his picture gallery, as a traveler to the Black Forest, and in his on-the-ground reporting of New York City's sights and sounds in *Frederick Douglass' Paper*. Wilson thus partakes in what Sarah Jane Cervenak identifies as a rich tradition of the philosophical ramble in Black letters and philosophy. She writes, "Despite and in the face of dispossession and of being disentitled from material landscape, black philosophers made terrain through wandering," thus countering the Enlightenment's rendering of people of African descent as "ungeographic," as Katherine McKittrick terms it.[2]

While the first installments of the Picture Gallery follow an ordered format, unfolding as a lively, yet contained tour of the gallery's collection, in the third and fourth installment of the series, readers are suddenly transported outside the gallery, where the plot takes an unexpected detour. Breaking with the series' ekphrastic form, in which Ethiop carefully describes a series of paintings hung on the walls of the gallery, here Wilson offers readers an account of Ethiop's voyage to a mysterious locale, where he meets an African American artist in exile, practicing his craft deep in the forest. By installing the Black Forest tale in the center of his Picture Gallery, Wilson publishes one of the earliest, if not the first, work of fantasy fiction in the African American literary tradition.[3]

In what follows, I am interested in how the seemingly nonpolitical dimensions of a quest fantasy—in which Ethiop takes a journey to a distant forest to visit a hermit artist and political exile—allow Wilson to express ambivalence in a time of abolitionist immediatism and agitation. In general, political propaganda does not allow for messy feelings or uncertainty. I argue that the Picture Gallery—like the Black antebellum epistolatory cultures to which it was deeply connected—becomes political insofar as it is a site where contradictory views, half-formed positions, and deep ambivalences can be held without neat or easy resolution.

I first turn to an early short story by Wilson titled "Terance Ludlam" (1854) that anticipates the itinerancies and themes of the Picture Gallery's own Black Forest tale in several ways, revealing some of Wilson's longstanding writerly preoccupations. I go on to consider the Black Forest tale's relationship to the tradition of fantasy writing and the role of the fantastical more broadly within the space of Wilson's speculative gallery. From there, I trace how forms of movement in the Black Forest tale intersect with the politics of Black mobility, migration, and emergent forms of queer movement in the period. I conclude by showing how the Black Forest narrative registers not political dogmatism but a decided nondecidedness around the question of Black emigration. This chapter builds on this project's interest in the contours and interventions of Black aesthetics in the late antebellum period, especially within Black fiction writing in the 1850s. The question of what African American literature *does*, or seeks to do, in this particular historical moment—especially narratives that were not slave narratives—remains a somewhat open question. Why did writers who were otherwise active in the political sphere retread and refract political questions through fiction writing? While the history of nineteenth-century emigration and colonization has often been split between "pro" and "anti" camps, Wilson's fantasy tale registers that emigration was a deeply contested site that Black activists had complicated feelings about. Throughout this chapter, I also suggest that the speculative, visioning genre of the fairy tale—and the act of fiction writing more generally—provided a narrative space not only for ambivalence but also for daydreaming, breathing, and rest: affects and practices otherwise little available to Black activists in the turbulent years immediately preceding the Civil War.

Early Perambulations

Like much of his periodical correspondence, Wilson's earliest fiction writing is interested in narrating racial capitalism's reorganization of space, time, and populations, and does so on foot. Published in two installments in *Frederick Douglass' Paper* in August 1854 and billed as an "Original Story" by William J. Wilson, "Terance Ludlam" opens with this observation from the narrator:

> We, who reside in crowded cities, talk of comforts, yet know but little of them. We deplore our condition, yet do comparatively little to change it. We complain of burdens[,] the unavoidable accumulations of city life[,] yet seldom seek rightly for the means whereby to lighten them, or look beyond for a refuge to which we may flee for relief. In fine, we wed ourselves to the habits, fashions and gaieties of city life, (though under protest we do it;) and yet never once seek for a bill of divorcement therefrom, which the dictate of our reason would most readily grant.

He says that he himself had rarely sought refuge outside the city, but sometime "in the summer of 184–, it occurred to me that a little cruise somewhere outside of the city would not prove profitless; and accordingly, I resolved to take it." From there, readers follow the narrator "descending to the street," "saunter[ing]" downtown, and "stepping on board the first steamer I found firing up, without inquiry when or whether bound." Moving slowly away from the "din and confusion" of the city, the narrator describes the receding shoreline as a kind of moving landscape, or even a panorama: "As each wave separated us, first from the living active masses about the wharves, next the hulls and masts of the ponderous ships within them, and then the more ponderous warehouses above them, I felt it was really a separation for the better. At last, the tall spires, tho' pointing high towards heaven, receded from view: and to close the scene, pensive evening unfolded and spread her curtain, thus shutting out altogether any further glimpses of the place where, for years, I had witnessed so much rioting and misery."

Once on land, presumably somewhere upstate, in a town only called "R——," the narrator offers another picture to contemplate, this time not an urban seascape, but a quaint country village, a "vale beautifully studded with neat little cottages the inhabitants of each astir, busied in, or preparing for the labors of the day." After approaching a "winding stream of water, about two hundred feet wide" and "finding no crossing," the narrator "followed a half-blind pathway along its banks some distance, when, suddenly, it spread into a broad and placid expanse, and almost as suddenly terminated into a deep glen, just above which rose the first of the group of hills I had descried from the village, and was in pursuit of." "What a lovely spot!" the narrator remarks, as his city worries fall away and his system becomes regulated by the "tranquility" of the countryside and the "salubrity" of its "morning air."

Wilson's "Terance Ludlam" is one of the many stories of nostalgic pastoral escape from the city that filled urban newspapers in a period marked by urban alienation, dispossession, and migration from the countryside.[4] But crucially, Wilson will almost immediately racialize this pastoral fantasy, noting the "nut-brown faces" of children playing in the yard of a cottage where he soon meets Terance Ludlam in the flesh, a "fine athletic-looking man," father to this crew of happy, playful children, and owner of the beautiful plot and farm laying before the narrator. Through the narrator's journey from Brooklyn to rural upstate, the story's frame narrative maps a city-to-country trajectory, thus reversing the pattern of urbanization happening across the United States and in other industrialized nations in the period.[5] However, Terance Ludlam's retelling of his life story, which occupies the rest of the narrative, will actually take readers *back* to the city, narrating his own migration as a youth from his rural hometown to New York, where he lived for many years before settling upstate in "R——." Ludlam recounts the tribulations he encountered migrating from his "backwater" hometown to the bustling city as a young man. Where the narrator had given us a sublime image of the New York skyline receding from his view from the deck of a steamer, Ludlam describes his impression of first seeing the city come into his view through an eerie metaphor signaling both urbanization and the regimes of deforestation and ecological ruination that undergirded it. He says, "What in my ignorance seemed to me an old dead forest, but proved to be the great city of New York, hove in sight."

Likely echoing Wilson's own initial feelings after arriving in New York from New Jersey as a young man, Ludlam tells of his initial loneliness in the "cold, gay, and unconcerned" city, his feelings of disorientation and "extreme anxiety" navigating the city, and the absolute necessity of finding a job. Like other Black New Yorkers, Ludlam needed to secure a wage for himself in a city with a notoriously biased and segregated employment landscape. Ludlam's account points to the ways that even nominally free Black people were treated as objects of exchange and exploitation in the city, used, objectified, and even sexualized at whim by white people hungry for social status, wealth, and titillation: "Being fresh from the country, and with testimonials of good character, I was soon sought after by ladies of wealth and fashion. Don't be startled, sir, (said he;) it was only to become their domestic; and if once obtained, judiciously broken in, and properly trained, I would be invaluable as such." Ludlam's language of being "broken in," as well as his coy joke about interracial sex, suggests that New York's formal economy was always a racial and sexual economy that depended on the illicit consumption and exploitation of Black labor and flesh.[6]

Being thrown into New York's cutthroat world of waged work gives Ludlam intimate access to New York's upper class, and much of his story offers salacious details about the excesses of a growing urban bourgeoisie benefiting from white supremacy and constant access to cheap or indentured labor. In addition to working as a domestic, he talks about his time laboring as a carriage driver with a family of "gay Quakers," from whom, Ludlam says, he learned the power of thrift and saving. At the same time, Ludlam satirizes the hypocrisy of his employers, who pass along heavy-handed moral lessons about the importance of thrift and humility while at the same time living a life of wealth and excess.

Ludlam's story certainly relates incidents from Wilson's own migration from New Jersey to New York City and the first jobs he worked as he sought to establish himself there and secure "some means" for himself. "Terance Ludlam" is tellingly subtitled "FOUNDED ON FACT," and readers of *Frederick Douglass' Paper* would have been acquainted with Wilson's travels and adventures in the other columns he contributed to the paper as its Brooklyn correspondent. Thus, in a kind of character doubling that mirrors Wilson's projection of himself as "Ethiop" into the text of the Picture Gallery, both characters in "Terance Ludlam" may be read as figures for Wilson himself, at different ages and stages of life. It's also possible to understand the story as one in which Wilson meets a version—or fictional avatar—of himself (Ludlam) who had escaped the city for his own country plot in the name of financial autonomy.

Ultimately, this queer little story offers a window into the exploitation of Black workers in New York while making visible some of the fantasies that kept Black urbanites going and sustained their visions for a better and less alienating future. Setting out on his journey, the narrator says that "the pleasure of the undertaking lies in the absence of any arrangement how or where to go, time and liberty being the only requisites." The narrator's wanderings give him occasion to comment on a changing, industrializing landscape based on his own observations on the ground, but the narrator's meandering trajectory at the same time challenges the ideological entrenchment of time and space by the capitalist workday and its disciplining of the movement of both mind and body. Rambling, thinking, and thinking about rambling are all ways that Wilson, as well as his avatars in both "Terance Ludlam" and the Picture Gallery, maintain liberty in a context of racial subjection, exploitation, and surveillance in American's most racist city north of the Mason-Dixon Line. In "Terance Ludlam," the narrator notes that periodic journeys outside the city are crucial for refreshing the senses, making it easier to be a keen and accurate observer of the city upon one's return home.

Holding interest on its own, "Terance Ludlam" also looks forward to the strollings and migrations that make up the Picture Gallery, especially in the series' Black Forest installments, while connecting to Wilson's ongoing interest in engaging in radical forms of "plotting," or the creation of alternative landscapes even within the city itself.[7] In moments like when Ludlam conjures New York as an "old dead forest"—pointing to both his country ways and the genocidal and ecocidal destructions of settler colonialism—he also gestures to what Sylvia Wynter calls the "plot." J. T. Roane says Black migrants carried the plot with them and would continue to shape their understandings of place and place-making in the city.[8] The Black flaneur's country "cruise" in "Terance Ludlam" gives us an idea of how Wilson may have understood his own relationship to space, time, and desire in Brooklyn. It also points to how his writing participates in the world-making powers of what Roane calls "black queer urbanism."[9] Roane's concept of Black queer urbanism simultaneously articulates the intimacies between the figure of the Black migrant and the Black dandy.

I open with Wilson's 1854 short story because it shares many thematic similarities with the Black Forest tale that Wilson places in the middle of the Picture Gallery. Beginning in the third installment of the series, the Black Forest tale transforms the text from a gallery tour to a work of fantastic flight and speculative fiction. The Black Forest tale echoes several of the tropes and themes charted in Wilson's "Terance Ludlam," including its city-to-country trajectory, its interest in what is made possible by going north/leaving the city, and its featuring of a (homosocial) form of storytelling that takes shape through an exchange between two masculine protagonists. The Black Forest tale might be understood as a continuation of Wilson's earlier writing in "Terance Ludlam," but it also marks a radical departure from the format and plot of the Picture Gallery itself. The quest, in this way, operates as a kind of fugitive line of flight within the text. Moving from a present rooted in industrial capital's standardization of time and space to a mythic, fairy-tale place, the Black Forest tale also partakes in the forms of rhetorical deceleration I have discussed elsewhere in this book.

Ethiop's Quest Fantasy

The Picture Gallery's fugitive quest fantasy begins with Ethiop's viewing of a beautiful and mysterious landscape painting in the gallery titled "Black Forest." The gallery's assistant, Tom, soon runs in to give Ethiop a letter that extends an invitation to come visit this very Black Forest and "examine some of the Pictures and other curiosities there."[10] Readers next follow Ethiop's journey, in which he travels through the actual landscape represented on the walls of the picture gallery: "Here in all its grandeur and wild sublimity was the native landscape spread out before me, the same that I saw in beautiful miniature but a day before hanging on the walls of our Afric-American Gallery."[11] The next several installments abandon the picture gallery for a tale about Ethiop's journey through the Black Forest. Yet even in this part of the narrative in which readers are taken far beyond the walls of the gallery itself, Wilson presents new characters and scenes to readers as if they are also works of arts titled and captioned back in the gallery (see, e.g., "Picture No. XIV—Portrait of a Man—Bernice").

In the forest, Ethiop meets Bernice, the mysterious letter writer who had invited Ethiop to the forest and a Black artist who has his own collection of pictures located in a studio set deep within a mountain cave. Surveying the walls of Bernice's cave gallery, Ethiop stumbles upon on a "fine duplicate portrait" of Tom, "our Gallery Boy," which was painted by Bernice himself. The cave gallery is revealed to be a kind of doppelganger, or mirror, of the picture gallery. Bernice, readers soon learn, left the "restless, busy crowd" of city life to produce his work in solitude; he has long labored "far from man's baseness, and man's vile injustice," but hopes that his work will one day "command the just approbation of even the enemies of my race." Ethiop's visit includes a tour of Bernice's studio, the discovery of a mysterious tablet excavated from a forest mountaintop that recounts the downfall of the white race, and, most spectacularly, an encounter with a terrifying-looking white man held captive by Bernice as an act of retribution for holding his own family in chains. Readers aren't told how the slaveholder came into Bernice's "possession," but we do learn that this man shot and killed Bernice's son (and possibly sold away the rest of his family). Bernice intends to keep his captive chained in this cave cell, his "prison-house," until the day he dies, after which he intends to "cast his carcass forth to gorge the *Vultures* that sit upon the mountain peaks of the Black Forest." When the slaveholder pleads for his rights, Bernice, ironically echoing the 1857 *Dred Scott* decision, informs him "he had no rights that I was bound to respect."[12]

There are many things to say about the Black Forest narrative's relationship to fantasy writing. Generically, this section of the text draws on the fairy-tale tradition, especially the Grimm Brothers fairy tales, which appeared in many English translations during Wilson's time. In the tradition of all good fantasy, the Black Forest is both of and not of this earth: Wilson gives this mystical-magical place an otherworldly quality, but at the same time, the forest is still connected to known geographies, including the United States. Transported from New York to this mysterious, quasi-Germanic geography by stagecoach and then by foot—but not, significantly, by ship—Wilson constructs a fantasy world that is somehow both inside the United States and outside it. Ethiop also contributes to the mysterious aura of the Black Forest by refusing to disclose its precise location: "As it is no part of my purpose to disclose the precise locality of the Black Forest, nor fully the manner of people dwelling there, nor yet their doings, I shall reveal no more of the contents of this letter."[13] The narrative follows the format of a quest fantasy, in which readers accompany Ethiop as he travels to and then through the Black Forest. Finally, both Bernice and his captive are described in highly fantastical terms. For example, Bernice is described as being "tall and erect, strong like a forest tree, this man of the Black Forest, for such he was, was a glory to look upon. The frost of at least ninety winters must have fallen upon his head, and yet had not chilled him, nor had their winds bowed him, nor their cold dimmed the fires of his eye."[14] Ethiop's characterization of Bernice, a kind of giant magic woodsman, echoes the woodland characters of the fairy-tale tradition.

While the Black Forest tale draws on a long tradition of fantasy in literature, fantasy is also critical to understanding the space of the gallery itself. Ivy Wilson calls the gallery a "fantastic" space, one in which Wilson is "continually imagining (both artistically and institutionally) that which does not quite exist in these almost-there forms as a way to present alternative ways of seeing for his black readers."[15] An intimate link between art and fantasy is forged in the series, since both allow Wilson to glimpse, in Ernst Bloch's terms, the realm of the "not-yet," or a future to come for Black America.[16] For Ivy Wilson, this is an important function of landscape painting itself in the Picture Gallery. He writes, "Wilson's depiction of landscape painting suggests that a putative 'here' might consistently elude African Americans and continually compel them to fantasize about a would be 'there' on a different horizon altogether."[17] In the Black Forest fable, landscape art becomes a transporting medium, operating as a portal that transports the viewer to distant scenes, lands, and times (outside that "putative 'here'" to which Ivy Wilson refers). Remember that it is the painting of the Black Forest itself that initially gives Ethiop access to the fantasy world of the Black Forest.

But this transporting effect of art is not just restricted to the Black Forest tale, it also plays a key role in Wilson's description of the gallery's works. For example, in his description of a painting titled *Sunset in Abbeokuta*, which I discuss in more detail below, Ethiop notes that "one could almost wish to be there," a wish that looks forward to the fantastical voyage to the Black Forest later in the series.[18] Indeed, with the gallery's inclusion of "happy" pictures from Canada, Haiti, and West Africa, Ethiop subtly suggests something about the potential promise of other types of voyages to far, distant lands. In this way, Wilson reframes Black emigration in terms of the utopian transport of fantasy.

Thinking about art as a transporting medium is one way of understanding the future-oriented aspects of the Picture Gallery. But fantasy is also a method through which Wilson collates, mediates, and transforms US print culture within the gallery itself. In this way, print becomes another kind of portal in the text. As I have discussed in earlier chapters, some of Ethiop's "sketches" were surely inspired by Wilson's viewing of original paintings and portraits, but many more were drawn from reproductions that appeared in print. For example, Wilson's description "A Head of Phillis Wheatley" most certainly referred to the iconic engraving of Wheatley that appeared as a frontispiece to her 1773 book of poems, *Poems on Various Subjects, Religious and Moral*. Wilson's source may have been one of the many reproductions of Wheatley's portrait that appeared in print in 1855, just four years before the Picture Gallery appeared in the *Anglo-African*.[19] These 1850s images of Wheatley were likely drawn from the frontispiece of the 1834 publication of *Memoir and Poems of Phillis Wheatley*, which included a reproduction of the 1773 frontispiece.[20] While "Head of Phillis Wheatley" could certainly signify a portrait in nineteenth-century parlance, in the virtual space of his gallery, Wilson simultaneously invites readers to imagine the possibility that many of these works could be sculptures.[21] At one point, Ethiop describes the presence of a statue of Ira Aldridge, the famed Black Shakespearean actor, transatlantic celebrity, and New Yorker who also attended the African Free School with James McCune Smith. In the picture gallery, Aldridge is posed as Aaron from *Titus Andronicus*. A year later, the 1860 bound volume of the *Anglo-African* would also feature a handsome engraving of Aldridge: one of only two images to appear during the magazine's run (figure 4.1). In short, by asking readers to imagine gallery works across media and forms, and to transform print objects into art objects, Wilson's ekphrastic descriptions require the harnessing of the reader's imaginative capacities. Fantasy is central not just to the Black Forest tale but also to Wilson's transfer of a variety of print sources onto the gallery walls and into its space.

Black Antebellum Cruising, Coasting, Dreaming

Over the past several years, the concept of fugitivity has become a preferred if not hegemonic paradigm for scholars seeking to articulate forms of freedom that are wrested, expressed, and exercised from within the contexts of racial subjection and unfreedom. Spanning a range of different histories, one discrete historical reference point for this critical lexicon can be found in the 1850s United States, when freedom seekers were becoming increasingly legible to a national press and public culture because of their own journeys to escape slavery and their juridical capture and criminalization in the wake of the passage of the Fugitive Slave Act in 1850. In the 1850s, the fugitive became a central object of political discourse in the United States and across the Atlantic world. But several other words were concurrently being used in that moment to describe states of fugitivity.[22] I have already at length discussed the figure of the dandy and its relationship to forms of unencumbered racialized and gendered movement made in opposition to the state's criminalization of both. Flaneurs like Wilson, his avatar Ethiop, and other Afropolitans, including James McCune Smith, similarly challenged a racial state organized through a dialectic of surveillance and abandonment through bold and nonapologetic displays of both physical movement and expressions of freedom of the mind. Setting such intention around highly visible and sometimes even flamboyant movement is part of what I see as being part of an early Black queer aesthetic, following J. T. Roane's argument about how queerness might be understood, not as the expression of discrete

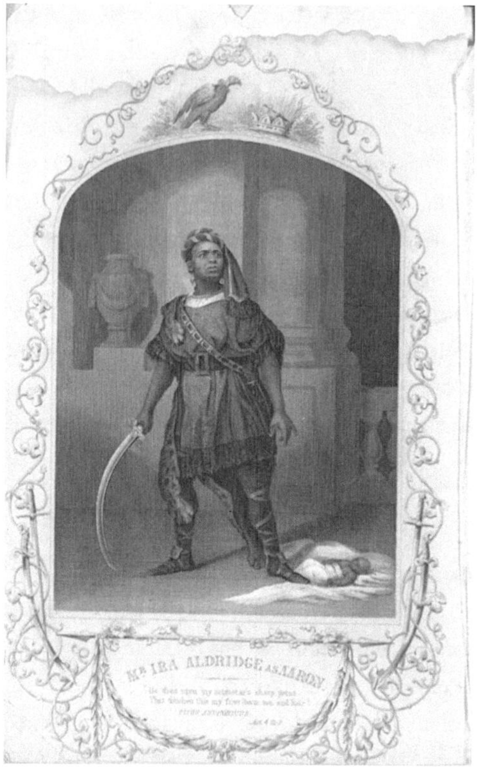

4.1 Ira Aldridge as Aaron in *Titus Andronicus. Anglo-African Magazine*, vol. 2 (New York: Thomas Hamilton, 1860), frontispiece.

sexualities but as a non-normative relationship to space as it was being actively constructed by racial capitalism and heteropatriarchy.[23]

Cruising was another term that operated adjacent to *fugitivity*. Wilson's use of the term *cruise* to describe the travels of his narrator in "Terance Ludlam" glimpses intersections of fugitive flight and emergent forms of queerness in the period. Although our contemporary understanding of this term as it takes shape in gay men's sexual cultures did not solidify until the early twentieth century, by the mid-1850s *cruise*, as a verb, already had a number of different meanings, most of which were nautical in nature but also emphasized forms of waywardness and a kind of activity taken with pleasure rather than a particular goal in mind: "To sail to and fro over some part of the sea without making for a particular port or landing-place, on the lookout for ships, for the protection of commerce in time of war, for plunder, or (in modern times) for pleasure."[24] Here we can think about Terance Ludlam's cruising as being akin to that of the ship he boards, knowing neither when it would leave port nor where it was headed.

As a roving, nonteleological form of movement, cruising also resonates with *coasting*, another nautical term from the period that referred to the kind of sea-based work and ocean harvesting that happened closer to the shore rather than in deep waters. Oystering was an important and profitable form of labor for African Americans in the coastal Northeast. It was a relatively open trade during a time of widespread segregation and discrimination in the labor market. According to Ayasha Guerin's fascinating study of Black oyster-harvesting communities in nineteenth-century New York, by mid-century "coasting" had become the preferred work of Black mariners with families, as it allowed them to stay closer to home and invest in their communities rather than going out to sea for months at a time.[25]

Practices of "coasting" and "cruising" illuminate how Ethiop's movements took shape in proximity to deeply entangled estuarine and terrestrial environments in antebellum New York. Wilson had a particularly intimate connection to nautical practices of coasting: Donald Yacovone says that Wilson's family operated an oyster boat near Shrewsbury, a coastal area in New Jersey that was connected to Brooklyn's shore by water.[26] Wilson traveled across that water when he first migrated to Brooklyn as a young man seeking to secure a professional and economic future. In a moment of memory and reverie in his writing for *Frederick Douglass' Paper*, Ethiop further reinforces the importance of New Jersey waterways in his life, noting, "When a boy, nothing to me was more refreshing than to wade the stream that passed in gentle ripples, near by the home of my childhood."[27]

Ethiop's journey to the Black Forest draws from the fairy-tale tradition as well as serialized stories of rural retreat in urban periodicals, but it also resonates with the fantastical dimensions of fugitive slave narratives and other Black travel narratives from the period, as well as with the forms of fugitivity, coasting, and cruising they contained. Narratives of fugitivity were often shrouded in a sense of mystery and opacity: This was a method for propelling the action and heightening the drama of stories of escape, but also one that strategically hid the actors and routes furtively used by fugitive slaves. At the beginning of his 1845 *Narrative*, Frederick Douglass famously critiqued other fugitive authors for disclosing key details of their own escape, thus closing those secret pathways for future runaways. In relaying escape through realism, or even documentary, Douglass says that these publicity-hungry narrators threatened to make the Underground Railroad into an "upperground railroad."[28] Thus, in the rendering of his escape from Baltimore in his second autobiography, *My Bondage and My Freedom* (1855), Douglass replaces stagecoaches and steamships with a "flying cloud or balloon": a mode of speculative transport that conceals the specifics of Douglass's escape while igniting the imagination of the reader.[29] Douglass's "flying cloud or balloon" also serves as a fantastical trope that interrupts the realism of his documentary account, a narrative irruption not unlike the portal of the Black Forest painting and of Ethiop's slumber that seems to transport him to the Black Forest. Douglass's speculative narrative trick in *My Bondage and My Freedom* would also feed the imagination of other Black writers: Martin Delany titled chapter 24 of his serialized novel *Blake; or, The Huts of America* (1859–62) "A Flying Cloud." Four years after the publication of his second, more militant slave narrative, Douglass's cloud floated onto the pages of the *Anglo-African* through Delany's contribution to the magazine. While Douglass's and Delany's flying clouds are connected to political struggle insofar as they describe the on-the-ground movements of fugitive enslaved people, this is also a utopian image that in other ways feels far away from politics, literally floating above the earth.[30] Such speculative figurations suggest the importance of fantasy, rest, daydreaming, and even distraction for Black activists and writers in the period.

Dreaming and fantasy were also important modes in African American travel writing in the 1850s. For example, David Dorr's *A Colored Man Round the World* (1855) uses a dreamlike mode of narration while straddling the genre of the slave narrative and the travel narrative. Like Wilson's creation of various fictional avatars, Malini Johar Schueller notes that "Dorr uses travel writing to project a leisurely, gentlemanly self and to fashion an aristocratic selfhood through the display of inherited 'cultural capital.'"[31] Born enslaved in New Orleans, for three years Dorr toured Europe with Cornelius Fellowes, the man who presumed to own him. When Fellowes refused to manumit Dorr upon their return to the United States in 1854 as he had promised to do, Dorr escaped to Ohio. There he published not a typical slave narrative, but a wide-ranging account of his European travels. A fugitive who had traveled the world, Dorr constructs a Black cosmopolitanism from within the state of slavery. Offering readers a panoramic view of the culture, history, and taste of the countries he visited, from Paris to Egypt, Dorr constructs, as William W. Stowe puts it, a "counterfactual narrative persona. . . . He uses travel writing as a dry run for freedom, a vehicle for fantasy, a way to dream what it might be like to be free, to imagine himself into an equal relationship with everyone he meets."[32] Indeed, Dorr frames his entire narrative as a dream—"let me dream of what I saw"—and offers confusing textual cues so that readers are often unable to parse dream from reality.[33] While the dream-narrations of Anglo-American travel narratives were deeply connected to the Orientalist, othering fantasies of European colonialism, here we see Dorr using dream-narration to escape surveillance back in the United States.

I want to suggest that the Black Forest tale is Wilson's own dream narrative within the broader text of the Picture Gallery, akin to those kinds of sequences in the narratives of Dorr, Douglass, and Delany. Wheatley, too, dreamed in verse. See, for example, her articulation of mental roving as a form of freedom in "On Imagination": "Now here, now there, the roving *Fancy* flies / Till some lov'd object strikes her wand'ring eyes."[34] After climbing up a ladder to his room in Bernice's cave, overlooking a majestic mountainous scene, Ethiop finds himself drifting into a deep sleep:

> I shall never forget the scene that burst upon my view. The peak of the Black Forest Mountain, for such it was upon which the solitary house stood, touched the very clouds, while the Ocean with here and there a massive ship upon its dark green bosom, though many miles distant, seemed to roll at its base. Crag on crag lay piled on every hand and vale outstretching vale; and beyond as it was early autumn, the sere and yellow leaf painted the otherwise vast green forest top with indescribable beauty. The morning breeze with a purity and freshness known only to mountain regions, sighed forth its soft music, so sweetly, that the feathered tribe, and they were legion—were constrained to join in with their unerring notes. . . . A few moments, and the sun, like a mighty angel came hastening up, as it were, from out of the Ocean; and with his strong presence gilded the whole scene in an instant. So, impressed with what I saw, ere I was aware, a reverie stole over me; and I know not how long it would have held me, but for a voice from below, calling me away.[35]

Ethiop's meditation of the landscape before him so impresses him (literally, his senses are impressed by the view) that a "reverie stole over" him. Ethiop's deep slumber registers something crucial about the importance of rest in 1859 for African Americans living and working in New York City. Indeed, periodicals, educational records, and convention minutes show how busy Wilson was. His advocacy for educational equality in Brooklyn was a particularly taxing effort, requiring constant battles with the city's board of education. I don't want to dismiss the real possibility that writing the Picture Gallery, especially its fairy-tale section, was a leisure activity for Wilson, a form of distraction that helped him to restore and recalibrate himself. Indeed, Wilson wrote for his own satisfaction throughout his life, even "compos[ing] several unpublished romances and sketches" during his retirement from public life.[36]

Ethiop's journey to the Black Forest, like the narrator's country escape in "Terance Ludlam," offers a much-needed rural retreat that refreshes him for his return to the bustling city and enables the flourishing of his interior life. In this way, the Black Forest tale captures something like the "sovereignty of quiet" that Kevin Quashie traces across African American literature and culture.[37] While scholars have tended to focus on the African American literary tradition as one of protest and oppositionality, Quashie says there is a quieter tradition that clears space for contemplation and interiority, a necessity in the context of a white supremacist culture that diminishes and denies Black humanity at every turn. It also feels important to note here that in the preceding passage Wilson's "feathered tribe" is a "legion" of birds that simultaneously conjures an image of those Indigenous tribes actively being dispossessed in Wilson's moment, a reminder of how even Black antebellum travel narrative fantasies could traffic in colonial imaginaries of conquest and colonization.

There was also at least one real-world referent for Wilson's Black Forest in Brooklyn itself. Weeksville was a free Black community founded in 1835 in an area that was at that point still on the rural outskirts of the recently incorporated city. Judith Wellman notes that "Weeksville's founders intentionally created in the 1830s a race-based geographically separate community, advertising land 'for sale to colored people.' Nestled among steep hills and valleys of the Bedford Hills in eastern Brooklyn, Weeksville was figuratively (and parts of it were literally) a city upon a hill."[38] One major motivation for founding Weeksville lay in the desire of Black Brooklynites to exercise full rights as citizens. By purchasing a parcel of land in Weeksville or elsewhere in the city, Black men could meet the state's property qualification to register as voters. This was a model of home ownership more connected to political participation than to the markers of bourgeois life. According to Wellman, the founding of Weeksville met a range of additional community needs, including "physical safety, education, economic self-sufficiency, and political self-determination."[39]

Weeksville, along with other Black enclaves in the city, provided Wilson with an important set of imaginative resources for his Black Forest, a protected space where one could rest, think, and create in peace. Places like Weeksville were also kinds of fantasy spaces carved out within the city itself. And in this period, one didn't have to go to Canada or even upstate to temporarily escape the thrum and chaos given a still-growing Brooklyn's proximity to the rural. Weeksville was figured by its own inhabitants as a bucolic retreat from the city. Junius C. Morel, a Weeksville founder and the principal of Colored School No. 2, paints this "half romantic fantasy" of his home there: "If it be any satisfaction to him to know who Junius is, I would lead him to a lonely cottage, surrounded with shrubbery of native growth, where birds flit through the boughs, and warble their sweet notes. The books he studies are first the Bible, and second Nature."[40] Morel figures his "lonely cottage, surrounded with shrubbery of native growth," as a quiet, protected space where he can study both the Bible and his natural surroundings.[41] Wilson was connected to Weeksville through his relationship with fellow principal Morel and because it was a hub of Black political activity in the city. Morel's description is one that cannily mirrors Ethiop's experience in Bernice's mountain home and art studio. And it's no coincidence that Wilson's wooded utopia is a *Black* Forest. This was a moment of historical transition when rural retreats could still be found at the edges of the city itself. Such rural and agricultural spaces on the margins of the city, like Brooklyn's estuarine environments, were life-sustaining for marginalized peoples seeking autonomy and dignity in antebellum New York. Weeksville's history is also a reminder that, in the contexts of white supremacy, the rural could itself be political, rather than a flight from it. This is an idea that Wilson picks up and runs with across his fiction writing.

Freedom Dreams and the Specter of Slavery

Despite the Black Forest tale's fantasies of unencumbered travel, movement in the Picture Gallery is always shadowed by the confinements of chattel slavery and the desperate flights of fugitive slaves. Travel in the United States and across the globe in 1859—in a post–Fugitive Slave Act, post–*Dred Scott* world—was especially risky for African Americans. In 1850, the Fugitive Slave Act had legally authorized the apprehending of any person of African descent suspected of having fled from slavery. It also authorized citizens to act as the police. African Americans like Solomon Northup, born free in upstate New York, were captured and sold into slavery under the authority of the Fugitive Slave Act. In 1857, *Dred Scott* would further reinforce the criminalization of Black personhood and denial of Black existence in the United States.

Wilson himself lived in a community that sheltered and housed fugitives. As Jesse Olvasky shows in his study *The Most Absolute Abolition*, the struggles and movements of fugitives on the front lines were always shaping abolitionist practice and thought.[42] Such was the case for Wilson and his cohort in New York. The omnipresence of fugitives in Wilson's midst is directly registered at the very end of the "Afric-American Picture Gallery." Relaying a story from the "early days" of the Underground Railroad in the "seventh paper" and final installment of the series, Ethiop recounts a day when a towering man named Bill came running into the gallery "in a towering rage."[43] Bill was hiding from his former owner, whom he had just seen walking on the street. This was in the early days of the gallery, during a time when "its quiet was seldom disturbed by visitors of any kind." From here, Ethiop delves into Bill's history and learns that this strapping, broad-chested, and clever man—a "real bull of Bashan"—managed to escape his master not once, but twice. In an especially dramatic moment, we learn that in a confrontation with two slave hunters, Bill only managed to escape after killing them both. As a sensationalist narrative filled with adventure, escape, and even murder, Bill's story may very well have been drawn from Wilson's frequent periodical reading. Or perhaps his story derived from a firsthand account from a fugitive who had escaped to Wilson's Brooklyn.

This final installment of the Picture Gallery closes with Ethiop noting that a portrait of Bill has been hung on the walls of the gallery: "The portrait of our sable hero, in all the flush of manhood, hangs on the north side of the Gallery, for the inspection of the curious."[44] It's significant that the final image we read in the Picture Gallery is a portrait of a fugitive slave. But of course, the act of bringing Bill into the field of representation was an ambiguous one: The fugitive's transformation into a word portrait stops his movement, places him in a frame, and potentially opens him up to recapture.

Thus, with fugitives and the threat of kidnapping as their immediate surround, even free Black cosmopolitans like William J. Wilson could not shake the specter of enslavement from their fantasies of travel and adventure. The harrowing journeys of fugitive people first appear much earlier in the series, when Ethiop describes "Pictures 5 and 6.—The Under Ground Railroad." Pictures 5 and 6 are a diptych depicting a group of fugitives escaping to the North on the Underground Railroad. The two paintings are placed side by side and labeled "A" and "B." Ethiop notes that they are large and represent "both the Southern and Northern portions of that mysterious road."[45] As on earlier stops on the tour, Ethiop plays with the geographical mapping of US slavery and freedom along a north–south axis, noting that although paintings "A" and "B" are hanging next to each other on the south side of the gallery, he would suggest that "B be changed over to the north wall, as a more appropriate place." While picture B depicts the group of fugitives safely arriving in the North, picture A is a Southern scene, depicting "a dark road leading through a darker forest, along which is seen merely some twenty pairs of fine stalwart human feet and leg—male and female—of all sizes, hurrying northward. Every muscle and limb indicates firmness and resolution." The diptych represents a diverse group escaping bondage; indeed, this is the first work on Ethiop's tour to mention any women at all. The group escapes at nighttime, the journey is hard, and the scene is dark, except for one bright beacon: "Far distant through the forest is faintly seen the north star—small but bright and unfailing, and to the fugitive, unerring." Picture B is filled with more light, a "north view" depicting "some twenty bold heads and fine robust faces, each of which is lit up with a joy no pen can portray, and nothing but the pencil of the master could have reached. The exclamation of each must be 'we have found it!!!'" Ethiop moves us from the joyful faces of the fugitives to the panting's foreground—a lake—and then to the background, "a Canadian forest, through which here and there you can perceive a small rustic cottage."[46] Is this a vision inspired by Morel's cottage from Weeksville? Or one of the other rustic homes occupied by African Americans along the water and on the outskirts of Brooklyn? Or Terance Ludlam's upstate country estate? Either way, it is a fascinating moment that looks forward to the Black Forest tale, even suggesting that Wilson's Black Forest may be located in Canada, a crucial destination for African Americans seeking freedom in the 1850s.

Wilson is keen to emphasize the Underground Railroad's secrecy and reliance on covert communication networks, and thus the difficulty of bringing it into the purview of the visual realm. Ethiop introduces the Underground Railroad as "that mysterious road," later mentions that "both of these pictures sustain well that air of mystery which envelopes the Under Ground Rail Road," notes the "mysterious manner in which those feet and legs move bodies toward freedom," and, in closing, emphasizes once again the "undefinable" nature of the "Road."[47] The group's destination is not the US North, but farther north, in Canada. Writing from his home in New York City, Wilson was very much aware that the portrayal of the US North as a haven for the fugitive was a fantasy, if not a delusion. In "The Under Ground Rail Road," as in both the Black Forest tale and in "Terance Ludlam," Wilson holds out hope that some form of relative safety might be secured for Black people north of New York City.[48]

Reader-viewers might also notice the title of this diptych splits *underground* into two words: *Under* and *Ground*. Such variability in spelling was common in the 1850s, when the Underground Railroad was still solidifying as both a signifier and as a network of cooperation and organization.

Under-ground Railroad, with a hyphen, was also commonly used. As with "Anglo-African" and "Afric-American," Wilson's Under Ground Railroad is part of the experimentation with abolitionist and racial nomenclature that was happening in years leading up to the Civil War. The Picture Gallery thus participates in an evolving political language developing alongside the accelerationism of abolition in the late 1850s.

Pictures 5 and 6 largely depart from the dominant visual grammars of runaway slaves as depicted in landscape and genre painting. For one, Wilson does not give us the full bodies of the fugitive figures; painting A represents their legs—or their "physical machinery," while painting B scans upward, giving us the heads and faces of the group.[49] This kind of figural splitting resonates with how enslaved people's bodies were commodified, calculated, and also anatomized, from the auction block to the plantation fields.[50] Fugitives were also a common specimen type in antebellum periodicals. Two stock images—a runaway woman and a runaway man—routinely appeared at the beginning of the fugitive slave advertisements that filled newspapers on both sides of the Mason-Dixon Line. These runaway ads also anatomized Black bodies, noting scars, disabilities, and other unique physical features that could help secure the capture and return of fugitives to the people who claimed to own them. But Wilson's fugitives arguably work as a critique of such regimes of violent anatomization. Ethiop notes that in representing part-bodies across the two canvases, the artist is making a point about the exploitation of enslaved people's bodies within the machine of slavery: "The head, the recognized seat of the mind, is useless to the slave, or, if of service to him, this thinking apparatus is not his own; it belongs to his owner; hence he makes use of his feet and legs, or the physical machinery; while in the second view, at the northern end of this undefinable Road, where liberty is, the head or mental part is presented to view. The slave,—the chattel,—the thing is a *man*." Wilson thus maps the enslaved body itself along a north–south axis, since in the South, his "thinking apparatus is not his own."[51]

There does not appear to be any one ekphrastic reference for "Under Ground Rail Road." There are some paintings from the period that depict fugitives in dense forest settings, as Wilson does. *Harper's Weekly* often published illustrations of escaped slaves, as well as maroons and rebels, in these kinds of scenes. Thomas Moran's *Slave Hunt* also resonates with what Wilson describes here, although it was produced in 1861, during the Civil War (plate 13). Wilson's painting depicting fugitive rebellion and escape through a treacherous and dangerous Southern landscape also hints at an event that had not yet come to pass: the raid on Harpers Ferry, led by John Brown and coordinated by a group of unnamed Black leaders in the North. "Under Ground Rail Road" appeared in the *Anglo-African* in February 1859, eight months before John Brown's raid on Harpers Ferry in October. However, Wilson was certainly privy to Brown's visits and planning with African American political leaders and actors across the Northeast. In moments like this, one can feel the thrum of revolutionary plotting and planning underneath the surface of the text.

The possibility of revolt to topple the enslavers' power—and the necessity of using armed self-defense to do so—is addressed directly when Bill runs into the picture gallery with his fist clenched around a "double-barrelled pistol."[52] Ethiop's subsequent note that in this earlier period "Colt's revolvers were not then in fashion" points to the fact that even the most cultured and elite African Americans in the North had knowledge of—and often themselves owned—guns. Wilson was part of a vanguard that did not rule out the necessity of force in fighting and dismantling white supremacy.[53] Seething with fear and anger, Bill suggests that if he sees this man again, he will kill him. That threat, interestingly, is issued under a kind of erasure in the text, with Ethiop saying he's relieved he did not hear the end of Bill's utterance: "The balance of this terrible utterance, happily, was lost on my ear . . . leaving me to supply my imagination what I could not ascertain by inquiry."[54] As in the world outside this text, it was enslaved people themselves who radicalized the abolitionist movement and moved abolitionists to advocate for the immediate end of slavery, by any means necessary.

Emigration, Ambivalence

The politics of movement in the Picture Gallery—including emergent forms of queer movement like flaneuring, coasting, and cruising—were thus deeply connected to escapes from slavery, and the conditions of terror, fear, and violence that accompanied them. Plots in both the Picture Gallery and "Terance Ludlam" also connected to larger-scale debates about Black settlement and emigration outside the United States. The question of emigration was an especially important and unavoidable topic in the political scene of Black Brooklyn in the 1850s. That energy culminated in 1859 with the founding of the African Civilization Society, an organization that was established to promote the founding of a colony for African American emigrants in Liberia. Wilson himself engaged in emigration debates in his capacity as a representative at Black state and national conventions. He was also a member of the Committee of Thirteen, which took an explicitly anticolonization stance.

Black advocates for emigration insisted that their intentions and goals were different from organizations like the American Colonization Society, which counted enslavers among its members and sought to rid the nation of African Americans who were free or freed, and thus bound to stir up trouble, in the hopes of preserving the enslaving republic. But even Black-led plans to emigrate outside the United States were clouded by this earlier history of white-controlled, anti-Black colonization efforts. In *Frederick Douglass' Paper*, Wilson compared the emigration movement to a contagious illness, saying, "A *distemper* long prevalent among the whites, has broken out here among the Blacks. It must be speedily cured: aye, if need be, burned out with *caustic*, ere it spread, and drink out the very life-blood of the people."[55] While Wilson vocally opposed emigration in his public life, his Picture Gallery registers the profound ambivalence that attended emigration debates in his community. Similarly, while scholarship has tended to understand the history of Black emigration in binary terms (people were either anti- or pro-emigration), the reality on the ground was much more complex.

As historian Ousmane Power-Greene has chronicled, debates over Black emigration and colonization in the 1850s were a site of active debate and division among African American communities.[56] Organizational records and minutes of the period also register emigration as a site of profound ambivalence. As Judith Wellman notes, Henry Highland Garnet was in 1858 delivering fiery anti-emigration speeches; by 1859 he had changed his mind, setting sail for Liberia and becoming a vocal proponent and leader in the movement to emigrate to that country. Power-Greene's more recent research focuses on the auxiliary societies of the American Colonization Society, which were often doing different kinds of work and serving local communities in all kinds of ways.[57]

The minutes of the Colored Conventions are especially helpful documents for understanding the ambivalence that surrounded plans for the mass resettlement of African Americans outside the United States. They are also documents that reflect how even anti-emigrationist positions could seed Black imaginaries of flight, fantasy, and utopian transport. On September 4, 1855, the Colored Men's State Convention of New York in Troy convened to fulfill a "sacred obligation resting upon the colored citizens of this State, to give the ear of our Legislature no rest till every legal and political disability, with all its depressing and degrading tendencies, shall be swept from the Empire State."[58] More concretely, the meeting was assembled to organize in opposition to New York State's suppression of citizenship rights through a property qualification that made voting rights contingent on the ownership of private property, a classic tool of disenfranchisement under racial capitalism that continues under other guises today, most notably through mass incarceration, ID laws, and gerrymandering. The proceedings also concretized the formation of the New York State Suffrage Association, with Frederick Douglass appointed as president, James McCune Smith as one of two secretaries, Wilson as part of the board of managers, and other Black leaders filling out the roster of officers. Wilson was Brooklyn's delegate to the Troy Convention.

The minutes of the Troy Convention offer much insight into the rhetorical and affective complexities that swirled around debates about emigration in the 1850s. Amid the rote bureaucratic details and formulaic resolutions presented and debated throughout the proceedings, most of which focused on fighting the rollback of Black voting rights in the state, one resolution stands out as exceptional in both topic and tone: "Resolved, That it is important that two sailing vessels, owned by the Grand Council of this State, be fitted out to reach the grievances of our deluded brethren who have emigrated to Africa or any other unhealthy clime, to give them an opportunity to return at any reasonable expense." The resolution clearly marks out the convention's stance on emigration, but it does so in a surprisingly performative way, one that moves the meeting resolutions from the terrain of administrative tedium to the horizon of speculative transport. The convention doesn't ask the state to ban emigration; it doesn't establish an anti-emigration speaker's bureau, as it did on the question of the Black franchise; it audaciously proposes that the state of New York outfit two sailing vessels to convey "deluded" emigrationists back to the United States. The resolution also implicitly asks attendees, and readers of the minutes, to form an image of these ships in their heads. It is thus a brief yet arresting moment of Black ekphrasis, expressed in a register that resonates with Douglass's own students-as-ships imagery in "Claims of the Negro, Ethnologically Considered," delivered just a year before the 1855 Troy Convention.

This surprising resolution-cum-speculative demand operates as a fascinating kind of rhetorical excess within the convention proceedings. It is further marked by the kind of dry wit and sardonic humor that characterizes much Black writing in the late antebellum period. What I want to note here is how even anti-emigrationist stances could take shape through the metaphorical resources made possible through the seafaring imaginary of emigration itself. Black emigration debates were raging in the mid-1850s and were dividing activist communities. But emigration—always traversing the memory and imagination of the slave trade itself—also opened up a space for Black expression that could accommodate the complex feelings that circulated around the question of uprooting families and leaving friends and communities behind. The emigration debate was thus fraught, not just with political dogmatism but also with opacity, hesitance, and ambivalence.

Political ambivalence also marks the literature of colonization and emigration in the 1850s. As a topic that many African Americans were anxious about, many writers worked through the question of emigration with fictional forms and other forms of rhetoric that were adjacent to, but not collapsible with, political speech and writing. Thomas Hamilton was sure to signal the anticolonizationist stance of the *Anglo-African Magazine*, but it is a topic that is taken up in multiple, and sometimes opposing, ways throughout the magazine. For Wilson, the genre of fantasy allowed him to explore the question of emigration without committing to a particular ideological position. Indeed, as a work of utopian writing, the Black Forest tale refuses transparent positions on politics.

The ambivalence characterizing Black emigration debates is especially clear in Ethiop's ekphrastic description of a Nigerian sunset, the fourth picture to be visited on the text's gallery tour. Shifting from the first colonial settlement in Jamestown in picture 1, to the first African American newspaper editor in picture 2, to the beginnings of the Revolutionary War in picture 3, Ethiop's gallery tour opens with a cascade of origin stories. This procession of "firsts" suggests themes and tropes that were of great importance to Wilson: slavery's horrors and the slave trade's degrading influence on the American republic, the rise of the Black press as an essential advocate for African American rights and building of political power, and the central role that African Americans have played in the nation's origins. These first three pictures also operate as a frame through which readers are encouraged to view the rest of the gallery's collection. But Wilson's sly repetition of firsts also impresses a fact central to the realities of nineteenth-century development and well known to all newspapermen and women of the period: that it's difficult, if not impossible, to find a single beginning in a society increasingly defined by commodification, capitalist exchange, and the rapid and promiscuous spread of news and reprinted stories across the print sphere.

In front of picture 4, Wilson moves readers away from polemical firsts and toward more ambiguous historical and political terrain. "Sunset in Abbeokuta" is a landscape, one that idealizes the Nigerian coast, and by extension, the entire continent of Africa. Abbeokuta—present-day Abeokuta—is situated on the Nigerian coast, about fifty miles north of Lagos. Historically a site of conflict between the Dahomey and the Igbo, in the mid-nineteenth century it became a battleground among British settler colonists, European and Anglo-American missionaries, and the local population. In other words, Abeokuta was a hotly contested territory in Wilson's own time, a space where settler colonial experiments and fantasies were relentlessly projected onto the land and its people.

Wilson's "Sunset in Abbeokuta" imagines a time before settler colonial violence and conflict over African territory and resources. A landscape, "rich, beautiful, [and] varied," "Sunset" envisions Abeokuta in an Edenic, precontact condition, before its devastation by European slavers and the Atlantic slave trade. Here, instead, is a mellow scene marked by beauty, peace, and rest: "The sky has all the warmth of hue and softness of tint, and all that gorgeousness (changing seemingly with every instant,) for which an African sky is so much noted. . . . The last touches of the artist's pencil has made the glow of the coming evening to softly spread itself over here and there a dusky inhabitant reclining upon the banks of an unrippled lake."[59] Ethiop, here, is describing golden hour, that "glow of the coming evening . . . softly spread[ing] itself," a moment of beauty and tranquility right before the nighttime descends. Ethiop goes on to say that no rainbow could compete with the variety of color and hue in the African sky: "No rainbow with us, in its full splendor, is so variegated or so wide in its range of colors."[60] Abeokuta was known as a mountainous refuge from slave hunters, and in this way, also connects to the histories of maroonage that interested Wilson in other places in the Picture Gallery.

Although it is depicted as a warm and welcoming scene that invites viewer-readers in, this is an idyllic landscape on the verge of invasion. In this moment in the late 1850s, the coast of Nigeria was also a place of much interest among African Americans advocating for a mass exodus to West Africa, including Martin Delany, who traveled to the Niger Valley in 1858 and 1859 under the auspices of the African Civilization Society to explore the possibility of African American resettlement there. A frontispiece from an 1854 missionary text appears to be a direct reference for Wilson. Titled *Abbeokuta; or, Sunrise Within the Tropics: An Outline of the Origin and Progress of the Yoruba Mission*, and authored by one Sarah Parker, the book traces the British colonial occupation of Abeokuta through both imperial force and missionary work, seeking to give readers "an 'outline' of the origin and progress of the Missions in Yoruba." The book also includes a frontispiece that approximates the scene that Ethiop describes (plate 14). This, then, is one of the objects in the picture gallery that has a real-world referent, an image taken directly from the print sphere and ekphrastically represented in Wilson's print gallery. It is significant that the frontispiece appears in full color in a time when that was rare. Perhaps this fact accounts for Ethiop's own emphasis on the color of his ekphrastic portrait. Wilson's mention of a rainbow also plays on the fact that the book's title page notes that "Miss Parker" has authored another work, titled *Rainbow in the North*. Wilson's transformation of Parker's *Sunrise Within the Tropics* into his "Sunset in Abbeokuta" demonstrates that this ekphrastic landscape seeks to be a part of the discourse on African American colonization and Christian missionary work on the African continent.

Despite its brightness, Wilson's welcoming scene is also shaded by darker hues. This, after all, is a landscape representing not a sunrise but a sunset. Perhaps Wilson is suggesting that the emigration movement is itself headed toward its own sunset, a dimming of former potential and activity. Ethiop's description is ultimately colored by a sense of doubt about the "civilizing" influence of African American missionary expeditions in West Africa. "Sunset in Abbeokuta" is, in this way, part of Wilson's broader ambivalence about the emigration movement. At the end of his description of this scene, Ethiop notes, in his characteristically dry tone, "The whole scene is so charming that one could almost wish to be there." Almost, but not quite.

An extant letter by William J. Wilson, a four-page piece of correspondence addressed to a Brooklyn historian and housed in the collections of the Brooklyn Historical Society, further suggests the complexity of the politics of movement and emigration on the ground for both Wilson and his community.[61] The letter details many departures from Wilson's school, including that of Augustus Washington, Wilson's predecessor at Colored School No. 1 and an early Black photographer who took famous daguerreotypes of John Brown and prominent Black leaders and families. Wilson was appointed principal after Washington emigrated to Liberia in 1852. Wilson's anti-emigrationist position feels implicit in the letter, but for reasons that are more practical than ideological. Throughout this letter, which is offered as a brief history of Colored School No. 1, Wilson conjures the ghostly absences of teachers, students, friends, and family swept up in the tides of late antebellum emigration, dispossession, and movement.

Our narratives about migration tend to focus on destinations, rather than the people and places left. Wilson's letter instead encourages us to consider the local dimensions of migration, especially the ways that departures from the community produced waves of grief and absence behind them. The building of a movement around leaving the United States also paradoxically required the establishment of local spaces that supported and nurtured those efforts. Black emigration in the 1850s was thus defined by a very particular dialectic of setting up an institution (putting down roots) to eventually leave it (emigration). Such a dynamic produced forms of ambivalence that were difficult to articulate in political and civic discourse. A seemingly nonpolitical genre, the fairy-tale tradition ultimately offered Wilson a generative space through which to grapple with those affective and emotional complexities, behind the scenes of official debates and public controversy.

Conclusion

William J. Wilson and his family joined the exodus of African Americans who left their homes and communities during the Civil War, throwing themselves into the war effort in various capacities and leaving behind hard-won conditions of relative stability in the North. Activists and educators went south to aid slaves-turned-refugees and war "contraband" as they fled from plantations and Confederate regiments to Union camps and makeshift free towns. Wilson was among the hundreds of Black New Yorkers who traveled south to educate former slaves, teaching in freedmen's schools founded independently by Black communities, Christian missionary organizations, and by the Freedmen's Bureau.[1] Fellow writer, educator, and activist Harriet Jacobs was also a part of this exodus from New York State.

In Wilson's Brooklyn, the African Civilization Society (ACS) was central to efforts to organize and move Black educators south. While the ACS was originally founded with an aim to resettle African Americans in Africa, during the war its focus shifted back to the national front as it mobilized to provide mutual aid and education to former slaves. The ACS's contributions also included their publication of the *Freedman's Torchlight*, which Elizabeth McHenry describes as a "schoolbook in newspaper form."[2] Published in Brooklyn beginning in 1866, the paper was explicitly designed to serve as a tool for literacy—complete with printed alphabets—and as a portable, cheap textbook of sorts, intended for use by Black teachers in formal classrooms and for adults who were working on their own to gain literacy and were engaged in other forms of self-study.[3] Thus, with the coming of the war, many Black Brooklynites turned their sights on the US South, committing themselves to the various needs of formerly enslaved people as they escaped captivity.

The outbreak of the Civil War was certainly an impetus for Wilson's migration out of the city, but there were other factors at play too. Donald Yacovone says that Brooklyn's board of education forced Wilson to resign from his position after he gave several antislavery speeches at the Cooper Institute in response to Lincoln's Emancipation Proclamation in 1863.[4] Even before this incident, Wilson experienced persistent surveillance and discrimination from the board of education. His school was also the frequent target of violence and harassment: In 1863, he reported to the board that his school faced constant vandalism and "mobbing" from antagonistic white residents who did not want a Black school in their neighborhood. White youth and adults threw stones into the school's windows at night, and on their way to school, students were harassed, bullied, and even beaten. In one especially painful moment Wilson talks about children having their books slapped out of their arms as they walked to school. As a result of these incidents, attendance at Wilson's school dwindled. Many parents kept their children at home because they didn't feel safe sending them to a school constantly being attacked by white people. Other parents pulled their children out of Colored School No. 1 and sent them elsewhere.[5]

The late 1850s were an especially destabilizing time for Black New Yorkers, and waves of harassment, violence, and forced displacement also contributed to periodic waves of migration *within* the city. In 1857, the city razed Seneca Village to clear space for the construction of Central Park, dispossessing the historic Black community who called it home. Wilson's report about the terrorizing of his students and school was published only a few days before the beginning of the Draft Riots of 1863, a protest waged by white immigrant workers against Civil War draft laws that turned into a violent mob that terrorized Lower Manhattan's African American community and ultimately killed over 120 Black New Yorkers.[6] The brutal violence and chaos of the Draft Riots initiated another round of migrations of New York's African American population, with many individuals and families choosing to leave Manhattan for Brooklyn.[7] For others, the Draft Riots proved too traumatizing to remain anywhere in the city: In their aftermath, many Black New Yorkers decided to migrate permanently outside the city. The 1850s were a decade in which African Americans in New York built unprecedented amounts of power and became highly organized as communities and political actors. As such, it was also a decade that witnessed vicious forms of backlash by white elites who benefited from a rigid class hierarchy in the city and by lower-class white workers who saw African Americans as competitors in the labor market. It was in response to these conditions of destabilization, violence, and dispossession that Wilson and his family decided to pack up and leave Gotham for good.

Given his interest in being at the center of both culture and politics, it's perhaps no surprise that Wilson moved with Mary and Annie to DC, the seat of federal power and the heart of formal Black politics in the Reconstruction era. In the summer of 1863, Wilson had traveled to DC, toured the nation's capital, and written about his trip in a series of letters to the *Weekly Anglo-African*, the weekly successor to the *Anglo-African Magazine*.[8] What he saw there must have been central to his family's decision to move south. In DC, Wilson would join many of the nation's most prominent African American leaders and activists, including Frederick Douglass. He also directed the school established at Camp Barker, one of the refugee camps established for recently emancipated slaves who had fled the Confederacy. That school would come under the direction of the American Missionary Association (AMA); Mary and Annie also taught formerly enslaved youth at Camp Barker. In 1864, Wilson accepted a position as principal of the Third Street School, another AMA school. As in Brooklyn, Wilson's teaching activities were paired with many civic and political activities. He was a member of a committee of African Americans that worked to memorialize Lincoln before the Lincoln Memorial would become a federal project, and he served as a delegate at the National Convention of Colored Men in 1869. He was active in advocating for and funding Black schools in DC and was also a founding trustee of Howard University.[9]

Wilson also continued to make contributions to African American periodicals after the Civil War. Literary scholar Benjamin Fagan has recently uncovered Wilson's contributions to Douglass's *New National Era*, where he wrote columns under a new pen name: Old Boy in "Spects." Wilson's column was titled "Notes from the Capital," and it ran in the paper in the spring and summer of 1874. "Notes from the Capital" bears much resemblance to Ethiop's jaunty, on-the-street reporting for *Frederick Douglass' Paper* in the 1850s. The column's subtitle, "To My Townsfolks 'Afar,'" suggests that Wilson was particularly interested in reaching readers outside the nation's capital, perhaps even directly addressing his friends and former colleagues in Brooklyn. Wilson's columns in the *New National Era* are characteristically witty and deeply attuned to happenings in DC culture and politics. They apprise readers of recent congressional appointments and debates happening in the government. They also relate Wilson's encounters on the street, both humorous and racially charged, and give glimpses into Black DC's high society, detailing a glamorous world of galas, dinners, soirees, and literary meetings among the city's most educated and well-connected African Americans. Wilson calls this world "fashionable colored young society," and he characterizes its members as participating in a "gay, young life" that was marked by horseplay and giddiness, rather than intemperance and vice: "They are intelligent but pleasingly giddy; not intemperate, yet innocently gay."[10] This class of youth in DC, Wilson emphasizes, expressed their new conditions of freedom through good, innocent fun. Of course, one may wonder why Wilson felt the need to emphasize the innocence of Black youth interested in testing freedom by following their desires.

As Old Boy in "Spects," Wilson also experiments with genre and form, playfully combining his own writings in prose and poetry. In addition to his street reporting, he includes humorous sketches and dialogues along with a few of his own poems. Old Boy refers to one of these poems as a "little winter scene" and goes on to suggest that readers "frame it and hang it up in your best room for next winter and all the winters that shall be spared to you."[11] In such moments where poems are imagined as frameable scenes of art, Wilson revisits the stylistic terrain of the "Afric-American Picture Gallery." Wilson also wants readers to connect his postwar writings as "Old Boy" to his earlier writings and pseudonym. In one column, he even outs himself as Ethiop. Introducing an illustrious cast of attendees at a recent meeting of the Lotus Club in the parlors of Douglass's home, he closes with a word portrait of a fashionable figure who should be familiar to readers: Donning a "blue coat, gilt buttons, and high standup collar, may be seen your old friend Ethiop quietly located among this self sustained and peculiar crowd."[12] In moments like this one, Old Boy slyly winks at his readers.

Across his columns "Notes from the Capital," Wilson stylizes himself as a skilled commentator on fine art and high culture. It should come as no surprise that Old Boy is keen to keep track of Black buyers of fine art. In his first column as Old Boy in "Spects" he informs readers that a much-discussed portrait of the late Charles Sumner has just been privately acquired by James Worsley, a successful entrepreneur and prominent member of DC's "colored aristocracy."[13] Worsley was the proprietor of a popular hotel in the city, and in 1871 he became a crucial force in getting Congress to fund the city's first public elementary school. It would be named the Sumner School.

With this new pen name, Wilson sought to construct himself as a venerable, bespectacled elder. But the columns are also marked by a youthful playfulness characteristic of all Wilson's writings. Grappling with the realities of aging and facing questions about his own relevance in a changing world, Old Boy circles around several scenes that meditate on his relationship to a younger generation of African American aesthetes in DC, who were not embarrassed by their desire to feel good and find pleasure where they could.[14] Old Boy will accept his status as elder in one column and in the next will insist on the relativeness of age, saying that anyone who has vigor, purpose, and determination should be considered young.[15] Old Boy's position is thus a vacillating one, marked by playfulness and cheer in some moments, and by ambivalence and even resignation in others.

Positioning himself as both an insider to DC's glamorous world of Black socialites and a trustworthy observer for those outside that world, Old Boy gives readers glimpses of the many galas, balls, and other social soirees being held in the city. For example, in his account of a "Grand Supper of the Waverly Club," he catalogs the "epicurean satisfaction" of the dinner and the superiority of the night's fashion, music, and dancing.[16] Ever the gentleman, he says that there was no one belle or beau of the ball. Everyone looked fabulous, and all who attended were captivating dancers and conversationalists. Wilson's role as an educator placed him in proximity to youth across his life, and it is from this vantage point that he offers views of DC's fashionable high society of African Americans in a new age of freedom.

As an educator and as someone deeply invested in the social scene, it's also the case that Wilson, more so than most of his male colleagues, circulated in a world of women. Many of his columns highlight the fashions and social activities of young Black women in the city, based on his firsthand observations and circulation in this world.[17] Falling into the traps of feminine stereotyping of his age, one column ascribes the passing of a recent bill funding the city's schools to the sympathetic, imploring body of women teachers in the city who "melted" the frigid hearts of Congress. The ever-dramatic Wilson says that "we are all in ecstasies" over the passage of this bill.[18]

While still attracted to the glitz, glamour, and secrecy of the well-connected, Wilson's Reconstruction-era writings also register a new attention to conditions of poverty and deprivation among his community, something that is not a focus of his prewar writings. For example, in a moving poem, "The Beggar Girl," he relates a tragic tale about the death of an indigent young woman, imploring readers to not forget the poor. Wilson's increasing sensitivity to the existence and experiences of the Black poor was certainly connected to his witnessing of the struggles of the formerly enslaved as they sought to gain a foothold in the nation's capital after the war.

Wilson's deepening class consciousness was also connected to his appointment in 1865 as cashier of the Freedman's Savings Bank, a position that put him in proximity to the city's population of former slaves as they struggled to find employment and save their pennies in a "free" economy striated by racial subjection and haunted by slavery. Established by the US government as a safe place for the formerly enslaved to deposit their earnings and for soldiers to deposit their pensions, the bank would ultimately fall victim to predation and corruption by white bankers and speculators, leading to its collapse in early July 1874. In *Black Reconstruction*, Du Bois said that the story of the Freedman's Bank was so disgraceful and shameful that it was "a chapter in American history which most Americans naturally prefer to forget."[19]

Serving as cashier of the Freedman's Bank befitted a man who believed that the liberation of the race was impossible without complete economic autonomy. Wilson's work in this new role was focused on receiving deposits, but he was also charged with building trust with the community, promoting the bank, and assuring former slaves and soldiers that the Freedman's Bank was a safe place for their savings. Of course, such trust building was essential for a people who had been betrayed by the American government time and time again. A fascinating feature in the December 14, 1874, issue of the *New National Era* relays several stories that seek to mythologize the founding of the Freedman's Bank and Wilson's role in building both its reputation and its coffers. The article opens with a proud announcement of the bank's recent move to a grand, opulent building across the street from the Treasury Department on Pennsylvania Avenue. It goes on to emphasize how far the bank had come from its humble origins: In its early years the bank was housed in several ad hoc locations, including in rented rooms in a woman's home. The origin story narrated here centers Wilson and the first deposit of a humble freeman:

> His first announcement [of the bank] was to his own pupils, and one of them, a son of a freedman named Hill, told him his father's box had been broken open the previous night and some two hundred dollars carried off. The boy said his father had still twenty-four dollars, and asked Mr. Wilson if he would put that in his bank. The answer being in the

> affirmative, his father was brought back after school recess and made the first deposit of $24, and so the freedman Hill, laid the foundation of an institution which struck deep root in the soil, and whose branches now spread over a large portion of the Union.[20]

During these early years, Wilson was known to carry the bank's capital "on his own person." Seeking to emphasize his dedication and intrepid commitment to a bank built for African Americans, the feature also details Wilson's hair-raising adventures while working on the ground to build confidence in and capital for the bank. The article relates one apocryphal story about Wilson recruiting depositors in a regiment camp in DC: After successfully convincing several soldiers to give him their pensions, he slept in a tent in the middle of the camp with all of the deposits. This was clearly a tense situation: In the morning, some soldiers changed their minds and demanded their money back, guns cocked at Wilson.

Such stories of Wilson carrying bank deposits "on his own person" and risking his life by doing so signal the priority that he and his colleagues placed on the amassing of Black wealth after the Civil War. Given Wilson's lifelong interest in the building of economic power as a pathway to freedom, it's striking to see newspaper accounts where he has money laminated literally to his body. In his columns for the *New National Era* we can feel Wilson selling the bank hard, puffing up the institution and presenting it as a monumental sign of progress for African Americans after the war. An 1873 article in the *New National Era* reported that Wilson left DC with some frequency, traveling across the South and "instructing" freedpeople on "economy and frugality" as part of his financial evangelism for the Freedman's Bank.[21]

The relocation of the Freedman's Bank across from the US Treasury Department held much symbolic significance for Wilson and his interlocutors. It must have felt like an auspicious sign for African American activists and political leaders in DC who were seeking visibility and political power within the parameters of a largely untested citizenship in the first years after emancipation. This was a federally supported Black institution housed alongside federal offices in the nation's capital. The December 1873 feature in the *New National Era* also offered readers a virtual tour of the new building (not totally unlike Ethiop's tour of the picture gallery), highlighting the opulence of the space, the quality of its furnishings, and the impressiveness of the bank's vault. Wilson's room, "the cashier's room," is described as a "fine one," and designed for "the transaction of a large business." It is designed to project richness and wealth: "A beautiful solid marble counter, paneled and moulded, extends along the entire length. This is surmounted by Black walnut desks, guarded by railings of the same material, behind which stands the cashier and his assistants. Beyond this room is the office of the actuary and his clerks, and within it is the vault for the valuables. This is protected by a massive metal door, which is secured by a ponderous combination lock. Within the vault is an immense safe, constructed to resist fire and burglars." Such descriptions of the Freedman's Bank are meant to instill trust and confidence in readers of the paper, who might themselves become depositors. At a larger, more symbolic level, the article conjures an image of a Black institution that is grand, secure, and opulent, auguring a rich future for the nation's freedpeople.

Given all we know about Wilson—especially his belief in the powers of Black wealth and conspicuous consumption—he must have felt proud to serve in this distinguished position as cashier of the Freedman's Bank. He must have been particularly delighted by the bank's move to a respectable and highly visible location on Pennsylvania Avenue. Loan receipts and other ephemera in his hand display a flamboyant handwriting style, as well as small drawings that served as visual embellishments (figure C.1). A surviving letter in the Freedmen's Bureau archive also records Wilson's request for a handsome desk and platform to be made for the bank in its new location (figure C.2).

But this moment of fortuitous beginnings and hope would soon come undone. The collapse of the Freedman's Bank in 1874 included the termination of Wilson's position as cashier. It also coincided with the end of his "Notes from the Capital" column in the *New National Era*. It's likely that the bank's closure was experienced by Wilson as a personal devastation that produced disillusionment and threw into question his belief in racial liberation through the accumulation of wealth in a capitalist system. The tragic collapse of the Freedman's Bank at the hands of greedy bankers and speculators showed that the nation's capitalist postwar economy was a setup, structured through racial hierarchy and exploitation in which white elites were designed to win, and African Americans were destined to lose. The bank's collapse was also an extension of the suffering, poverty, and illness that plagued former slaves in the nation's capital. In 1863, Harriet Jacobs wrote about her firsthand witnessing of how smallpox had devastated a refugee camp in Alexandria, Virginia, where she was doing relief work, noting, "The misery I have witnessed must be seen to be believed."[22] Indeed, rampant disease and illness were among the most real and immediate afterlives of slavery.[23]

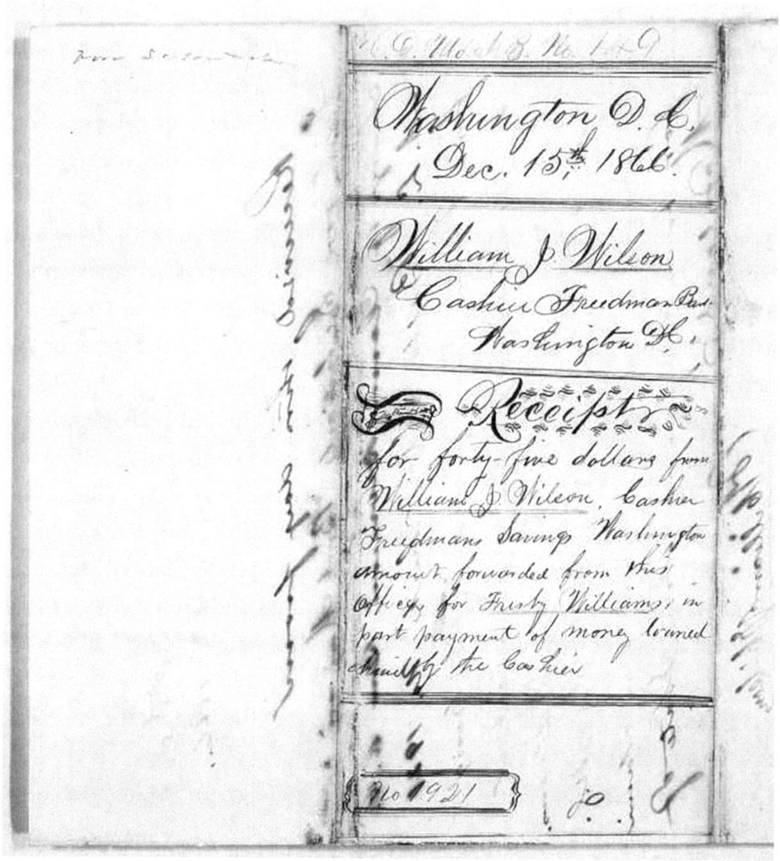

Washington D.C.
Dec. 15th 1866.
William J. Wilson
Cashier Freedman Ban[k]
Washington D.C.
Receipt
for forty-five dollars from
William J. Wilson, Cashier
Freedmans Savings Washington
amount forwarded from this
Office for [illegible] Williams in
part payment of money loaned
the Cashier
No 1921

C.1 Loan receipt written by William J. Wilson, cashier of Freedman's Bank, Washington, DC, December 15, 1866. Freedmen's Bureau Records, National Archives.

Wilson's last column in the *New National Era* appeared on July 16, 1874, and with it, Old Boy chooses not narrative but verse to decry the tragic fall of the Freedman's Bank, which he calls "the institution of my people." Indeed, he says he's able only to write a poem in such distressing times: "Much to say to you, my dear Townsfolks 'Afar,'" but "the sad event of this week forbids me, and I can only say now—." What follows is a seven-stanza poem that offers sorrowful scenes of misery, hunger, and desperation among those who lost their precious earnings in the bank's failing. The poem suggests that the closure of the Freedman's Bank threatened to deepen conditions of deprivation as well as feelings of hopelessness in the age of so-called emancipation.[24] It also foregrounds

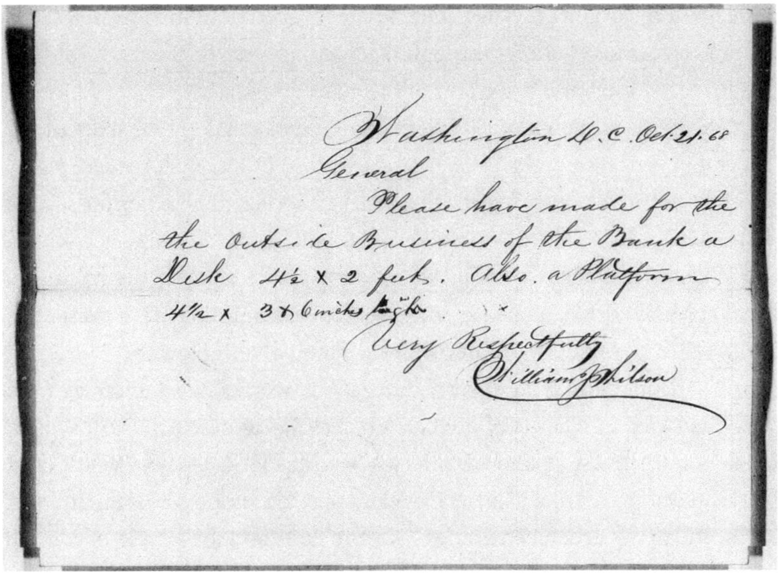

Washington D.C. Oct 21. 68
General
Please have made for the
the Outside Business of the Bank a
Desk 4½ x 2 feet. Also a Platform
4½ x 3 & 6 inches high.
Very Respectfully
William J. Wilson

C.2 Letter from William J. Wilson, Washington, DC, October 21, 1868. Freedmen's Bureau Records, National Archives.

Wilson's own feelings of despair, while suggesting, subtly, that he himself is not to blame for the bank's mismanagement and closure ("I was slain unawares"):

> A great and mighty institution has fallen!
> And I am undone!—I am clean gone!
> My purposes are broken off!
> The institution of my people,
> The tower whence cometh their strength,
> Has suddenly come to naught,
> And their substance is scattered.

It's certainly possible to read this poem, his last in the *New National Era*, as being about Wilson trying to save face, possibly even pleading for mercy and forgiveness from his community. It appears that the Freedman's Bank's failure tarnished Wilson's reputation among the city's Black professional class. The *People's Advocate* noted that many directed anger and indignation at "Mr. Wilson" that should have been directed at those "white rascals" who "*profited* and still profit *by the stealings*."[25] It is telling that the bank's failure corresponds with the end of Wilson's writing career: He was never to be heard from again in the periodical sphere. Wilson's name can still be found in Howard's Catalog of Trustees and Officers through 1878, but in these final years of his life, there are few other archival traces of the man or his activities.

Wilson passed away on November 26, 1878, at the age of sixty after a "short illness of two weeks." His funeral was held in DC at St. Luke's Episcopal Church on Fifteenth Street, where he had served as an elder for several years. Alexander Crummell—pastor of St. Luke's, sometime emigrationist, and Wilson's friend since his Brooklyn days—presided over the memorial service. Many distinguished members of the community were present to honor Wilson, including Robert Purvis, faculty from Howard, Mary and Annie Wilson, and surely several other Black women whose names were rarely included in records of events and meetings in newspapers.[26] Wilson was laid to rest in Graceland Cemetery, a historic Black cemetery where both Maria Stewart and Anna Murray Douglass were also interred. Graceland was one of the many urban cemeteries—for the poor and for people of color—that were closed as cities expanded and required more space. Most of the people laid to rest in Graceland, a cemetery that included many of DC's most prominent Black citizens, were disinterred over a series of decades and moved to other burial plots.[27]

Wilson's obituary notes that the collapse of the Freedman's Bank bankrupted him and caused him to lose his property on Q Street. Friends subsequently helped him to secure a position as justice of the peace, followed by an appointment in the Treasury Department. The paper's editor goes on to suggest that Wilson's "poems, sketches and romances might form the basis of a volume entitled Ethiop," with the proceeds going to his "widow and his daughter." Although the Picture Gallery series was not a "begging book" like Harriet Wilson's *Our Nig*, here the editor says that the publication of a posthumous collection of Wilson's writings as Ethiop could provide much-needed financial support for Wilson's widow and daughter. Marked by financial struggles and housing and employment insecurity, Wilson's final years point to the precarity of class status for even the most educated and professionally established Black Americans in the period. This turn of events both affirms and points to the limits of Wilson's lifelong commitment to the accumulation of capital as a political strategy for African Americans. Prithi Kanakamedala notes that after William's death Annie and Mary were both still working as teachers and lived together at Hannah Peck's boardinghouse, near Logan Circle.[28] By the early 1880s, Mary Wilson was listed in DC city directories as being a widow, living on U Street. Annie Wilson, now Annie Boston, and her husband, Thomas S. Boston, would join the exodus of Black Americans to the Midwest, eventually resettling in Chicago. And Kanakamedala shares this surprising and telling detail: By 1904, Mary had apparently returned to Brooklyn and was living at the Wilsons' former home at 23 Greene Avenue in Fort Greene.[29] She was eighty-two years old. Her migration back to the Northeast suggests that even some forty years after their departure, the Wilsons still regarded Brooklyn as home.

William J. Wilson and the Origins of a Black Queer Aesthetics

It would be against the spirit of Wilson's writing—especially its life-affirming creativity and playfulness—to end this book with themes of tragedy, demise, and death. Instead I want to conclude by suggesting that with Wilson we can locate the beginnings of a Black queer aesthetics as it began to develop within cultures of Afropolitanism and bohemianism in late antebellum urban cultures; those cultures were themselves deeply shaped by the practices and cultures of the enslaved as well as ideas about labor, leisure, and the refusal of work itself. Indeed, given Wilson's sardonic wit, his dandyism, and his interest in dragging and "reading" his closest friends in print, we might place his writings within the beginnings of a genealogy of queer writing that is often dated to the New Negro Renaissance but that has roots in this earlier moment in the late 1850s. As early as 1851, Wilson was experimenting with narratives and tropes that we associate with queer lexigraphy and practice.

Wilson's life and writing in the postwar period also helps us to track how midcentury dandyism and cultures of the urban flaneur would be transformed into more modern queer identities later in the nineteenth century. Wilson's postwar writings as Old Boy in "Spects" help to connect the dots between 1850s bohemianism and more modern queer identities and cultures that were starting to emerge in the 1870s, alongside social scientific and sexological discourses invested in categorizing and capturing sexual "inversion." As Siobhan Somerville has argued, "Simultaneous efforts to shore up and bifurcate categories of race and sexuality in the late nineteenth and early twentieth centuries were deeply intertwined."[30] Somerville argues that the emergence of homosexuality in the late nineteenth century depended on the entrenchment of the color line. It's no accident that the homosexual was "invented" in 1896, the same year that the US Supreme Court upheld the legality of racial segregation across the United States.

Wilson's writings are an archive of Black pleasure, decadence, and desire, practices of freedom the state would increasingly attempt to suppress through law, custom, and vigilante justice after the fall of Reconstruction. Old Boy in "Spects" offered readers of the *New National Era* a glimpse into a glamorous world of Reconstruction-era sociality, parties, and merry-making. But underneath this only partially public world of Black socialites and heterosexual courtship documented by Wilson thrummed an underground scene of Black drag and ball culture. In 1880s DC, the formerly enslaved brothel owner William Dorsey Swann was known as the "queen of drag" and founded something that looked very close to the house culture that would be central to drag cultures in the twentieth century, especially for young queer and trans people of color. Swann's secret balls for Black queer men and trans women in the city provided crucial spaces for self-expression, collectivity, and pleasure, but they also were subject to police raids and suppression.[31] Although Wilson's reporting did not extend to drag balls and Black gay cultures, his proximity to women's fashion and style is a pronounced part of his reporting as Old Boy in "Spects." And the semiunderground world he portrays—one that centers pleasure, joy, and "carousing"—helps us to see that Black queer forms of writing and expression in the United States did not appear out of thin air during the Harlem Renaissance; they only became more public at that moment, with a more substantial platform for publication and a broader mainstream curiosity (that could veer into fetishism) about countercultural practices and forms of life in urban areas that would soon be labeled "slums."

Thus, I want to conclude by suggesting that with Wilson's writing we can trace an early arc of Black queer aesthetics across the nineteenth century. The "Afric-American Picture Gallery" deserves our attention today in part because it marks the beginning of an aesthetic genealogy that was just taking off the ground in the late 1850s. Indeed, one goal of this project has been to broaden and deepen our attunement to Black bohemian and queer aesthetics in the nineteenth century, from William J. Wilson's bohemian antebellum Brooklyn to William Dorsey Swann's world of post-Reconstruction drag balls. Even if not everything he saw made its way into the respectable space of the newspaper, Wilson was a close observer of the world of both polite society and a more underground world of queers, cross-dressers, and free lovers. His work is positioned to enrich our understanding of how Black intellectual cultures in the nineteenth century intersected with more countercultural forms of expression and belonging.

At the same time as Wilson's writing helps to construct a queer genealogy of pre-1900 African American literature attuned to both inchoate queer cultures and styles, it would be an error to see this as a homogeneous and uninterrupted history stretching from the 1850s to the 1920s. Timothy Griffiths notes that "black queer genealogy building" resists both "triumphalism" and "linear progression." In contrast to the "out of the closet and into the streets" paradigm of queer studies, "it is difficult to anoint specific epochs, authors, and texts in African American culture as breakthrough points for an idealized and consecrated Black queer desire ethos." He goes on to note that the streamlining of African American literary history in an efficient line from the antebellum era to the present "does not account for all the ambiguities, regressions, radical imaginings, and failures that make up" this genealogy.[32] A too-rosy account of Black queerness is also complicated by the fact that, as Darieck Scott notes, "blackness is primarily associated in Western culture with perverse, nonnormative sexuality"; Fanon, as Scott writes, recognized that "Negrophobia is essentially a sexual phobia."[33] Aliyyah Abdur-Rahman has shown that early African American literature is rich with narratives about sexual transgression and perversion, and that these representations do important political work. However, this body of literature is a world away from the "out of the closet" paradigm of visibility and respectability that has been traditionally used to describe the development of (white) queer literary history.[34] This is all to say that any account of Black queer aesthetics in the nineteenth century must contend with the hypersexualization of Black subjects under and after slavery as well as with the ways that Black sexualities and desires often resist mapping onto triumphalist narratives about "coming out of the closet" into full, public visibility. In a society structured by white supremacy, domination, and sexual terror, opacity and dissemblance have been—and remain—crucial strategies for survival.[35]

Indeed, Wilson's own trajectory and history of migration reflects the tenuous, halting, and ephemeral nature of Black bohemian and intellectual networks in the period, as well as their relationship to forms of grief and loss. Black New Yorkers who moved south during and after the Civil War made important contributions to the Freedmen's Bureau and to efforts led by African Americans on the ground, but their exodus also left something of a haunting absence in New York itself. Indeed, the Civil War would radically transform the landscape of Black activism and politics in places like Brooklyn. The war also transformed the terrain of Black creativity and expression as political priorities shifted, in a very real way, from aesthetics to war.

Wilson would reemerge as a writer, with a new nom de plume, after his migration to DC at the end of the Civil War, but we should also pause to reflect on the forms of expression and creativity that were foreclosed by that war. Our narratives of migration tend to focus more on destinations than on the places left. The departure of Black New Yorkers at the beginning of the Civil War resulted in a renaissance of Black letters and activism in places like DC, and later in Atlanta, but it also produced forms of grief that are registered in documents written by people "left behind" in the North. Wilson's own unanswered mail sitting at a Brooklyn post office gives us a very real sense of the forms of writing and exchange that were halted by the war. This is all to say that as we grapple with the counters of Black queer writing before the Harlem Renaissance, we have to view it as a punctuated and sometimes halting tradition, one that comes to us in brief, precious glimpses across different historical moments, and in response to shifting regimes of regulating race and sexuality. What better model for understanding this underground genealogy as it becomes visible in intermittent bursts across the nineteenth century than in the playful panoramic optics and forms of experimental spectatorship modeled in the Picture Gallery itself?

Acknowledgments

I began this project over a decade ago, and my research and writing has been supported by many friends, colleagues, and institutions during that time. Due to the duration of this research, as well as its concurrence with a pandemic, child-rearing, and other forms of care work, I am sure to have left out some names. For that I apologize.

I want to begin with gratitude for the scholars and friends who have been part of ongoing efforts to recover William J. Wilson's writing, family, community, and activism: They include Ivy Wilson, John Ernest, Derrick Spires, Ben Fagan, Leif Eckstrom, Carla Peterson, Rian Bowie, Radiclani Clytus, Lara Langer Cohen, members of the *Just Teach One: Early African American Print* initiative, the Colored Conventions Collective, Jonathan Michael Square, and Prithi Kanakamedala. It has been so rewarding to be part of a collective effort to restore Wilson to historical memory.

I am grateful to the following institutions for fellowship support: the American Council for Learned Societies, the National Endowment for the Humanities, the American Antiquarian Society, and the Hutchins Center for African and African American Research at Harvard University. At the Hutchins Center I have a whole magnificent cohort to thank—for both their intellectual camaraderie and for their fellowship—as well as gratitude for research assistance from Aneesa Kneeland. I want to thank Henry Louis Gates Jr. and Sarah Lewis for their enthusiasm about this project while I was in residence at Harvard. Many thanks to Krishna Lewis, Abby Wolf, Velma

DuPont, and the rest of the staff at the Hutchins Center for their administrative support and generosity. At the Antiquarian Society, I have many people to thank, including Nan Wolverton, Scott Casper, Lauren Hewes, Georgia Gigi Barnhill, Ashley Cataldo, Vince Golden, Elizabeth Pope, John Garcia, Dan Boudreau, Brianne Barrett, and long-term fellows, Susan Schulten, BJ Lillis, Michelle LeMaster, Andrew Jay Chung, and Ilana Larkin.

I have benefited immensely from the expertise of librarians and archivists at the Houghton Library at Harvard, the Moorland-Spingarn Research Center at Howard, the Brooklyn Public Library, the New York Historical, and the W. E. B. Du Bois Library at UMass Amherst. I am grateful to the College of Humanities and Fine Arts at UMass for its support through research and travel funds, and for a subvention grant. Thank you to Tricia Loveland for administrative support, and for her kindness. Thank you to my students over the years, who have approached the "Afric-American Picture Gallery" with curiosity and creativity.

I am grateful to audiences who generously engaged with this work and to the colleagues who invited me to speak. They include Bob Levine, Edlie Wong, and the Local Americanists Lecture Series at the University of Maryland; Michael Ortiz, Christopher Rodelo, and the Harvard American Studies Workshop; and Seth Rockman and the US History Workshop at Brown University.

Thank you Cameron Awkward-Rich and Signe Predmore for being my Esselon writing buddies. Thank you to those of you who have talked through parts of the manuscript or read sections of it: Jordy Rosenberg, Tanisha Ford, Zoe Tuck, Mia Bagneris, and Jina B. Kim. My parents, Jim and Diane Rusert, are an endlessly steady wellspring of love and support. Kris Cirullo, thank you for taking such good care of Lucy while I was writing.

It has been wonderful to work with Ken Wissoker, whom I first met when I was a first-year graduate student at Duke University over twenty years ago. Thank you to everyone else at Duke University Press who supported this publication, including James Moore, Kate Mullen, Olivia Schmitz, and Livia Tenzer, as well as to the anonymous readers of the manuscript for their keen insights and encouragement, and to Christi Stanforth for careful copyediting. I am grateful to Jude Hayward-Jansen for indexing the book and to Mario Ontiveros for a late-stage art consultation.

Mark Wunderlich's workshop "Writing the Ekphrastic Poem" at the Fine Arts Works Center (FAWC) in Provincetown changed both this project and my life. FAWC has become such a warm and supportive environment for my work. So has the *Massachusetts Review*. Being in community with creative writers and artists over the past few years has been transformative for my writing practice. It has also enriched my life, immeasurably. My writing was deeply shaped and sustained by participation in the George Floyd protests, mutual aid and care webs forged in the wake of the pandemic, and organizing in support of Palestinian liberation.

To my comrades in western Massachusetts: Friendship and organizing in the Valley has given my life so much meaning, and I feel grateful to be part of this beautifully weird and queer little corner of the world. I'm not sure if she knows it, but Mia Bagneris got me over the finish line. Jina Kim, you are a model friend: caring, brilliant, ethical, and so damn funny. You keep me grounded and safe. And finally, to Lucy, my beloved kid and budding writer: Your joy and fearlessness inspire me every single day. You make me so proud. Keep going.

Appendix

ETHIOP [WILLIAM J. WILSON], "AFRIC-AMERICAN PICTURE GALLERY," *ANGLO-AFRICAN MAGAZINE*, FEBRUARY–OCTOBER 1859

Edited by Leif Eckstrom and Britt Rusert

Note: The following text and notes were prepared by Leif Eckstrom and Britt Rusert. This edition first appeared as part of the *Just Teach One: Early African American Print* project (no. 2, Fall 2015) and is available at https://jtoaa.americanantiquarian.org/welcome-to-just-teach-one-african-american/afric-american-picture-gallery/. Reading the "Afric-American Picture Gallery" in an isolated, continuous format represents a dramatic excision of innumerable details—from the lively context of the articles printed alongside the Picture Gallery in the *Anglo-African Magazine* to the experience of reading this text as a monthly serial, printed in the magazine's double-column format. For this reason, we encourage readers to consult the digital images of the magazine provided at the *Just Teach One* website: A rich resource, they complicate and further enliven Wilson's Picture Gallery.

February 1859

Afric-American Picture Gallery.

BY ETHIOP.

NUMBER I.

I always had a *penchant* for pictures. From a chit of a boy till now, my love for beautiful, or quaint old pictures has been unquenched.[1]

If an ever abiding love for any branch of *Art* is indicative of a fitness to pursue it, then I should have been a painter. Even when so small as to be almost imperceptible, I used to climb up, by the aid of a stool, to my mother's mantle piece, take down the old family almanac and study its pictures with a greater relish than ever a fat alderman partook of a good dinner including a bountiful supply of the choicest wines. All this however, never made me a painter. Fate marked out a rougher, sterner destiny for me. But the habit of rambling in search of, and hunting up curious, old, or rare and beautiful pictures, is as strong as ever.

It was in one of these rambles, that I stumbled over the Afric-American Picture Gallery, which has since become one of my dearest retreats wherein to spend many an otherwise weary hour, with profit and pleasure[.]

The collection is quite numerous, having been sought from every quarter of the American continent, and some from abroad; and though as a *Gallery of Art*, if not highly meritorious, still from its wide range of subjects and the ingenuity with which many of them are presented, it must, to the lover and curious in such matters, afford much for amusement, and to the careful observer and the thinker much that is valuable and interesting.

In style and excellence these pictures vary according to the fancy or skill of the artist. Some are finely executed, while others are mere rough sketches. Some are in oil, some in water colors, and India Ink shadings, a few statues, statuettes, and a few Crayons and Pencilings possessing a high degree of merit; others are mere charcoal sketches and of little worth beyond the subjects they portray.

But without pursuing this general outline further, let the reader, with me enter into this almost unknown Gallery. Well, here we are, and looking about us.

The first thing noticeable, is the unstudied arrangement of these pictures. They seem rather to have been put up out of the way, many of them, than hung for any effect.

The walls are spacious, and contain ample room for more, and, in many instances, better paintings; and many niches yet vacant for busts and statues; and just here, let me make an humble petition in behalf of this our newly discovered Gallery.—It is that generous artists, will, at their convenience, have the goodness to paint an occasional picture, or chisel a statue or bust, and we will be sure to assign it to its appropriate place. But let us take a survey, and speak only of what strikes us most forcibly in our present mood.

PICTURE NUMBER 1.—THE SLAVE SHIP.

This picture hangs near the entrance, on the south side of the Gallery, and in rather an unfavorable light.

The view is of course Jamestown harbor, Virginia, in 1609, and has all the wild surroundings of that portion of our country at that period; the artist having been faithful even to every shrub, crag and nook. Off in the mooring lays the *slave ship*, Dutch-modeled and ugly, even hideous to look upon, as a slave-ship ought to be. On the shore is a group of emaciated *Africans*, heavily manacled, the first slaves that ever trod the American continent; while in the fierce and angry waters of the bay, which seem to meet the black and dismal and storm-clad sky, is seen a small boat containing another lot of these human beings, just nearing the shore.

If the artist's general conception of this picture may be regarded a success, in its details, beyond all question, this is its crowning point. The small boat struck by, and contending with a huge breaker, is so near the shore that you can behold, and startle as you behold, the emaciated and death-like faces of the unfortunate victims, and the hideous countenances of their captors; and high and above all, perched upon the stern, with foot, tail and horns, and the chief insignias of his office, is his Satanic Majesty, gloating over the whole scene.

What is more truthful than that the devil is ever the firm friend and companion of the slave ship?

PICTURE NUMBER 2.—THE FIRST AND THE LAST COLORED EDITOR.

This small, but neat picture hangs on the north side of the gallery; and though simple in its details, is so well executed that it has much attracted me.

The Last Colored Editor,[2] quite a young man, with a finely formed head and ample brow—thoughtful, earnest, resolute—sits in chair editorial, with the first number of the Freedom's Journal, the first journal ever edited by, and devoted to the cause of the colored man in America, held in one hand and outspread before him, while the other, as though expressive of his resolve, is firmly clenched.

Surrounding him are piles of all the journals edited by colored men from the commencement up till the present, among which the Freedom's Journal, Colored American, People's Press, North Star, and Frederick Douglas[s]'s paper are the more prominent.[3] The First Editor is represented as a venerable old man, with whitened locks and placid face, leaning on a staff, and unperceived by the Last Editor, is looking intently over his shoulder on the outspread journal.[4]

It is his own first editorial, and the first ever penned and published by a colored man in America. The scene is the linking together of our once scarcely hopeful past with the now bright present.

PICTURE NO. 3—THE FIRST MARTYR OF THE REVOLUTION.

This is a head of Attucks. It may not be generally known, and it may not be particularly desirable that the public should know, that the First Martyr of the American Revolution was a colored man; that the first bosom that was bared to the blast of war was black; the first blood that drenched the pathway which led up to American liberty, was from the veins of a colored man.[5]

And yet such is the fact; and the artist has done a service in the execution of this head. It hangs at the north east end of the Gallery, and is a fine likeness of a bold, vigorous man,—just such, as would be likely to head a revolution to throw off oppression. May the name of Attucks and the facts connected therewith never perish.

PICTURE NO. 4. SUNSET IN ABBEOKUTA.

This is a fine painting. The landscape is rich, varied, beautiful. The sky has all the warmth of hue and softness of tint, and all that gorgeousness (changing seemingly with every instant,) for which an African sky is so much noted. No rainbow with us, in its full splendor, is so variegated or so wide in its range of colors.

The last touches of the artist's pencil has made the glow of the coming evening to softly spread itself over here and there a dusky inhabitant reclining upon the banks of an unrippled lake. The effect is fine, and the whole scene is so charming that one could almost wish to be there.

PICTURES 5 AND 6.—THE UNDER GROUND RAILROAD.

In these two pictures the artist is certainly quite up to our idea. They are of large size and represent both the Southern and Northern portions of that mysterious road. They hang beside each other on the south side of the Gallery and are marked A and B. I would suggest, that B be changed over to the north wall, as a more appropriate place. Picture A, or the south view represents a dark road leading through a darker forest, along which is seen merely some twenty pairs of fine stalwart human feet and legs—male and female—of all sizes, hurrying northward. Every muscle and limb indicates firmness and resolution.

The scene is night-time, and far distant through the forest is faintly seen the north star—small but bright and unfailing, and to the fugitive, unerring.

Picture B on the north view consists of some twenty bold heads and fine robust faces, each of which is lit up with a joy no pen can portray, and nothing but the pencil of the master could have reached. The exclamation of each must be 'we have found it!!!'

In the foreground is a lake and the back ground is a Canadian forest, through which here and there you can perceive a small rustic cottage. Both of these pictures sustain well that air of mystery which envelopes the Under Ground Rail Road.

In the first view we have but the feet and legs; indicating the mysterious manner in which those feet and legs move bodies towards freedom, or pass along that undefined and undefinable Road that leads to liberty.

There is another thought. The head, the recognized seat of the mind, is useless to the slave, or, if of service to him, this thinking apparatus is not his own; it belongs to his owner; hence he makes use of his feet and legs, or the physical machinery; while in the second view, at the northern end of this undefinable Road, where liberty is, the head or mental part is presented to view. The slave,—the chattel,—the thing is a *man*.

(To be Continued.)

March 1859

Afric-American Picture Gallery.—Second Paper.

BY ETHIOP.

PICTURE VII.—TOUISSANT L'OVERTURE.

Pictures are teachings by example. From them we often derive our best lessons. A picture of a once beloved mother, an almost forgotten grandfather whose image perhaps we bear, or a long lost child, once the centre of our affections; such a picture occasionally taken down from its hiding-place, and looked at, calls up associations and emotions, and produces troops of thought that paint the memory afresh with hues the most beautiful, touching, beneficial and lasting. A picture of a great man with whose acts we are familiar, calls up the whole history of his times. Our minds thus become reimpressed with the events and we arrive at the philosophy of them.

A picture of Washington recalls to mind the American Revolution, and the early history of the Republic. A picture of Thomas Jefferson brings before the mind in all its scope and strength that inimitable document, the Declaration of Independence; and in addition, carries us forward to the times, when its broad and eternal principles, will be fully recognised by, and applied to the entire American people. I had these conclusions forced upon me by looking not upon either the picture of Washington or Jefferson in the gallery. Far from it; but by a most beautiful portrait of one of the greatest men the world ever saw—TOUISSANT L'OVERTURE.[6] This painting hangs in the south east corner of the Gallery in a favourable position and in good light as it ought; as it portrays the features of one of God's and Earth's noblemen long since retired.

Far be it from me to venture to a description of either the picture or the man. I have no pencil and no pen with which I can do it. Some future historian in other times, will yet write the name of Touissant L'Overture higher and in purer light than that of any man that has lived up to to-day. But the special point to which I wish to call attention, and upon which I may venture a remark, is the long and interesting train of historical facts in relation to Hayti, that gem of the sea, this portrait associates in the mind of the intelligent beholder. To say nothing of him who led the breathings of this people after liberty; the breaking in pieces the yoke that galled them their heroic struggles, the routing finally and utterly from the soil their oppressors; their almost superhuman efforts thereafter, to rise from the low state in which the degradation of slavery and chains had placed them and their final triumph over every obstacle; in fine the whole history from first to last of this Island and this people is so vividly brought before the mind, by merely this likeness of the inimitable Touissant L'Overture, that it is reimpressed with the extraordinary, *useful and touching lesson it teaches.*

PICTURE VIII.—SOLOUQUE AND HIS COURT.

If any thing else was needed to carry the mind over the field of Haytian events, and complete our history; or in leading us for the first time to study that history, this additional picture ought to be sufficient. It is of largest size, consisting of portraits of the sable Emperor and the magnates that move round his Imperial person;[7] and hangs beside that of L'Overture. The various descriptions given me of these persons lead me to believe, that these likenesses, unlike many that have been gotten up for the *American prejudice Market*, are genuine and up to the originals. That of the Emperor's is superior as he is known to be a superior looking man.

PICTURE IX.—MOUNT VERNON.

Our artist must have taken time by the forelock in the execution of this picture; as MOUNT VERNON has become of late the great popular theme of the American people. Mount Vernon just now enters into everything. It has something to do with every spring of the machinery of American society; social, political, and religious. It is Mount Vernon in the pulpit, Mount Vernon on the rostrum, Mount Vernon from the Press, Mount Vernon from every lip.

The boys in the streets busily cry out Mount Vernon; the fashionable young belle simpers Mount Vernon.

Mount Vernon exclaims the breast-laden patriot; Mount Vernon echoes the good old ladies, Mount Vernon is piped, Mount Vernon is harped; Mount

Vernon is danced; Mount Vernon is sung. Even men walk by the aid of Mount Vernon canes, manufactured from some of its decaying relics. And what is Mount Vernon?

MOUNT VERNON as the readers must know is a spot of earth somewhere in Virginia, and once the Home of the Father of his Country. How careful ought we to be, then, in word or deed about Mount Vernon.

I must plead in excuse, therefore, that in the conception of this picture, the Artist has simply failed; if not in faithfulness to the original, certainly in gratifying the popular American feeling. The Picture hangs on the south side of the Gallery, and in excellent light.

It is of largest size, exhibiting the grounds, the mansion, out-house, slave huts and all; once planned, laid out, and erected with so much care by *Washington*; but now alas, all in a state of dilapidation and decay. Decay is written by the Artist's pencil more legibly than in letters, on everything—On the house top, on the door sill is written decay. On the chimney, on the gables, on the eaves, is written decay. The consuming fingers of decay and dilapidation mark each and every out house.—Every old slave hut, like so many spectres shadows forth decay.—Decay stands staring in the gateways, staring in the porches, staring in the cellars.—The very wind which bends the here and there scattering tree-tops, (land marks of the past) seem to creak through the many visible crevices of the Old Mansion and sigh decay, decay! decay!!

I never saw Mount Vernon; and as I gaze upon this Picture I ask myself is it true? Is this the home of the *Father of his Country*? Is it, that, every thing Washington possessed should so perish? Or, so perish the all, that we should have left to us, but his name; and yet with a tendency to forget names however great, I am at a loss to know how we shall preserve even the name of Washington many years longer.

But there is another feature in this Picture besides the stern solemn passing away, that I desire to direct attention to. The Artist has located, and I suppose correctly enough, on the banks, where sluggishly glides the Potomac's waters, the TOMB OF WASHINGTON.

The first thing that here arrests the eye is the recently dug up coffin of Washington; just behind which stands the ghost of his faithful old slave and body servant; while in front, a living slave of to-day stands, with the *bones* of Washington gathered up in his arms, and labelled 'For Sale' 'Price $200,000; this negro included.' 'Money wanted.'—A number of other slaves, men, women, and children, are placed in a row along the bank just beyond, bearing about the neck of each the following inscription: [']*These negroes for sale. Money wanted.*'

Proceeding from the Old Mansion to the *Tomb*, are two elderly, portly, aristocratic looking gentlemen, bearing unmistakable evidences of being the present proprietors of the Mount Vernon estate, and celebrated relatives of the great Virginian, and Father of his Country; and a noted son of Massachusetts. These gentlemen are followed towards the tomb by a few pious looking old ladies.

Such is but a faint description of this picture of Mount Vernon; and as obscurely as it is hung in our midst, Edward Everett the distinguished limner of Washington should see it, and if any, point out its defects.

Our Gallery begins to draw. Numerous have been the inquiries about it, and two individuals who after sundry searchings and pryings have found out our *secret*.—Our pleasant hiding-place, where we have so often and so long shut up ourselves from the blast and chill of the world, is no longer our own. The luxury of solitude is even gone, gone forever!

Just as I had finished the sketch of the last picture, (luckily for me) and pointed my pencil for another, the little brown-faced boy in attendance, bowed in, to my great surprise, a very respectable appearing gentleman—a little seedy, though very genteel with all notwithstanding—and not Anglo-African, but Anglo-Saxon, or Anglo-American or something of that sort; botheration, I never could get the hang of these Angloes! but no matter, he was genteel in manner and intellectual in appearance.

'I read your Picture Sketches in the last number of the Anglo-African Magazine, and have sought out your Gallery,' said he. 'Well, what do you think of it?' said I. ' Your Gallery? well, I must examine it,—but your Magazine!!!' 'Magazine,' rejoined I, 'yes, that is the question.' 'Your magazine,' said he (not regarding the interruption) 'is uncalled for.' I started up. 'I am a well-known friend to your race.' I started a little more up-right, and said, 'my dear sir, if you mean Anglo-Africans, well; but do not say "your race."' [H]ere I brought my fist down on the table, added—'there is but one *race of men on the face of the earth, sir!!!* ' Our visitor colored a little. 'I was about to remark,' he said, 'that if your men had capacity they might write for our anti-slavery journals and other ably conducted magazines in the country, such as Harpers' or the Atlantic Monthly. It would be more creditable. You don't want a separate magazine and pen up your thoughts there.' 'The "Anglo-African" is not such as you designate it,' said I, 'it is simply headed by colored men, but excludes no man on account of his color from its pages, and it were unfortunate,' I said this with emphasis, 'that since colored men are the oppressed, it were unfortunate that every *anti-slavery* journal in the country is not edited by colored men.' This was a little too sharp, and our new friend colored more deeply than before. 'What do you think of that statue of Ira Aldridge,[8] just over on the other side of the Gallery, there?' said I, as anxious to turn the conversation as he was. He examined it a few moments and said, 'It is quite a clever attempt for—' he was about to add something more, but suddenly turning asked who modelled it. 'All I know,' said I, 'is, Mr. Aldridge went from this country to Europe when quite a young man, took to the stage, his color being no bar to eminence there, and step by step he has ascended until now he stands on the very highest round of the actor's ladder. He stands to day, as an actor, the most renowned in the world. The statue before us I believe was modelled in Europe.' Our visitor hastily glanced at it again, and pronounced it excellent, adding a few criticisms about its breadth of forehead and a few doubts about its want of faithfulness to the original, he passed around the Gallery. I sat down again to make a sketch of this plaster statue of Aldridge, the world-renowned actor (by the way, an excellent model of him as Othello), when our little brown-faced boy bowed his head in the doorway, and announced this time a lady—a colored lady. I laid down my pencil, and though much confused, tried my hand at politeness. The lady, plainly, but neatly attired and rather stiff, was all politeness, but it was of that kind that first chills, and then freezes you. Eye-glass up, and with sarcastic smile, she hurriedly scanned several of the pictures. Her air was a dissatisfied one in the outset; she had come to find fault and quarrel with our poor Gallery from the first. I felt this, and determined on revenge. 'What nonsense is all this! ' she exclaimed, and proceeded to criticise quite freely. I caught up my pencil, and wrote: 'An old maid; a little dimmed in sight; somewhat faded, but a few good traces of beauty yet left: face a little too sharp, and eye too restless and a little prudish with all: quite ready in speech, but rather too second-hand in opinion.' I stopped. A kind of nervous feeling came over me, and I began to fumble for my knife, to scratch the words *old, dimmed*, and all the other unpleasant adjectives I had thrown into my sentences, for in truth she was not old, though I learned afterwards she was a maid. My lady friend perceiving my embarrassed manner, laid it to her own superciliousness, and her eye dilated at the supposed effect and proceeded freely with her criticisms. My old revenge came back upon me: 'Madam, or mam,' said I at last, 'these pictures, as a whole, make no claim to the high artistic merit you look for in them, though I think some of them rather clever as works of *art*; but they serve as simple reminders of what the people of color were, now are, and will yet be. What they have gone through, are going through, and have yet to go through.' This last speech of mine had the desired effect. With glass still to her eye, she passed on in her strictures, and on, too, in the

Gallery. I adjusted myself again to make the sketch of *Aldridge*, and taking position, looked up for the purpose. Lo, and behold! my visitors were both gone. I was alone. My paper for my intended sketch was scribbled out, and my pencil whittled away. Bothered and puzzled, I snatched up my hat and started for the door, bidding the boy at the same time to bar it against all further intruders, I rushed into the street.

April 1859

Afric-American Picture Gallery.—Third Paper.

BY ETHIOP.

PICTURE NO. X.—A NEW PICTURE.

Our gallery Boy who barred its doors so firmly against intruders, has just entered the Gallery with his own likeness, and desires that it may be hung up; and, for more reasons than one he shall be gratified. The picture comes to us in mien pleasant, smiling, and as fresh as nature itself.

This boy *Thomas Onward* (I call him *Tom* for shortness,) though he has seen all of life—yea more, is not an *Old Tom* by any means; nor an *Uncle Tom*, nor a *Saintly Tom*, nor even what is commonly deemed a good Tom; but a shrewd little rogue, a real live *Young Tom*, up to all conceivable mischief and equal to all emergencies. He is a perfect model of a little fellow in his way, and a fair representative of his class. Sound in limb, symmetrical in form and robust in health, jovial, frank, easy mannered and handsome—infinitely so compared with even the likeness I hold, one would scarcely conclude that this boy has come down to us through nearly three hundred years of hard trial.

And yet it is true. Such is his story. He was almost whipped into existence, whipped into childhood, whipped up to boyhood. He has been whipped up to manhood, whipped down to old age, whipped out of existence. He was toiled into life; he has been toiled through life; toiled out of life. He has been robbed of his toil, robbed of his body, robbed of all but his soul.

He has been hated for what he was, hated for what he was not, and hated for what he ought to have been. He has been dreaded because of his ignorance, and dreaded because of his knowledge, dreaded for his weakness, dreaded for his strength.

Noble, innocent boy! hadst thou been able to remember a tithe of the hard things done to thee; or hadst thou known a tithe of the hard things said of thee; or of the hard feelings entertained towards thee, it would be difficult to conjecture the result. But out of all these mountains of dust and ashes without one bit of sackcloth upon thee, hast thou come forth fresh, smiling and free. *Tom, Tom!!!* Who shall write a fitting apostrophe to thee and thy rising fortunes.

What sorry figures do the hard, grave, iron, half savage and half barbarous faces of Washington and Jefferson, of Clay, Webster and Calhoun, present beside the fine expressive likeness of this rising little fellow. The American Nation, if it can, may try its hardened hand yet a few centuries longer upon our live little Tom; but it will hardly mould him to their liking. Like gold ore he will lose but the alloy and become brighter and brighter in the oft passing through the furnace of their oppression.

PICTURE NO. XI.—THE BLACK FOREST.

Two days after I had hung up the picture of the Gallery boy Tom, I sat examining another marked the *Black Forest*, which from its grand and beautiful scenery, dark back ground shadows and the air of profound mystery which seemed to pervade it, so attracted me that I intended to make a sketch, but my mind turned towards the boy and my eyes towards the portrait, and I sat gazing upon its beauty, and meditating upon its superior excellence as a *Work of Art*, and the probable whereabouts of the unknown Artist, and also upon the destiny of the Boy himself, when his shrill, merry, musical voice rung out: 'a letter sir.'

Taking it from his hand, I instantly broke the seal, and by a single glance discovered it was from an unknown source, and on further perusal that it was from the *Black Forest*; a place and name then wholly unknown to me, except as the landscape painting just alluded to in the gallery. The purport of the letter was an invitation to visit this inhabited or uninhabited part of the globe. Let me give the reader one paragraph of this curious epistle. It ran thus: '*Come over to the Black Forest and examine some of the Pictures and other curiosities there. Two days journey by stage and by foot for a man, and none others are asked!* ' As it is no part of my purpose to disclose the precise locality of the Black Forest, nor fully the manner of people dwelling there, nor yet wholly their doings, I shall reveal no more of the contents of this letter than to say it pointed out the route so minutely that no careful observer could mistake it; while without such a description, the keenest mind could not by any process penetrate even the recesses of the Black Forest, much less the precise spot in question. 'Come over to the Black Forest and examine some of the Pictures and other curiosities there. Two days journey by stage and by foot for a man, and none others are asked!'

This paragraph I read over a dozen times ere I laid down the letter, and then all my old love of adventure, of ramble and of picture hunting came back upon me.

Filled now with new thoughts and new projects, I repaired to my lodgings, wrote a few hasty lines to a friend, and retired for the night. But the sentences 'Come over to the Black Forest. Examine some pictures and other curiosities. Two days journey by stage and by foot for a man. None others are asked,' had fastened themselves in my mind and insisted so pertinaciously in remaining there, that it was with unusual effort sleep could take entire possession of me.

Early next morning I commenced preparations for my journey, and my arrangements completed, I started on what to many might have seemed [a] not only hazardous but profitless undertaking. But to him who bears perseverance about with him in his breast and determination in his face, and holds communion with all things around him, nothing is hazardous, nothing profitless.

PICTURE NO. XII—TWO PORTRAITS THAT OUGHT TO BE HUNG UP.

The forepart of my journey contained little of interest if I except the appearance and movements of two travellers whose portraits ought to be hung up in our Gallery for the benefit of both Afric and Anglo American.

One by one the stage emptied its passengers till these two individuals and myself only were left. Let me give a rough pencilling of each. One of them, and by far the most attractive of the pair, was a lean, sallow-faced, lantern-jawed, hyena-looking little man, standing about four and a half feet in his boots, with a long, narrow, retreating forehead, heavy brow and small piercing black eyes and long black hair. His nervous excitability rose and fell with every jolt of the stage coach, and with every whiff of the wind.

The other was an animal of yet a meaner cast. Though not a greyhound, nor a blood, still a kind of hound, a two legged one of a genuine American stock.

He was large in frame and bloated in flesh. His hands resembled a pair of oyster rakes, and his feet shovels, such as are used by ditchers. Upon his large bullet head, which was closely cropped of its coarse bristly hair, jauntingly sat a low slouched hat, from beneath which his blood-shot eyes, when they dared to look directly at you, seemed truly terrible. His coarse, vulgar mouth contained a quid of tobacco nearly as large as your fist—genuine Virginian—the juice of which he squirted freely in all directions. His clothes were loose and slovenly, and his linen dirty. From his trousers' pocket obtruded a pair of shackles, from his vest a revolver, and from his inner shirt a dagger.

Reader, here surely was a pair of portraits for you. I would have given the half of all I ever possessed to have had these two rare specimens of Anglo humanity for our *Afric-American Gallery.* I was certainly in a menagerie.

They eyed me and I eyed them. Incidentally I learned that they were a *Slave Holder* and a *Slave Catcher* in search of runaways, and mistook me for one. I prepared myself accordingly, and should have made summary work with them, had a hand to hand encounter taken place, just such as fugitives should make in a like case.

To assure themselves that their suspicions were correct, they struck up a conversation in good Old Virginia style, and I, willing to enliven or drive away I cared not which, the dull hours of the stage coach, readily joined in.

They were not long in discovering not only their mistake but were soon routed. White men generally, and slave holders in particular, dislike nothing so much as to stumble over and wake up black men capable of a single thought, much less intellectually equal, and none laugh more heartily than common sense black men over the extreme folly of the continually assumed or imagined mental superiority of white men over them.

In this instance matters began to look quite serious, and I began to fear something more than a wordy encounter, as fingers began to twitch and pistols move from their places, but by dint of chewing and spitting and frothing and hard swearing and round ponderous oaths, affairs assumed their wonted state. But so chagrined were my companions at their sad discomfiture, that I verily believe had it been possible, they would have crawled into the harness of our horses and took their places if thus they could have passed from observation.

Thus ended my first day's journey towards the Black Forest. The second was to be mostly the pedestrian's task.

The stage coach sat me down by ten o'clock next morning, and my two companions eyed me so wistfully till the thick tangle wood separated us, that I was well satisfied that their desire to make me their prey, was strong to the last.

PICTURE NO. XIII.—A PICTURE OUTSIDE OF THE GALLERY

Freed from this cage of wild beasts quite as miraculously as was Daniel from the lion's den, I s[e]t out in good earnest, and for a time made fine headway; a cold drizzling rain however s[e]t in late in the day and the travel became bad.

The afternoon wore away, and still I found myself wending towards a huge mountain forest, whose crest loomed up blacker and blacker as the clouds of coming evening rolled up from below the horizon. Here in all its grandeur and wild sublimity was the native landscape spread out before me, the same that I saw in beautiful miniature but a day before hanging on the walls of our Afric-American Gallery. Cold and wet, dark, gloomy night at last overtook me still plodding my weary way, now alas, through a dense and pathless forest in the direction of a solitary light. Dim at first, now brighter as I passed on and on.

Three hours more gone, and now dancing still more brightly through the trees this solitary light to my unspeakable joy, suddenly revealed itself fully in a small open space, but almost as suddenly disappeared.

A low growl of a mastiff told me that I was quite near the place of my search. Down, down sir! said a gruff voice to the dog, and all was silent and dark as the grave.

Used as I was to adventure and a stranger to fear, I confess a peculiar sensation now passed over me in this reign of deathlike stillness, and I for a moment hesitated. 'Men only are asked over to the Black Forest,' whispered a still, small voice in my ear.

I boldly stepped forward, and in a few moments came directly upon the steps of a small and unpretending log *hut*. I lingered a moment on the landing; all was quiet within, but a gentle rap soon brought to the door a man who bade me enter.

A cheerful wood fire was blazing on the open hearth, while three vacant chairs quite rural in aspect surrounded it, and a small table and an old fashioned settee completed the furniture of the apartment.

PICTURE NO. XIV.—PORTRAIT OF A MAN.

Tall and erect, strong like a forest tree, this man of the Black Forest, for such he was, was a glory to look upon. The frost of at least ninety winters must have fallen upon his head, and yet had not chilled him, nor had their winds bowed him, nor their cold dimmed the fires of his eye.

What a treasure, thought I, as I looked upon him, would this old man's portrait be in our Gallery.

'From G——?' said he, as he fixed his searching eyes upon me. I answered in the affirmative, and a brief but satisfactory conversation ensued. Mine host soon after set before me some cold meats, brown bread, an excellent dish of coffee and a bowl of delicious milk; thus with the aid of the cheerful fire, making me feel quite comfortable and at home, and the conversation was resumed. I shall not attempt even an outline of it. If I except my own part I could not if I would.

I have listened to many men. It has long been my privilege to converse with men of intelligence, and men of mind on all topics common to the day, but never before did I witness such a flood of knowledge poured forth from the lips of man. I am no *Paul*, but surely I sat at the feet of *Gamaliel*. Who was this *man*? How came he here? From whence did he come? What hidden treasures are there in this place? What mysteries hang over it? These interrogatories irresist[i]bly came up in my mind as the *old man*, with lamp in hand, began to ascend a rude ladder to a single upper chamber, bidding me follow. Here on a clean bed of rushes, I laid down, wondering at first, but soon buried myself in sound beneficial sleep.

(*To be Continued.*)

June 1859

Afric-American Picture Gallery.—Third Paper.

BY ETHIOP.

The reader will remember, that we parted company in the upper chamber of a lone Hut, in the midst of the Black Forest at the dead of night to take rest and repose. Ere the dawn of the next day, both eyes were wide open and I started on a tour of observation.[9]

Through a small window, so high, as to be beyond reach, the only aperture discernable to the outer world, came a grey streak of morning light to my pillow, and roused me from my bed. I up and hastily made my toilet such as it was, the best perhaps that could be made in a mountain fastness, and ascended by a ladder to the roof. I shall never forget the scene that burst upon my view. The peak of the Black Forest Mountain, for such it was upon which the solitary house stood, touched the very clouds, while the Ocean with here and there a massive ship upon its dark green bosom, though many miles distant, seemed to roll at its base. Crag on crag lay piled on every hand and vale outstretching vale; and beyond as it was early autumn, the sere and yellow leaf painted the otherwise vast green forest top with indescribable beauty. The morning breeze with a purity and freshness known only to mountain regions, sighed forth its soft music, so sweetly, that the feathered tribe, and they were legion—were constrained to join in with their unerring notes; while the deer, the squirrel, and the rabbit danced and skipped o'er steppe, crag and glen with laughing joy. A few moments, and the sun, like a mighty angel came hastening up, as it were, from out of the Ocean; and with his strong presence gilded the whole scene in an instant. So, impressed with what I saw, ere I was aware, a reverie stole over me; and I know not how long it would have held me, but for a voice from below, calling me away. It was the old man of the Forest summoning me to the morning repast; which to be brief, was all the most fastidious taste could have desired, and far beyond any thing I could have imagined.

Breakfast over, the old man *Bernice*, for such was his name, retired; but returned after a few moments, garbed in a red flannel gown, blue cap and black sandals; giving a grotesque, yet a most commanding appearance. Holding in his hand a lighted lantern, he advanced and mildly said; now my son, if you like, you may accompany me. So saying he led the way through a narrow passage to what appeared from the house top, a mere adjacent outbuilding. A stranger might have passed through this passage a thousand times without so much as imagining that the huge rough stone laying almost in his pathway covered the mouth of a famous cave.

At a slight touch from the old man's hand this stone rolled away as if by magic, and revealed a deep, dark *Cavern*. With a firm step he began to descend a ladder and I followed. Down, down, down we went. Down, down, down; and long was it ere we reached the bottom; and when we did so, we were brought directly upon a massive door which like the stone above, yielded to the touch of the old man's magic hand. We entered a dark and spacious apartment through which old Bernice grouped to the centre and held the lighted lantern up to a large lamp which depended from the ceiling. What a transition!!! The dark and sandless cavern now revealed all surroundings of the most studied and life long *Artist*. Bust[s], statues, statuettes; landscapes, portraits, fancy pieces; paints, pencils, pallets, mallets, chisels; half finished sketches, studies in plaster; all, all lay in profusion on every hand.

Prominent on a table near the lamp lay a fine duplicate portrait of our little *Tom*; our Gallery Boy, which I hung up just before I left for the *Black Forest*. The whole truth flashed upon my mind in an instant. Mine host was an *Artist*; and the executor of that beautiful likeness. "My son" said the old man as he perceived my astonishment, "though I have long since left the restless, busy crowd, I have not been unmindful of its jostlings. In this place, far from man's baseness, and man's vile injustice, have I labored; and it has been to me, a labor of love; a labor too, not without its reward. Much that I have done with both *pencil and chisel*—(I say it not in a boastful spirit,) will yet not only see the light, but command the just approbation of even the enemies of my race. I shall be gone, but these," said he, pointing to his *works* around him, "these shall live after me."

He then seated himself before his *Easel*, stretched his canvass, and with brush and pallet commenced the labors of the day;—saying at the same time in a manner as bland as it was touching.—"Oblige me my son and amuse also yourself by an examination of some of these my much *cherished creations* trifles—many of them—still I regard them with the affection of children.

Some of them recall to mind some of the dearest spots of earth to me; spots, which, if not for them, would long since have faded from my memory." I soon entered upon my survey; and for the hours, (and how swiftly did they fly,)—that the old man plied at his *work* I reveled and feasted my mind upon the splendours about me.

Here I found a statue or there a bust that might have done credit to the conception of a *Canova* or the hand of an Angelo.

Here hung a landscape, or half concealed, there lay a portrait or a Scripture piece or fancy sketch, that might have excited the envy of a *Raphael.*

Among other things, my attention was arrested by a new curiosity. It was a *Tablet* of stone which mine host informed me was dug out of the mountain peak of the *Black Forest*, but disclaimed all further knowledge of it. It is of brown sand stone, thirty-six inches square, and three in thickness, engraved on one side only; and having when found the engraved side downward.

The words are curiously spelt by the aid of 41 singular, new and beautiful characters, or letters, each representing a distinct sound; and so many only are employed as are necessary to make up each word.

I have by dint of hard study, been enabled to make out its contents; but of its history or origin, or aught else of it, I leave for the learned in such matters. It certainly challenges the attention of the Historian, the Ethnologist, and the Antiquarian. Is it fiction, is it history, is it prophecy? Who can tell?

I herewith present a duplicate of the copy I made on the spot.

YEAR 4,000.

THE AMECANS, OR MILK WHITE RACE

1 Now hear oh ye who dwell in this age of pure light and perfect liberty; and marvel not when I tell you that there were once such things as slaves in the land; since even the *word slave* is no more mentioned among the children of men.

2 And these same slaves were human beings held in bondage—yea cruel bondage, against their will, and against the dictates of common humanity; and were subject to purchase and sale, like unto beast of burden and like unto merchandise.

3 Nor marvel not that these slaves were whipped with great gads, and were driven to and fro in gangs and in chains, as we read of in our books, the beast of burden were in the *nineteenth and twentieth centuries*; yea they were whipped often without offense even unto death.

4 And be ye not puffed up nor proud in spirit, oh ye sons of noble fathers because ye now possess the land; and oh ye beautiful and refined daughters of virtuous mothers, be ye not vain overmuch because this land is now yours for an inheritance for ever.

5 Nor be ye enraged, none of you, because ye hereby learn that your *ancestors* were these slaves, and subject to this hard bondage.

6 And give ye heed now while from this Tablet of stone, which your fathers made; [and other tablets have they made also] I speak to you, and tell you what manner of people possessed the land and bought and sold and held your ancestors and so despitefully used them.[10]

7 And lo and behold, as one appeared, so appeared all of them. They had *milk white skins*, and their faces were like the chalk of foreign hills, yea like unto the evil spirit; and their hair was long and strait and uncomely; and in hue as the yellow or red clay of our fields.

8 And their faces were long and narrow, and their noses sharp and angular, and their nostrils thin; so also were the lips of their sunken mouths,

9 They had sharp white teeth, like unto the teeth of the shark; and their eyes were blue as the cloudless sky, and sometimes leaden as when it is overcast; and their brows were large even unto the hiding of their eyes; and they were terrible to look upon, yea even fearful.

10 And these people, long ruled in the land, and their hand was the hand of iron, and their hearts as the stones of our valleys.

11 And though they had great energy, and their wills were like unto the oaks of our forest, their unscrupulousness was great, yea as huge as our mountains; and their consciences were less than a span and harder than the diamond.

12 They built them large cities, and made great attainments in *science* and in *art*; and were cunning workmen, and wonderful tillers of the soil, making it yield its abundance.

13 And they made them great *ships* and many; so much so, that the seas were whitened with their sails; and they sent great burdens out of their land; and they got in return great riches.

14 And they builded also gorgeous *temples* in which they worshipped the *Gods* of their own making, while they professed to worship the true *God*; all of whose known laws they violated, and did but evil in his sight daily.

15 And your forefathers, they would not so much as permit them to enter the seats of their *temples* though they worshipped the true God, nor at their solemn feasts; but compelled them to stand afar off, because they had great hatred and prejudice against your forefathers.

16 And this people waxed fat and begat great pride, and clothed themselves in fine linen and black cloth every day; and their hearts became more and more filled with the world and the lust thereof.

17 And they said, who is like unto us? We are the great and the mighty ones of the Earth, and have a great mission to perform. We will level the hills and fill up the vallies; and will lay the mountains low, and make the path of the land straight, and they did so.

18 And we will lay on the path iron of our own workmanship and swift running vehicles will we put thereon, so that when the warm breath of the water puffeth at them they will run with swiftness and we will add to our cities and increase our comforts; and they did so.

19 And they wrapped themselves up in their ease and luxury in hopeful security; and their hand slackened; and great physical and mental weakness came over them; and many changes came in among them; so much so, that your forefathers looked upon them with much concern.

20 Yea their hair darkened, so also did their eyes and their skins; and they said unto your forefathers let us come in among you and be of you and partake of your substance les[t we die?] before our time.

21 And your forefathers did so; for they had increased much in substance and in numbers; and much in strength and in wisdom also; and had gained great possessions, yea all the land.

22 And these people dwindled at last to leanness; and their bones became small, and thin, and so did their statues; and their minds became feeble,

so much so, that they wist not what they did; and finally they disappeared
from among the children of men.

23 They staid no longer than to accomplish their *work* and then vanished;
yea as a cloud did they vanish from off the face of the whole land; yea
the land which your fathers have since possessed and enjoyed.

24 And it is a great grief unto this day that so little, beyond these *tablets*
of stone, your fathers have left unto you that so little is now known of
these *Amecans* or that a people once possessing so many peculiar traits,
should have passed away without leaving to your fathers some greater
memor[i]al of their existence.

25 But *wo* was unto them; and their works with their evil deeds seem to
have perished with them.

Simultaneous with my finishing this transcript, old Bernice rose from his labors. He lighted his lantern and saying 'come my son,' stepped to a side door hitherto unperceived by me but which like the first instantly yielded to his touch. We now turned into a narrow passage and continued in its subterraneous windings some fifty yards to another massive door, which like others swung back at the old man[']s bidding. But what a change!!!

From the artistic, the beautiful and the curious, we had just quitted, an object the most appalling my eyes ever beheld stood before us. Was it a man, was it even human?——When we entered he stood crouched in one corner of his cell. His figure was gaunt and tall; his head large and covered with long snow white hair, which hung in disordered masses over his pale and shriveled face; and through which his glaring eyes kept up a most terrible rolling; while his mouth was white with foam. He soon commenced an incoherent muttering the only words distinguishable was *Bernice, Bernice!*

Suddenly he made a fearful lunge for me. I started back. It was a useless start. A chain was there. He could go no further. Then he raved, he shrieked, he tore his hair; then he pronounced the most awful imprecations upon his captor, upon all mankind, upon his *Maker*; then he subsided into the same low and unintelligent murmur again, *Bernice* being the only distinguishable word.

Suddenly he knelt; then he prayed; then he sprang up, then he bounded the length of his chains, then he stamped them in the earth, then he gnawed at their links; then he begged, then he pled incoherently for something; I thought it was for deliverance and instinctively stepped forward as though to give it. *Stay!!* commanded *Old Bernice* in [a] voice that I shall never forget. A stout heart only saved me from immediate petrification on the spot; and when my eyes met his I confess I had some misgivings as to my own safety. And wherefore this man, said I.

'This man! he is a murderer' said he; and the old man's eyes kindled almost to a living flame. *'He is a murderer!!'* exclaimed he again.

'The wretch once had wealth and a[ll] the influence it brings; he once ha[d] power and he exercised it like a fiend. The oppressed and helpless were the victims of his fiendish spirit. Many, too many of God's poor have, alas, felt his diabolical hand. *I* was one of his victims, and dearly, dearly have I paid the cost. I had a wife and children.

'He held them as his property. Would you ask the fiend where they now are; or shall the sigh of the winds as they come up from the rice swamps answer? I had a son, a son dear to me, though he held him too as property. Despite oppression he had grown to beautiful manhood. Would you ask him where that son now is? Shall I answer that? Listen! That chained hand the wretch now lifts toward heaven and you for undeserved mercy, that chained hand struck down that son to the earth; and with that other hand withered as you see it, the wretch blew out the brains of my child without provocation and without warning; and would not so much as allow his body burial.' The old man made a pause, and I took advantage of it and said something about the law, redress, justice &c. *'Laws!'* exclaimed he almost frantic. *'Laws!!* what laws, what justice is there for the oppressed of our *class*? What laws except to oppress them harder? What laws except to pursue and rob them from the cradle to the grave, yea even beyond both. The wretch there,' said he pointing more significantly than ever at the miserable object before us, 'the wretch opulent in lands, opulent in human chattels, received the general approbation of his associate Tyrants for his *acts*.'

'But no matter,' continued he, 'I made my resolve and came hither. An interval was permitted to pass—a short one. He was brought hither, by what means I need not say. He was placed in my power. We confronted each other. It was a sore trial to him. We conversed much and freely. He spoke of the wrong done him; I spoke of mine. He spoke of his wife and children left behind. I reminded him of the sale and separation of mine. He spoke of his position in society and the wide difference between us. I told him that his superior advantage and position, so far from making him a wiser, and better man, had availed him little,—worse than little, since it had made him a robber of the helpless, an oppressor of the weak and a murderer of the innocent. He plead earnestly for his rights. I told him he had no rights that I was bound to respect.[11] He then begged hard for his liberty. It was a strange sight,' said he, 'to see a man begging for liberty from one of a class of whom he had his whole life long deprived of not only liberty but all that makes life worth having. He made large promises for that liberty. I told him that they were useless that he had now nothing to give; that he no longer possessed even himself; that his pleadings were now as useless as mine once were; that I was now the master and he the slave. I then assigned him his fate, and bid him prepare to meet it.

Long years have since gone by. I yet have him in my possession. I will not harm a hair of his head; but so long as he lives that gloomy cell shall be his prison-house, and these chains he is now bearing about with him in his sleeping moments and in his long waking hours, shall be his only earthly companions; and when he dies, as die he must, I will cast his carcass forth to gorge the *Vultures* that sit upon the mountain peaks of the Black Forest.'

'Bernice, Bernice,' imploringly murmured this white trembling *Felix*; and his knees smote together with very fear, as he stood before his *sable master* and heard his words.

The huge drops of perspiration rolled down my face as I said to myself what a terrible fate for a once proud tyrannical, wealthy white man who regards the black man as but a poor imbecile ignorant feeble thing, not so much even as the beasts that perish.

As the wretched fiend, for such I too now regarded him, commenced again his wild and loud imprecations, so loud that it seemed like a thousand voices, old Bernice drew himself up to his full height, and with a commanding gesture waved me to retire, and following said 'my son, thou hast as yet seen but little of this place;' and then turning round with one touch of his hand the heavy door sprang back to its place, and all sounds within that cell were hushed from the *world.*

(*To be Continued.*)

July 1859

Afric-American Picture Gallery.

FIFTH PAPER

BY ETHIOP.

——Home again, and in fine spirits.

> "Sound, sound the clarion, fill the fife;
> To all the sensual world proclaim,
> One crowded hour of glorious life
> Is worth an age without a name."[12]

So felt I, after my visit to the Black Forest, which has been among the most remarkable of my meandering life. A faithful recital of what I heard and what I saw, lengthened out in a dozen carefully collated and closely written volumes, would scarcely do justice to my three days' stay in that place of mysteries. But, as the pressure of other engagements called me from those never-to-be-forgotten scenes, so now, also, do the events of the passing hour require at my hands something else for my readers, reserving for another occasion a further chat about the famous Grotto Home of Old Bernice, one of Nature's noblemen and one of her noblest artists.

Home again, and in the Afric-American Picture Gallery, and seated in my big arm-chair. Dear old arm-chair! seated in thee I survey with renewed and increasing satisfaction this extraordinary Gallery.

My feelings are fresh and my eye clear, so that I can, perhaps, better take in the beauties and excellencies of a picture than give out anything like an accurate description of one.

Notwithstanding this, I cannot resist the temptation of a sketch offered by a pair of pictures just beneath my eye, on the south side of the Gallery. They are marked

Pictures Nos. XIX and XX.

PREACHING AND AFTER PREACHING.

The first represents the interior of a church—a negro church.

Locality—sunny South. The particular spot, I conclude from its surroundings, is among the best of the good old plantations.

The church is filled to overflowing with devout worshippers, and is being discoursed to, affectionately, of course, by a double-fisted, burly, white-faced old Southern Preacher—a genuine Hard Shell.[13]

The *artist* has caught him just in the nick of time.

The Preacher is just in the act of extorting his sable hearers to obey their masters—their kind, good masters.

"He that knoweth his master's will and doeth it not shall be beaten with many stripes."[14] These are his words. In catching the artist's conception, you feel them, you hear them—you put yourself in his audience, and then they are gracious words to you. They are unct[u]ous. On them your parson is feeling; he looks full of feeling; he looks unct[u]ous all over. Unction pours out of his mouth; it beams out of his eyes; it sticks out of his outspread fingers; it runs down his broad face in greater profusion than did the oil down the venerable beard of Aaron.

Just at this unct[u]ous point is our good man taken, and I heartily thank the artist for having done him such justice. A fairer exhibit of a Southern preacher is certainly nowhere else on canvass.

Nor has the artist lost any of his inspiration in the other details of his picture. The preacher's sable hearers, with eyes dilated, mouths agape, nostrils distended and ears alert, are intently leaning forward, that they may lose no word of the good admonition, while here a moody brow, and there a skeptical face, or yonder a defiant look, combine to form an admirable back-ground.

The second of this pair of pictures, entitled *After Preaching*, represents the congregation standing about outside the church in groups around the faithful leaders, who, being men carefully selected by the white piety of the sunny South, are of course, all of the Uncle Tom school.

By another masterly stroke of the artist's conception, they are taken just at the point of the extreme of their e[cs]tacies about the great and good sermon they have just heard, while the leaders are in earnest exhortation on submission and willing obedience to masters as the height of Christian duty.

In the back-ground may also be seen a few young, determined-looking faces, on which are expressed disbelief in, and detestation of, the whole affair. They are the same noticed in the back-ground of the former piece.

These young spirit-faces possess such a strong look of meaning that none need mistake it. A look so strong, so bold, so towering, that, like Monadnoc among the granite hills, it peers far above the scrawny frowns, and puny smiles, and jeers, and gibes, and sneers, and hates of the vulgar, the mean, the base; a look that will go up through all time, and, as light before the coming sun, so as surely will it be the forerunner of the great deliverance of long-'pressed humanity. The look and the meaning do actually exist, and the sooner the World knows it the better.

These faces, in contrast with the others of the congregation, give a most striking effect to the picture. They are the unruly, the skeptical, the worthless of the flock—the wicked ones, who would rather run the risk than be bound up in the religious love so feelingly and so faithfully proclaimed to them—the religious love of the land.

It is of this class comes our Nat Turners,[15] who laid a scheme for redemption, and the *man* in Georgia who received nine hundred and ninety-nine lashes by way of gentle compulsion, and then would not so much as reveal one particle of the *plan* laid by and for the uprising of his oppressed brethren. It is of this class come the Margaret Garners,[16] who rather than their babes even shall clank a chain, prefer to send them up to their God who gave them. It is of this class comes our Douglasses and our Browns,[17] and a host of other spirits now cast upon the regions of the North, as a Southerner once expressed it, "to wail in the misery of their sins, and lament in the wretchedness of their misunderstood liberty."

These are good views, and may be studied with profit by any Southern Preacher, master or monster who will take the trouble to visit the Afric-American Picture Gallery.

Picture No. XXI is

A HEAD OF PHILLIS WHEATLY.

It hangs in the north-east corner of the Gallery, and in good light, and is so decidedly one of the finest in the collection, whether viewed in an artistic light or in point of fact, that it is both a constant charm and study for me. The features, though indicative of a delicate organization, are of the most pleasing cast. The facial angle contains full ninety degrees; the forehead is finely formed, and the brain large; the nose is long, and the nostrils thin, while the eyes, though not large, are well set. To this may be added a small mouth, with lips prettily turned, and a chin—that perfection of beauty in the female face—delicately tapered from a throat and neck that are of themselves perfection. The whole make-up of this face is an index of healthy intellectual powers, combined with an active temperament, over which has fallen a slight tinge of religious pensiveness. Thus hangs Phillis Wheatly before you in the Afric-American Picture Gallery,[18] and if we scrutinize her more closely through her career and her *works*, we shall find her truly an extraordinary person. Stolen at the tender age of seven years from the fond embraces of a mother whose image never once faded from her memory, and ferried over in the *vile slave ship* from Afric's sunny clime to the cold shores of America, and sold under the hammer to a Boston merchant—a delicate child, a girl, alone, desolate; a chilly, dreary world before her, a chain on her feet and a thorn in her bosom, and an iron mask on her head, what chance, what opportunity was there for her to make physical, moral, or mental progress? In these respects, how get up to, or keep pace with, other and more favored people?—how get in the advance?—how ascend, at last, without a single competitor, the highest scale of human eminence? Phillis Wheatly did all and more than this. A sold thing, a bought chattel, at seven years she mastered, notwithstanding, the English language in sixteen months. She carried on with her friends and acquaintances an extensive and elegant epistolary correspondence at twelve years of age, composed her first poem at *fourteen*, became a proficient Latin scholar at *seventeen*, and published in England her book of poems dedicated to the Countess of Huntington at *nineteen*; and with the mantle of just fame upon her shoulders, sailed from America to England to receive the meed due to her learning, her talents, and her virtues at twenty-two. What one of America's paler daughters cotemporary with her, with all the advant[a]ges that home, fortune, friends and favor bring—what one ascended so far up the hill of just fame at any age. I have searched in vain to find the name upon the literary page of our country's record.

Oh! Wheatly!
What degrading hand, what slavish chain,
What earthly power could link thy nobler soul
To baser things, and check its eagle flight?
Angel of purity, child of beauteous song,
Thy harp still hangs within our sight
To cheer though thou art gone.

The lady visitors to the Gallery would do well to make the head of Phillis Wheatly a study.

*

I have never read a *treatise* on the art of pleasing, nor have I otherwise acquired it, and hence my imperfection in so important a matter. I never could well please; a lady friend says I have never tried. Be this as it may, permit me to observe that since my three days' visit to the Black Forest and three weeks' barricading of the doors of the Afric-American Picture Gallery against its many friends who have sought it out,[19] there has been brought upon me such a storm of choleric feeling as will serve for all of life to come. I had just finished the last sketch, and wrapped myself up in the happy consciousness of its justness, my old mood stealing over me, my mind traversing back to the days when Banneker lived and told of the stars and of the rising suns,[20] and Wheatly sung their praise to listening worlds, when a loud rap at the door brought me to a sense of the present moment and to my feet. Wondering who the intruder might be that dared to thus disturb me, I bade him enter. It was *Tom*—yes, Tom, with a package of letters in his hand. The little rogue's smile was as fresh and sunny as ever, and it was a pleasure to see him; but, somehow or other, there was a wicked twinkle playing about the corners of his usually wicked little eyes, that told me something in my absence had gone amiss. I concealed this discovery, however, and merely said: "Well, Tom, my good fellow, what has turned up since my absence?" "Oh! nothing much, only a plenty of calls, sir," said he. "Calls?" said I, rising, "I hope you have not permitted, sir, any one to enter the *Afric-American Gallery* during my absence?" "Why no, sir," said he, provokingly, "but then there has been such a knocking at the door!"

I perceived how it was in an instant. The little rogue had been operating on his own hook, and pointing out the Gallery to the various magnates around for his own special amusement.

"The doctor has been here," he added, without paying any heed to the embarrassment in which he had placed me; "and the Professor has been here, and the Philosopher with him; and a little lady in black, and a tall lady, and a fat lady, and a strange nice lady from abroad have been here; and a number of other ladies, and some queer ones, too, have been here; and a crusty old gentleman, (white,) with a cane, has been here, too; and two colored gentlemen, in white cravats and long black coats all buttoned down before."

Tom's odd description of so strange a group really put me in good humor. I took the package from his hand, and throwing it on the table, wheeled round before the statu[e] of Benjamin Banneker, for the purpose of a few *notes* for the readers of the *Anglo-African Magazine*, when rather a loud and unusual noise in the outer hall interrupted me. In looking up, lo! and behold, advancing and bowing, hats in hand, who should my eyes meet but the *Doctor*, the *Professor*, and the *Philosopher*, closely followed by the little lady in black, and the tall lady, and the fat lady, and the lady from abroad, and the two gentlemen in white cravats and long black coats all buttoned down before, fetching up the rear. Dumbfounded at so many and such imposing visitors, I could only rise and make my best bow, which was awkward enough at best. Of course I was cheated out of my reflections on Banneker, and so are my readers.

The conversation of my visitors, which was free, characteristic, and remarkable, I must reserve for my next, reader.

(*To be Continued.*)

August 1859

Afric-American Picture Gallery.

SIXTH PAPER

BY ETHIOP.

It may not be forgotten by the reader, that I was last seen standing bolt-upright in the middle of the Afric-American Picture Gallery, surrounded by quite a number of the notables of our times, who had been attracted thither by the notoriety the Gallery has recently assumed.

"What a singular picture," exclaimed the "little lady" in black as she fixed her attention upon a small picture just opposite. This, to my own relief, drew the attention of the entire party. "It is singularly sad, even distressingly so," said the "lady from abroad;" "and yet," she added, "it is susceptible of improvement. Such a condition, though it tax our best energies, should be rendered better." "I much doubt, if such a sorry subject as that could be improved in condition," broke in the "tall [not fat] lady." [Anglo-African Magazine must father that appellation.][21] This last remark was backed up by the "stout lady," who always seemed but a necessary prop to the tall one—seemed made stout and strong, and short and broad, for that very purpose.

That the reader may better appreciate these remarks, I will here give a simple outline of the picture to which they had reference.

It is marked "*Picture 26*," hangs on the North wall of the Gallery, and is entitled "CONDITION." The subject is a *colored youth*, sitting upon the bank of a rapid river, beneath a huge tree much resembling the *upas*,[22] and surrounded by abject wretchedness. Rags and their concomitants cover his body; poverty and want stare him in the face—a face marked with ignorance and the indifference of stolid content.

All else is vacancy.—Pale and emaciated he sits; and at this vacancy alone he stares. What the amount of intelligence he has, or what he is capable of acquiring, is for the speculative, the philosophic and philanthropic to ascertain. On the opposite bank of this river however, are green pastures, lowing herds and waving corn; while down the swift-gliding stream, are miniature fleets of heavy laden little skiffs and beautiful pleasure-yachts. The artist may be forgiven for over-drawing occasionally, as in the case of the main subject of this picture; for I am sure, it would be difficult to find within the whole range of our knowledge anything reduced to a *condition* compared with it.

And yet the question put by the "tall lady" and backed up by the "stout lady," and oft repeated on the tongue of nearly all Anglo-Americans: "can such a subject be improved?" incidentally received a partial discussion, if not solution, in our Gallery.

The Doctor, who is a piece of a philosopher and a larger bit of a wag, was intent on a fine large picture of the "*First Colored Convention*;" and, overhearing the conversation as above noted down, turned round to the company. "What do you think of that, Doctor," asked a dozen voices together; pointing to poor little "*Condition*" on the wall. The Doctor, after a few hurried glances at the picture through his *turtle shells*, said, "you may improve the condition, if you change the nature."

An opinion—though it meant nothing—from so high an authority, and so deliberately given, was not without its weight; and the "Skeptic" shook his head doubtingly; while the "Philosopher" with thumb and finger, and outstretched hand, launched out on hair-splitting subtleties, to prove the amount of labor necessary to make even the "Doctor's" proposition good. He also entered upon a learned dissertation, upon the nature of the world in general, and our *poor little "Condition" in particular*; and wound up by saying that "whatever is, is right."

All this to me seemed so foreign from the point at issue, that, my impetuosity getting the better of my known modesty, with arm uplifted and fist clenched, I broke out with. "It is the youth's condition, not his nature, that demands a change. He has all the great essentials common to humanity; hence, he neither wants more of this, nor less of that, within his composition, before he can be rendered susceptible of improvement." "Will our Gallery-friend inform us then, how he would effect that change," enquired one of the "white cravats," who had all this time been balancing like a rope-dancer, first on this side, and then on that—of the rail of the conversation—to see which would best bear him. "How would you proceed in so great an undertaking," said he, and concluded his own effort, by drawing himself up in an attempt to look dignified. "Put a lever in his hands, and he will proceed to raise himself from out of his own low Condition," said the "Philosopher."

This was not quite definite enough, and the "skeptic" added, "if the Philosopher will compose his *lever of means* and *intelligence*, I will agree with him. The youth wants first of all things, *means*, substantial *means—wealth*; such as the world values, and then intelligence enough to use it, and a fig for either his dull eye, his curly hair, or his *ebon face*.—The most repulsive of his features may laugh in derision at their sternest foe; for they will appear charming to the surrounding crowd, their possessor's friends. Beauty's eyes are wealth and power."

"I now perceive the point of the argument," chimed in one of the long black coats; and he buttoned it all down before. "It is the youth's disabilities, and not his color, that bind him there;" and as he said this, he significantly pointed to the picture with his ram's-horn cane, strongly reminding one of ancient Jericho and its falling walls. "Precisely so," said I; "you have it at last." Notwithstanding I thought him very slow to perceive a plain point, and came near telling him so.

At this point the "lady from abroad" mildly interposed, and said: "take that youth, forlorn and wretched even, as you there behold him; and let but the light of culture beam in upon him, change not his physical, but his moral, mental and religious state; and then possess him with *means—with wealth*; and you place beneath him a power, and put in his hands a force, that will be felt throughout the entire ramifications of human society."

This lady had such a neat way of putting her propositions, that it was not an easy task to disturb them without risk; and so the "Doctor," the "Philosopher" and the "white Cravats and long black Coats" deemed it best to keep quiet; but an old lady, who had hitherto been a quiet spectator to the whole scene, now threw up her *spectacles*, and sharply remarked; "you young folks' talk is altogether too metaphorical for me, as my good brother—a Philosopher,—yes, a Philosopher of the old school—a real Philosopher—used to say, when he overheard folks (he did not wish to offend), who did not know exactly what they were talking about. He always said to them, 'you speak too metaphorically for me,' and so say I to you, my young friends." "You are not understood[,]" ejaculated the old lady quite out of breath. She then drew her shawl a little closer, tossed back her hat, adjusted her *specs*, and began an examination of the picture in question, as she thought; but which was in fact one entitled "FARM LIFE IN WESTERN AMERICA."

The whole Party, which for the moment was put to silence, at this unexpected sally, stood a picture of suppressed mirth and hilarity, as they observed the "old lady's" careful scrutiny of what she believed to be the subject of their conversation.

"Bless me," said she at length; "what is this? Colored folks farming!! Ah now, that is it. This puts the question in a clear light; and if you young folks could only throw up your metaphorical veils, you could see it."

No one ventured to interrupt, and she proceeded:

"Now here are colored folks farming for themselves; and don't their grain grow as well as if they were white; and don't it sell as well?"

"Is not this a change only of condition? Talk of changing nature!!!"

"But where is the boy, that I hear you say so much about," inquired the "old lady," evidently puzzled.—"The Village?" said she. "Yes, yes; and here is its colored village blacksmith, shoeing his white neighbor's horse."—"What can't change our condition?"

"Fiddle-sticks and nonsense," exclaimed she again. "Talk of changing appearances!"

"And look here," cried she out again; "here is a colored man tending his own mill; and is not the flour as white as any other? and are not all the town, white and colored, running to procure it?"

"Welladay, welladay," said the "old lady," and shook her head disapprovingly.

Peering over the picture, she spied a splendid carriage, drawn by a span of spanking bays, driven by a boy, and containing the owner, a colored gentleman and his family, just entering the village.

"The Lord be praised," fairly screamed out the "old lady" this time; and she put up both hands, threw up her *specs*, and wheeled square round to the company, exclaiming: "and you would have them change the color of their faces, would you, before you would have them ride thus? This is your methaphysics, is it?" and "welladay, welladay," muttered she again.

A little farther on, and she espied a large mansion, in process of erection by colored, and white mechanics conjointly.

"The Lord be praised," ejaculated she again. "Now if this is not, what I call truly practical. For it is truly a practical operation where color is no bar," said the old lady.—"Away with your methaphorical, methaphysical nonsense, and give them plenty of the wherewith to do with, and they may wear their color without let [fret?] or hindrance." And as if doubly to assure herself and the company of the correctness of her opinion, she re-affirmed it, by saying, "possess them, all round, with money and all its pertainances; and no station is there so high and no power so great, but will, at their pleasure, be handed down to them." The "Doctor," whom the "old lady" eyed with a keenness evidently provoking retort, dared venture no reply, and only bit his lips. One of the "White Cravats" buttoned down his coat, elongated his face, and poised himself on both sides of the argument, manifestly anxious—since the "Doctor" said nothing—to jump down on the "old lady's" side of the argument; while the other "long black Coat" pulled up his cravat, and enjoyed vastly his friend's vacillating but uneasy position. The "little woman in black seemed" quite self-satisfied, that she had called attention to so grave a subject; for gravity and weight were her themes, her elements, her life, her all. In them she lived, moved and had her being.

The "tall lady" failed to see any convincing proofs; and so did the "stout lady," her friend and necessary prop.

The "Philosopher" archly enquired if the ladies saw at all?—

At this the "tall lady" grew taller, and the "stout lady" stouter; so much so, that I began to get anxious for the unfortunate "philosopher," and mildly suggested that the ladies would find some interesting views on the other side of the Gallery. The company, some satisfied, some self-satisfied and some dissatisfied, each in his own mood, passed over to where hung a series of small pictures labeled "CITY-LIFE." One of these, a *beautiful colored girl*, with a hideous monster of a white-faced doll in her arms, caught the "old lady's" eye; and she at once exclaimed, "That is more of your metaphorical nonsense—putting such prejudicial stuff into little children's heads—even before they know they have heads! Set your little boys and girls in the right way of thinking in the outset: that's what *I* say;" and the "old lady" threw herself back into our good old Gallery arm-chair, muttering to herself, "what stuff and nonsense these new-fangled colored folks are putting into the heads of our people. They are worse than white folks."

The "tall lady" and the "stout lady" and one of the "white cravats" were quite indignant, that such a picture was allowed a place on the walls of the Afric-American Picture Gallery. "It is a life-picture," provokingly chimed in the "Philosopher," forgetting his former risk.

"It is an insult to the children," sarcastically exclaimed the "tall lady." "It is an insult to the children," scre[e]ched out the "stout lady." "It is an insult to the children," blandly bawled out one of the "white cravats;" and he buttoned down his coat, and tried to look very dignified indeed; and then they all three looked daggers at the gaunt "Philosopher."

Turning round to the "lady from abroad," the "tall lady," with a leer said, "what would *you* have for our children, Madam?[" "]Yes, what would you have?" smirked out the "stout lady."

"Just so, what would you have," deferentially cold drawled out the "white cravat," and he again buttoned down his coat. The "lady from abroad" with some warmth answered: "Educate first of all things, and above all things, your children to have *true self-respect*: yes, I repeat it," said she with an energy that startled her auditors, "true *self-respect*; and then, upon this basis, and this alone, place all their future acquisitions. In the matter before us, I leave you to draw your own conclusions."

This fine proposition caused the "skeptic" to rub his hands with glee, while the wily "Philosopher" made a vain attempt to split it by one of his philosophical hair-splitters.

The "Doctor" and one of the "long black coats" by this time had got quite interested and rather warm over *Picture No. 27*, THE FIRST CONVENTION, the "Doctor" maintaining with much pith, that the leading minds of that time, who did most to advance the cause of Afric-America, were outside of the clergy; and pointed out the leading heads in this fine picture in evidence.[23] It was with a glow of delight, that—with stick in hand,—moving from the commanding form and strong head of Hamilton to the calm brow and ponderous intellect of Sipkins;[24] from the keen phiz and business-like air of Forten to the massive head and eagle eye of the fiery Grice, or the eloquent, yea almost now speaking lips of Hinton, the cool and determined Bird, the polished Burr, the vigorous and clear-sighted Bowers, the strong-minded Van Brackle, and the unswerving Vashon—all, all—and discanted upon their excellencies.

The "long black coat," cool, cautious, wily and earnest, with equal pertinacity pointed out the talented clergy, who led on the host of that day. He pointed to the far-seeing Bishop Allen, the able Watkins, the eloquent Corr, the learned and talented Cornish, the far-seeing Easton and the faithful Rush; all of whom stood to their posts in the dark hour of our trial.

Turning from these, he pointed to the mild and gentle face of Peter Williams, who so long led an intelligent people onward and upward to a higher state. This called up reminiscences of the past to the "Doctor's" mind; and if it did not convince, it certainly touched him, and he was silent. The "wily long black coat" then turned to the portrait of the lamented Theodore S. Wright, and set forth in strong light his vast labors and their results. He also pointed out others, who were prominent in that day, and finally exclaimed: "The good they have done, no man can estimate!!! Its influence will vibrate through time, and will continue up into eternity. There hang their portraits," said he, and he pointed round the gallery. ["]Let no man take them down. Let no ruthless hand disturb them; no polluted finger dare to touch them!!! There they hang, and there may they hang forever!!!"

This little patriotic conclusion elicited from the whole company, the "Doctor" included, a round of hearty applause.

"There is no metaphorical nonsense about that!" exclaimed the "old lady;" and she rose, put up her specs, gathered up the folds of her dress, and walked dignifiedly out.

"No metaphorical nonsense about that," echoed the other of the "white cravats," as the "old lady's" last foot-fall sounded down the gallery, and he felt again for his dignity, and buttoned down his coat.

The "Philosopher" pulled out his watch, and began to measure time. The "Doctor," suddenly jumping up out of a deep brown study, started for the door; and the "skeptic" took a stroll down the gallery. The "tall lady" turning up what nose she had, and the "stout lady" endeavoring to turn up what nose she had not, at the possibility of "colored folks" ever being improved, at least by their own efforts, they both indignantly strode out of the gallery, shaking the very dust off the soles of their feet.—

The "lady from abroad" proceeded to examine some pieces of statuary at the upper end of the gallery, and made some just criticisms; thereon, while the "little lady in black," self-satisfied and prime, sat a model of patience. The "white cravats" and "long black coats" adjusted their neckties, buttoned their coats down before, put on their hats, drew on their gloves (black ones of course), and quietly departed, wiser I trust for their visit; while I, unable to draw any thing but this imperfect sketch, hurriedly sent Tom off with it to the *Anglo-African Magazine*. (*To be Continued.*)

October 1859

Afric-American Picture Gallery.

SEVENTH PAPER

BY ETHIOP.

The Early Days of the Underground Railroad.

Bill came in one day in a towering rage. It was in the earlier days of the Afric-American Picture Gallery, when its quiet was seldom disturbed by visitors of any kind.

I started from my old arm-chair in much alarm, and somewhat hastily inquired what the matter was.

Bill's eyes (and I watched him closely) had all the seeming of a fiery demon. His large athletic frame seemed to expand with his increased emotion. His broad breast heaved to-and-fro like the surges of the ocean lashed with the fury of a storm; while his clenched fist continued its hold on a double-barrelled pistol (Colt's revolvers were not then in fashion) which lay hid in his left breast-pocket.

His countenance, hitherto of dark hue, was now pale, even to ashiness; and his teeth gnashed like one of the furies just let loose from the bottomless pit.

"What is the matter," said I, with increased alarm, "for heaven's sake, say what is the matter?"

"*I have seen him*!" said he, with an emphasis that made me shudder all over. "I have seen him!" exclaimed he again, still more emphatically, "and should he cross my path again, by the"——The balance of this terrible utterance, happily, was lost on my ear; and without abating anything either in appearance or manner, and without another word, he rapidly strode the floor, leaving me to supply with my imagination what I could not ascertain by inquiry.

Bill was a product of that famous plateau bounded by Pennsylvania, Delaware, the Atlantic, North Carolina, and the Alleghany Mountains; and which gives out to the country and the world men.

He was a large, strapping young fellow, just twenty-five, with the proportions of an ox, his chest alone having the breadth of two ordinary men. His head was large, his face round, his mouth wide, as were his nostrils, and his forehead broad. A real bull of Bashan; and yet the general aspect of his countenance was mild, and even pleasant, when not under excitement.

He had formerly been one of a large plantation of ill-used, badly-fed, overworked, and ignorant slaves. I say ignorant, because they knew nothing of the world beyond their plantation home, and Bill, at the time we now speak of, had never seen beyond his native hills. But he had a pair of quick eyes, two open ears, two strong legs, and a will of his own.

These, young as he was at that time, he determined to use for his own benefit; and if denied him where he was, to seek out some other spot where he could exercise this most natural intention.

How small a circumstance sometimes will turn the point, the vital point in a man's destiny, and so it was with our hero.

White young Northern adventurers, in those days, were in the habit of finding their way, summers, down South, seeking employments which paid better than in their own sterile New England, or among the cold blue hills of Northern New York.

One of these fellows, a carpenter, who found his way to the plantation on which Bill belonged, now and then, to the slave boys who chanced to be about him, would make occasional remarks about the North and New England, and especially his own native state, Maine. Bill, dull and indifferent, seemed always in the way. His seeming indifference to anything said in his hearing by the white help about the plantation gave him excellent advantages, and well did he improve them; for he kept up a most wonderful thinking and a strict reckoning, and in due time was fully prepared to step out and ascertain for himself if all the long yarns and handsome stories he had heard and overheard about the North were really true. Why should he not, like other boys, gratify a natural curiosity, even if he was only Bill and lived on a plantation; and though, too, it was said that he belonged to it? This latter saying, just here, we may remark, he never could, some how or other, fully make up his mind to believe; he never could lead his mind fully to believe that he belonged to the plantation or the master thereof. Reasoning thus, one Sunday morning, having made previously all due preparation, he obtained permission to go a distance in a southward direction, but like a naughty boy turned his face northward, not, however, till he had turned himself into a bale of tobacco, and took passage in the underground railroad. The road, then, not as now, had but one track, and it would have been a novel sight, methinks, to have seen this tobacco, alias our Bill, traveling, wheelbarrow fashion, upon the primitive underground railroad.

But such sights are, as a general thing, denied to mortal eyes, and our hero proceeded under the strict privacy of a gentleman incog; and arrived in due time North, and like a self-unwrapping mummy laid his tobacco, one night, quietly down upon the steps of a New England factory, and stepped forth to see the country.

Thus he got North; and staid North, till early one bright November morning he was suddenly roused from his slumbers by a heavy hand; and on rubbing out his eyes and looking up who should stand before him but his young master and a posse of officers.

The place where he was so unceremoniously woke up was in a humble but respectable lodging in Calais, Maine; the very place he had so often heard of in scraps of story and snatches of song, by the young white employee on the old plantation, and had pictured to himself in his dreams of liberty.

Alas, poor fellow! little did he think that a betrayer almost invariably lurks under a white skin; and that the same who seemed more civil than the ferocious Southerner, would be the one to send him back to his chains and to the prison-house of bondage for a little more than a mess of pottage.

Jakes, the carpenter, in his wanderings returned to Calais, his native town, and one day discovering Bill, conceived the idea of replenishing his nearly empty purse by the betrayal of a poor fugitive youth, in which he out-Judased Judas Iscariot; for he (Judas) covenanted for thirty pieces of silver, while Jakes got only twenty-five.

Poor modern Judas! Just as the last of his twenty-five pieces was expended, he blew out his own brains with a horse-pistol, and his body falling into a stream it swiftly drifted out to sea and was made food for the fishes.

"Come, Bill! don't you know me? What are you doing here? Get up you rascal, instantly, and come along! Get up, I tell you, or by"——

"Massa," said Bill, "I is so glad you come! for I is so sick and tired of this ere place."

"I is been most starved since I run'd away, and is been most naked, too. 'Tain't no use to try to get along without Marsar."

So saying he made ready and proceeded with all possible haste with his young master to a place of safety.

However unsound our hero's admissions and reasonings may have seemed to his real friends, they were perfectly philosophic to him, and so insured the confidence of his master that he dismissed his Northern menials, save one, who acted as a sort of lacquey, and forthwith repaired to the South with his man.

"Such complete disgust of this negro of the North will have a most salutary effect upon the rest of the negroes," said he. "He will be most valuable to the plantations round generally." Thus reasoned the master, as he sat the first morning after his arrival home, in his dining room, after perusing the morning paper.

Whoever will take the trouble to examine so far back as our story dates, will find this paragraph going the rounds of the Calais, Portland, and other New England and many other Northern journals of that day:

"*The beauties of Negro freedom.*"

"A negro, the property of J. D., Esq., of Maryland, who had, either through the machination of some of the enemies to humanity, or his own thick-pated folly, strayed away to the North—where the rigors of the climate and the pinchings of hunger had well nigh used him up.

His master, happily, however, arrived just in time to take his too-willing slave where, ere this, doubtless, he has been restored to his wonted comfort and happiness; and can brood at his leisure over the beauties of *Northern freedom*, we mean negro freedom.

When will the negro learn his simple mission, and his pretended or misguided friends learn wisdom."

Bill's arrival was hailed as a great triumph by the surrounding slaveowners, especially so when they were made acquainted with his sentiments of Northern negro freedom, and its horrors generally.

Never did poor plantations ring out so many doleful changes on the horrors of the North, with Bill, poor Bill, for a standing example; and very soon he was exalted to a kind of exhorter or lay preacher among his colored brethren.

But while the masters were thus teaching over Bill's back the horrors of Northern freedom and the North generally, Bill, wide awake, and adroit in manner, was instructing far more effectively in quite the opposite direction.

Such an unusual number of slaves decamped that summer, that a convention of the neighboring masters was held to enquire into the cause, and, if possible, provide an immediate remedy.

No one, of course, suspected Bill. His notions of Northern negro freedom, and earnestness in the interest of the master, continually and publicly expressed, placed him too high in general estimation for that.

Still decade after decade of the "Boys" foolishly forsook their kind masters for the unknown regions of the hated North.

In course of time Bill was also again missing. Yes, Bill, the faithful, penitent Bill, the negro exhorter.

Nothing could exceed the consternation, chagrin and rage among the plantation owners generally, and Bill's especially, when it became fully established that Bill, the least suspected, had, for the second time, betook to his heels for parts to them unknown.

Pursuit, hot pursuit, was the cry that ran along the line of the plantations, and two of the most celebrated, wreckless and daring of the negro catchers quickly volunteered to overtake and return, dead or alive, this daring and dangerous negro.

Without a moment's loss of time these fellows set out and pushed forward.

For a correct account of what followed from this point of our story we must extract from Bill's own narrative of the affair. He says, "Time and experience had taught me many things, and I was this time fully prepared for any and every emergency. I started under cover of a stormy winter's night and proceeded many miles ere the sun of another day broke the darkness. I then refreshed and rested myself in a well-retired place, resuming my journey soon after the next night-fall. After some three hours' travel, [I] came to a cross-bridge overhung by large beechen trees, with thick underbrush lining the sides of the deep chasm beneath.

"Just as I had got about midway of this bridge, I descried through the thick darkness two men stealthily approaching from an opposite direction, and so close upon me that retreat was useless.

"'Stand!' demanded the well-known voice of a most dreaded negro catcher, and quickly made for me, while I, with the rapidity of lightning almost, leveled my pistol at the other and remoter man, who in an instant rolled heavily over on the bridge without a groan.

"The first was now so near that there was nothing left for either of us but to close in the deadly hand-to-hand struggle[.] He, though a powerful man and used to conflict, finding his inability to overpower me, endeavored to draw his pistol on me, which I, either by tact or superiority of strength, averted, and it harmlessly exploded in the air.

"It was now my turn. Liberty or death with me, and life or death with him. The struggle was a fearful one. It was up, it was down; it was down, it was up.

"Not a word was spoken; not a murmur, not a whisper escaped either of us. He got me round the waist, I him by the throat. It was dark; but yet through that darkness so livid and changed became his countenance, and so glaring his eyes (I can see him even now), that, though knowing him well, it seemed it was the very devil with which I was dealing.

"But I held my grasp, increasing it only in tightness. I neither could, nor cared, to do otherwise.

"There seemed to be a charm upon me as I gazed into his livid face; a spell that worked upon my fingers as I held him.

"His limbs, which, for a moment, assumed the rigidity of iron, suddenly relaxed; his eyes, like an exploded lamp, suddenly flared out; his vice-like arms which bound me fell down. A strange emotion came over me. I knew nothing but one convulsive effort.

"I then listened: I heard a loud splash some thirty or forty feet below, which told me all I wished to know.

"Seized with the same spirit, I ran to the other lifeless carcase and gave it one heave, and with another splash it followed its mate to where no tales are told, and where earthly quiet reigns supreme."

"I had decided the question of my own liberty," says he, "this time, before I left the plantation; and because God had implanted the principles of liberty in my bosom, both in seeking and maintaining that liberty, I had determined to remove every obstacle that obtruded itself between me and it.

"I did, therefore, nothing more than my duty to myself, to my manhood, and to my God."

"After the incident of the bridge which I have narrated," says he, "no further impediments came in my way, and I soon found myself North, where I had determined, come what would, to take up my abode."

It was on the morning on which our story commences, when Bill entered our Gallery under the excitement we have described, and exclaiming, "*I have seen him, have seen him!*" that the man who claimed to be his owner passed him in the street, and fortunate for that man that he did not see Bill; fortunate for the community that they passed and did not meet.

The portrait of our sable hero, in all the flush of manhood, hangs on the north side of the Gallery, for the inspection of the curious.

Notes

The "Afric-American Picture Gallery" was a seven-part serial sketch published in 1859 over nine months of the *Anglo-African Magazine*'s fifteen-month run. Minor typographic and grammatical inconsistencies have been corrected silently for the sake of readability; a few additional edits and spelling corrections appear in brackets. Misspelled names have been retained because they reflect important spelling variations. We gratefully acknowledge EBSCO for providing the page images of the *Anglo-African* that were used in creating this text, which are accessible at the *Just Teach One: Early African American Print* website.

1 "Ethiop" was the pen name of Black activist, educator, and Brooklynite William J. Wilson. Wilson contributed to other African American periodicals under this name.

2 "The Last Colored Editor" refers to Thomas Hamilton, bookseller, printer, and editor of the *Anglo-African Magazine.*

3 Here Wilson is listing early African American newspapers: *Freedom's Journal* (1827–29); *Colored American* (1836–42); two of Frederick Douglass's newspapers, *North Star* (1847–51) and its successor, *Frederick Douglass' Paper* (1851–60). *People's Press* was Thomas Hamilton's short-lived weekly (1841).

4 The "First Editor" refers to Samuel Cornish, cofounder and editor, with John B. Russwurm, of *Freedom's Journal* (1827–29), the first Black newspaper published in the United States.

5 Crispus Attucks had recently been commemorated in William Cooper Nell's *The Colored Patriots of the American Revolution* (1855), a text widely read and cited by Black intellectuals in the 1850s. In 1858, Nell and Lewis Hayden organized a commemorative festival that recognized and memorialized Attucks's role in the Boston Massacre; he also collaborated with other Black activists to have a "Crispus Attucks Day" designated in Boston.

6 Toussaint Louverture, a former slave turned military leader, led the Haitian Revolution (1791–1804), the first and only slave revolt to result in the founding of a Black state in the Western Hemisphere. Note that here Wilson spells Louverture as "L'Overture." Toussaint also appears as "Touissaint" in a series on Haiti by J. Theodore Holly that appeared in the *Anglo-African Magazine.* See Holly, "Thoughts on Hayti," 186. This and all subsequent citations of the magazine are drawn from the Arno Press reprint edition of the first volume of the *Anglo-African.*

7 Faustin Soulouque ruled Haiti from 1847 to 1859. In 1849 he declared absolute control of the country and named himself Emperor Faustin I. He was overthrown by a coup in 1859. In J. Theodore Holly's "Thoughts on Hayti," Soulouque is referred to as the "Louis Napoleon of Hayti." See Holly, "Thoughts on Hayti," 220.

8 Ira Aldridge, an African American actor and playwright, emigrated to England in the 1820s, where he became a popular stage actor especially well known for

his performances as Othello and in other Shakespearean roles. In the 1850s and 1860s, Aldridge lived, traveled, and performed across Continental Europe.

9 Although called the "THIRD PAPER" here, this is the fourth installment of the Picture Gallery. The next installment, which appeared in the July 1859 issue of the *Anglo-African*, is correctly titled the "FIFTH PAPER."

10 The brackets appear in the original text.

11 Bernice's statement echoes the language of Supreme Court Justice Roger B. Taney's decision in *Dred Scott v. Sandford* (1857) that Black people "had no rights which the white man was bound to respect." The *Dred Scott* decision affirmed that neither enslaved nor free African Americans were citizens of the United States, thus they did not have standing under federal law. William C. Nell's "Colored American Patriots" in the *Anglo-African* also begins with this quote from Taney's decision. See Nell, "Colored American Patriots," 30.

12 These lines were composed by Thomas Osbert Mordant but popularized by (and often attributed to) Sir Walter Scott, who used the lines as an epigraph in his novel *Old Mortality* (1816).

13 "Hard Shell" is a slang term for fundamentalist Baptists.

14 Luke 12:47.

15 Born into slavery on a Southampton County plantation in Virginia in 1800, Nat Turner led a slave revolt on August 21, 1831, that extended to multiple plantations. The December issue of the *Anglo-African Magazine* reprinted the "Confession of Nat Turner" as a comparative touchstone to John Brown's attack on Harpers Ferry. See *Anglo-African*, 386–97.

16 In January 1856, Margaret Garner killed her two-year-old daughter and wounded herself and her three other children in a final attempt to resist their forced return to slavery. The subsequent trial tested the contradictions and limits of the federal Fugitive Slave Act (1850), since Garner was charged not with murder but with the destruction of property.

17 Frederick Douglass was the former slave, antislavery lecturer, writer, and editor who wrote the autobiographies *Narrative of the Life of Frederick Douglass, an American Slave* (1845) and *My Bondage and My Freedom* (1855), among other books, and edited and published *The North Star* (1847–51) and *Frederick Douglass' Paper* (1851–60) from Rochester, New York. William Wells Brown was the antislavery activist, writer, performer, and formerly enslaved man who published an early work of African American fiction, *Clotel; or, The President's Daughter* (1853). In 1860–61, a revised version of *Clotel* was published serially as *Miralda; or, The Beautiful Quadroon* in the *Weekly Anglo-African*, the newspaper successor to Thomas Hamilton's monthly magazine. Brown also included an entry on William J. Wilson and his picture gallery in his 1863 history, *The Black Man, His Antecedents, His Genius, and His Achievements*. The first edition of that text was published by Thomas Hamilton.

18 Phillis Wheatley was the enslaved Boston poet whose book *Poems on Various Subjects, Religious and Moral* was published in London in 1773. As with the variant spelling of Toussaint and Soulouque above, readers will note the spelling of Wheatley as "Wheatly" here and below. This spelling discrepancy raises fascinating questions about how Wheatley's name and legacy circulated in oral and written sources among African Americans in the antebellum period. Jefferson famously spelled Wheatley as "Whately" when he disparaged her poetry in *Notes on the State of Virginia* (1781; 1787), and enslaved poet Jupiter Hammon's 1778 poem dedicated to the poet was printed as "An Address to Miss Wheatly." Wilson's spelling is consistent with William C. Nell's entry on Wheatley in *The Colored Patriots of the Revolution* (1855).

19 This comment is a sly nod to the interruption of the Picture Gallery serial in May. The third and fourth installments of the series were published in April and June, respectively.

20 Benjamin Banneker, an eighteenth-century free Black mathematician, astronomer, farmer, and almanac-maker, lived in Baltimore County, Maryland.

21 These two sets of brackets appear in the original text.

22 The upas, a tropical fruit tree found in Africa, Asia, and the Pacific Rim, is used for many purposes, including, most notoriously, as a poison.

23 "THE FIRST CONVENTION" refers to the first Colored Convention, held in Philadelphia in 1830. The Colored Conventions movement took shape around state and national conventions organized by African Americans across the country over decades. The people listed in this and the subsequent paragraphs were participants in the Black convention movement, and many of them also appear in "The First Colored Convention" in the October 1859 issue of the *Anglo-African Magazine*, even if some of them didn't appear in the convention records themselves until later meetings. They include William Hamilton, Henry Sipkins, James Forten, Frederick A. Hinton, Hezekiah Grice, James Bird, John Bowers, John Emery Burr, Samuel Van Brakle, and John B. Vashon. The clergy mentioned by Wilson include the founder of the AME Church, Bishop Richard Allen, and ministers William J. Watkins, Samuel Cornish, Hosea Easton, Joseph M. Corr, Christopher Rush, and Peter Williams.

24 In the text, the *m* of *calm* has been set sideways. See W. J. Wilson, "Afric-American Picture Gallery," 246, and the image of this typographic anomaly on the *Just Teach One: Early African American Print* website, https://jtoaa.americanantiquarian.org/welcome-to-just-teach-one-african-american/afric-american-picture-gallery/.

Notes

Preface

1 For example, in correspondence from 1873, Wilson appends a note saying that he looks forward to a return visit to the Philadelphia studio of William Henry Dorsey, a Black artist, collector, and son of the prominent activist and early historian of African America, Thomas Dorsey. See William J. Wilson documents in Thomas and William Dorsey Collection, series B, box 132-2, Moorland-Spingarn Research Center, Howard University.

2 Cobb, *Picture Freedom.*

3 Wells, *Kidnapping Club.*

Introduction

1 Powell, *Cutting a Figure*, xvi.

2 For example, the influential *Black Portraiture[s]* conferences have brought together scholars, curators, gallerists, educators, collectors, and artists in different sites around the world for over a decade since 2013.

3 "From Our Brooklyn Correspondent," *Frederick Douglass' Paper*, March 11, 1853.

4 Lorang and Weir, "'Will Not These Days.'"

5 Peterson, *Black Gotham.*

6 W. J. Wilson (Ethiop), "Afric-American Picture Gallery," 53. This and all subsequent citations of the Picture Gallery are drawn from the Arno Press reprint edition of the first volume of the *Anglo-African Magazine.*

7 W. J. Wilson, "Afric-American Picture Gallery," 53.

8 W. J. Wilson, "Afric-American Picture Gallery," 53.

9 W. J. Wilson, "Afric-American Picture Gallery," 53.

10 Ernest, *Liberation Historiography*; I. Wilson, *Specters of Democracy*; Clytus, "Visualizing in Black Print"; Bowie et al., "Visionary History"; Spires, *Practice of Citizenship.*

11 This literature is vast and expanding. See, for example, Cohen and Stein, *Early African American Print Culture*; *MELUS*'s 2015 special issue on "African American Print Cultures," edited by Joycelyn Moody and Howard Rambsy II; Fielder and Senchyne, *Against a Sharp White Background*; Cobb, *Picture Freedom*; Gonzalez, *Visualizing Equality*; Wallace and Smith, *Pictures and Progress.*

12 See Helton et al., "Question of Recovery."

13 Mirzoeff, *Introduction to Visual Culture*; Mirzoeff, *Right to Look*; Lewis, *Unseen Truth*; Jay and Ramaswamy, *Empires of Vision*; Gould, *Mismeasure of Man*; Fabian, *Skull Collectors.*

14 hooks, *Black Looks*; Mirzoeff, *Right to Look.*

15 Plasa, "Ekphrastic Poetry and the Middle Passage"; Ford, "Notes on Black Ekphrasis."

16 Wilder, *Covenant with Color*, 52. My portrait of Brooklyn in this section is largely inspired by Wilder's richly textured account of the city's commercial expansion in the mid-nineteenth century.

17 Sharpe, *In the Wake*, 21.

18 *Frederick Douglass' Paper*, December 11, 1851.

19 *People's Advocate*, November 30, 1878.

20 Watson, "Free Blacks in Accomack County."

21 *People's Advocate*, November 30, 1878; mention of Wilson's boot-making shop appears in the September 16, 1837, issue of the *Colored American.*

22 Yacovone, "William J. Wilson," 400.

23 *Colored American*, November 18, 1837.

24 For more on St. Philip's Church and the lives of its congregants, see Peterson, *Black Gotham.*

25 Many thanks to Marc Landas for this new information on Wilson's residences and activities.

26 W. J. Wilson, "Public Schools for Colored Children," letter to Henry R. Stiles, ca. 1863, Henry Stiles Papers, Brooklyn Center for History, Brooklyn Public Library.

27 W. J. Wilson, "Public Schools for Colored Children." Wilson wrote that Mary took up this post after the previous principal of the department and possible family relation, Almyra Wilson, "from Boston Mass," passed away in 1862.

28 Kanakamedala, *Brooklynites*, 106.

29 Kanakamedala, *Brooklynites*, 4.

30 Wilder, *Covenant with Color*.

31 See city atlas holdings (*Maps of the City of Brooklyn*) in the Brooklyn Center for History, Brooklyn Public Library.

32 On shifts in racial nomenclature in the antebellum period, see Rael, *Black Identity and Black Protest*, 82–117.

33 Scholarship on the nineteenth-century Black elite includes Winch, *Philadelphia's Black Elite*; Winch, *Gentleman of Color*; Peterson, *Black Gotham*; E. D. Taylor, *Original Black Elite*.

34 Kanakamedala, *Brooklynites*, 175.

35 Peterson, *Black Gotham*, 286.

36 Records of the Colored Men's State Convention of New York, Troy, September 4, 1855, coloredconventions.org.

37 Spires, *Practice of Citizenship*, 158.

38 Spires, *Practice of Citizenship*, 294.

39 Yacovone, "William J. Wilson," 400.

40 I. Wilson, *Specters of Democracy*, 7.

41 I. Wilson, *Specters of Democracy*, 7.

42 Mitchell, *Picture Theory*, 156.

43 Campt, *Black Gaze*, 104.

44 Campt, *Black Gaze*, 27.

45 McHenry, *To Make Negro Literature*.

46 Douglass, *Claims of the Negro*, 7.

47 Spires, *Practice of Citizenship*, 28.

48 Spires, *Practice of Citizenship*, 28.

49 Spires, *Practice of Citizenship*, 28.

50 On the complex terrain of political aesthetics in Black antebellum writing, see I. Wilson, *Specters of Democracy*. Throughout this book, I am deeply

inspired by Wilson's careful attention to how Black writers in the antebellum period "conceptualized the relationship between art and politics" (7) as well as to his pathbreaking chapter on the Picture Gallery, which reads William J. Wilson's curatorial efforts as "the means though which he articulates a form of black subjectivity that is hemispheric and transnational" (146).

51 *Frederick Douglass' Paper*, October 5, 1855.

52 Miller, *Slaves to Fashion.*

53 Powell, "Sartor Africanus," 222.

54 Miller, *Slaves to Fashion*, 6.

55 Clytus, "Visualizing in Black Print," 54.

56 Smethurst, *African American Roots of Modernism.*

57 "Terance Ludlam," *Frederick Douglass' Paper*, August 11, 1854.

58 Foreman, *Activist Sentiments*, 7. See also Yao, *Disaffected.*

59 *Frederick Douglass' Paper*, February 9, 1855.

60 Quoted in Clytus, "Visualizing in Black Print," 45.

61 An exemplar in this regard is Hager, *Word by Word.*

62 D. Taylor, *Archive and the Repertoire*; Muñoz, *Cruising Utopia*; Phelan, *Unmarked.*

63 Battle-Baptiste and Rusert, *W. E. B. Du Bois's Data Portraits.*

64 W. W. Brown, *Black Man*, 235.

65 W. W. Brown, *Black Man*, 230, 233.

66 W. W. Brown, *Black Man*, 235.

67 W. W. Brown, *Black Man*, 235.

68 This literature is vast. Some relevant titles include Raiford and Raphael-Hernandez, *Migrating the Black Body*; Finley, *Committed to Memory*; Wood, *Blind Memory*; Fleetwood, *Troubling Vision*; Lugo-Ortiz and Rosenthal, *Slave Portraiture in the Atlantic World*; K. J. Brown, *Repeating Body*; English, *How to See a Work of Art*; Beach, *Sculpture at the Ends of Slavery*; and Deborah Willis's entire oeuvre, especially *Black Civil War Soldier* and *Reflections in Black.*

69 Thompson-Spires, *Heads of the Colored People*, 199.

Picture Number 1. The Slave Ship

1 W. J. Wilson, "Afric-American Picture Gallery," 53.

2 For more on the *Brooks* and its relationship to the abolitionist movement and visual depictions of the transatlantic slave trade, see Wood, *Blind Memory.*

3 For example, on the American Anti-Slavery Society's visual propaganda campaign, see Clytus, "'Keep It Before the People.'"

4 On the complicated history and provenance of Turner's *The Slave Ship*, see Lewis, *Unseen Truth*, 109–14.

5 Rediker, *Slave Ship*, 135; Smallwood, *Saltwater Slavery*, 1.

6 W. J. Wilson, "Afric-American Picture Gallery," 53.

7 Barthes, *Camera Lucida*.

8 W. J. Wilson, "Afric-American Picture Gallery," 53.

9 Finley, *Committed to Memory*, 5.

10 Finley, *Committed to Memory*, 16.

11 Finley, *Committed to Memory*, 16.

12 Junker, "Containing Bodies," 20.

13 Plasa, "Ekphrastic Poetry and the Middle Passage," 298.

14 See Brand, *Map to the Door*.

Chapter 1. "He Thinks He Will Submit": The Work of Black Art in the Age of Racial Capitalism

1 Wallace and Smith, *Pictures and Progress*; Stauffer et al., *Picturing Frederick Douglass*.

2 Clytus, "Visualizing in Black Print"; Spires, *Practice of Citizenship*.

3 Mirzoeff, *Right to Look*.

4 W. J. Wilson, "Afric-American Picture Gallery," 88.

5 On the centrality of Blackness to the iconography of George Washington, see Bagneris, "Illuminating the Shadows of 'Liberty.'"

6 W. J. Wilson, "Afric-American Picture Gallery," 88.

7 Meer, *Uncle Tom Mania*.

8 W. J. Wilson, "Afric-American Picture Gallery," 88.

9 Buck-Morss, *Dialectics of Seeing*, ix.

10 Buck-Morss, *Dialectics of Seeing*, ix, 47.

11 Eckstrom and Rusert, "Introduction."

12 Gardner, *Black Print Unbound*.

13 The attempts to suppress the circulation and reading of David Walker's *Appeal* through the passage of antiliteracy laws and by interrupting distribution networks have also been well documented. See Hinks, *To Awaken My Afflicted Brethren*.

14 Moten, "Black Op," 1743.

15 Buck-Morss, *Dialectics of Seeing*, 67.

16 Buck-Morss, *Dialectics of Seeing*, 67.

17 For Odell's memoir, see Wheatley, *Memoir and Poems of Phillis Wheatley* (1834), 9–29. I will not reproduce images of torture devices used on enslaved people in this text, but they were pervasive in the period.

18 Gonzalez, *Visualizing Equality*, 2.

19 Gonzalez, *Visualizing Equality*, 3.

20 See, for example, Bennett, *Birth of the Museum*.

21 Foucault, "Of Other Spaces."

22 W. J. Wilson, "Afric-American Picture Gallery," 218.

23 Bennett, *Birth of the Museum*, 6.

24 W. J. Wilson, "Afric-American Picture Gallery," 52.

25 W. J. Wilson, "Afric-American Picture Gallery," 52.

26 Quoted in Powell, *Cutting a Figure*, 31–32.

27 *Frederick Douglass' Paper*, December 25, 1851.

28 Henkin, *City Reading*.

29 Barthes, *Camera Lucida*, 76.

30 Barthes, *Camera Lucida*, 77.

31 Willis, *Reflections in Black*, xv.

32 Willis, *Reflections in Black*, 4.

33 McRee, "Mathew Brady."

34 For more on Augustus Washington's photography career, see Gonzalez, *Visualizing Equality*, 145–67.

35 Gonzalez, *Visualizing Equality*, 135–42, on Ball's panorama tour.

36 Quoted in Willis, *Reflections in Black*, 6.

37 Trachtenberg, *Reading American Photographs*, 34.

38 Trachtenberg, *Reading American Photographs*, 33.

39 Trachtenberg, *Reading American Photographs*, 33.

40 Trachtenberg, *Reading American Photographs*, 43.

41 W. J. Wilson, "Afric-American Picture Gallery," 87.

42 W. J. Wilson, "Afric-American Picture Gallery," 87.

43 Ernest, *Liberation Historiography*.

44 W. J. Wilson, "Afric-American Picture Gallery," 87.

45 W. J. Wilson, "Afric-American Picture Gallery," 87.

46 W. J. Wilson, "Afric-American Picture Gallery," 87.

47 W. J. Wilson, "Afric-American Picture Gallery," 87.

48 W. J. Wilson, "Afric-American Picture Gallery," 87–88.

49 Benjamin, "Work of Art."

50 Trachtenberg, *Reading American Photographs*, 32.

51 Trachtenberg, *Reading American Photographs*, 45.

52 Trachtenberg, *Reading American Photographs*, 33.

53 K. J. Brown, *Mortevivum*, xix–xx.

54 K. J. Brown, *Mortevivum*, xvii.

55 Benjamin, "Work of Art," 227.

56 Trachtenberg, *Reading American Photographs*, 22.

57 Fox-Amato, *Exposing Slavery*, 2.

58 For analyses of the Zealy daguerreotypes from multiple disciplinary and artistic perspectives, see Barbash et al., *To Make Their Own Way*.

59 W. J. Wilson, "Afric-American Picture Gallery," 100.

60 W. J. Wilson, "Afric-American Picture Gallery," 90.

61 Cobb, *Picture Freedom*.

62 On a rich tradition of interiority in African American cultural production, see Quashie, *Sovereignty of Quiet*.

63 Scholarship on Black women's friendship albums includes Cobb, *Picture Freedom*; Bagneris, "Radical Floriography"; and Rusert, *Fugitive Science*. Photograph albums were also collected by African American women in the period. See Buchtel and Best, *Framing Freedom*.

64 Trachtenberg, *Reading American Photographs*, 60.

65 "My Picture-Gallery" was published in *The American*, October 30, 1880, and subsequently incorporated into *Leaves of Grass* in 1881. Quoted here from Renner, "Leaves of Grass, 1881–82 edition."

66 My suspicion is that this column was an important seed for the writing that would become the Picture Gallery.

Chapter 2. "Our Essentially Aesthetic or Art-Nature": Late Antebellum Black Aesthetics

1 Blackwood, *Portrait's Subject*, 76.

2 Rusert, *Fugitive Science*; Hickman, "Douglass Unbound."

3 *Frederick Douglass' Paper*, October 5, 1855.

4 Thompson-Spires, *Heads of the Colored People*, 199.

5 Spires, "Seriality and Future Histories of Blackness."

6 Spires's book-in-progress is titled "Serial Blackness: Periodical Literature and Early African American Literary Histories in the Long Nineteenth Century."

7 *Frederick Douglass' Paper*, October 5, 1855.

8 Peterson, "Capitalism, Black (Under)Development," 562.

9 Sekora, "Black Message / White Envelope."

10 Peterson, "Capitalism, Black (Under)Development," 566.

11 Peterson, "Capitalism, Black (Under)Development," 560.

12 "Death of Prof. Wilson," *People's Advocate*, November 30, 1878.

13 H. Wilson, "Preface."

14 H. Wilson, "Preface."

15 V. Smith, *Self-Discovery and Authority*; Hartman, *Scenes of Subjection*; Leigh, *Loophole of Retreat*. On the aesthetic experiments of *Incidents*, see also Davis, "Harriet Jacobs's 'Excrescences.'"

16 Rusert, *Fugitive Science*.

17 Sanborn, *Plagiarama!*, 9.

18 Irving, "Guests from Gibbet-Island."

19 Stauffer, *Works of James McCune Smith*, xxxi.

20 Stauffer, *Works of James McCune Smith*, xxxi.

21 W. J. Wilson, "Leaf from My Scrap Book," 165.

22 Amy Matilda Cassey Album, 1833–56, Collections of the Library Company of Philadelphia.

23 W. J. Wilson, "Leaf from My Scrap Book," 168–70.

24 W. J. Wilson, "Leaf from My Scrap Book," 166–67.

25 Sharpe, *In the Wake*, 21.

26 W. J. Wilson, "Leaf from My Scrap Book," 167.

27 W. J. Wilson, "Leaf from My Scrap Book," 173.

28 Western Reserve College is now Case Western University and located in Cleveland, Ohio.

29 Douglass, *Claims of the Negro*, 4.

30 Duane, *Educated for Freedom*.

31 *Frederick Douglass' Paper*, January 10, 1852.

32 *Frederick Douglass' Paper*, October 5, 1855.

33 Sanborn, *Plagiarama!*

34 Kelly, "Frederick Douglass's Prospective Aesthetic Theory."

35 Casarino and Righi, *Another Mother*, 20.

36 On the pernicious intertwining of sexism and racism and its effects on Black femmes, see Bailey, *Mysogynoir Transformed.*

37 Quoted in Casarino and Righi, *Another Mother*, 20.

38 Quashie, *Black Women, Identity, and Cultural Theory.*

39 Lorde, "Uses of the Erotic."

40 McHenry, *To Make Negro Literature.*

41 On this point, see Ernest, *Chaotic Justice.*

42 Deleuze and Guattari, *Thousand Plateaus*, 204.

43 Buck-Morss, *Dialectics of Seeing*, 264.

44 Buck-Morss, *Dialectics of Seeing*, 263.

45 Buck-Morss, *Dialectics of Seeing*, 263.

46 Buck-Morss, *Dialectics of Seeing*, 262.

47 Gardner, *Black Print Unbound.*

48 Douglass, *Claims of the Negro*, 20.

49 Eiland and Jennings, *Walter Benjamin*, 41.

50 Eiland and Jennings, *Walter Benjamin*, 41.

Chapter 3. "Sung Their Praise to Listening Worlds": Two Ethiops Communing Across Time and Space

Parts of chapter 3 were first published in my essay "'The World Is a Severe Schoolmaster': Phillis Wheatley's Poetics of Domination and Submission," *Early American Literature* 57, no. 3 (2022): 779–96.

1 Wells, *Kidnapping Club.* As chapter 1 chronicled in more detail, there are many moments when the Picture Gallery is already anticipating Benjamin's theses in "The Work of Art in the Age of Mechanical Reproduction."

2 On models of aesthetic absorption and contemplation in American Romanticism, see especially Emerson, *Essential Writings*; and C. Smith, *Thoreau's Axe*, on the nineteenth-century attention economy.

3 Benjamin, "Work of Art," 240.

4 Campt, *Black Gaze.*

5 Wheatley, *Memoir and Poems of Phillis Wheatley* (1834). The memoir included in this book was penned by Odell, who was probably the great grandniece of John and Susannah Wheatley.

6 Spires, *Practice of Citizenship*, 131. Spires notes that Wilson's Ethiop persona "signals Wilson's dedication to building black communities and literary histories."

7 I. Wilson, "'Are You Man Enough?,'" 266.

8 Italics are Wheatley's. This and all subsequent citations of Wheatley's poetry come from Wheatley, *Complete Writings*.

9 To parse Wheatley's biting wit and caustic critique of the Christians who claimed to own her, one must pay close attention to the politics of italicization, capitalization, and parenthetical asides in her verse.

10 On the politics of race and age in the age of slavery, including how people of African descent were excluded from normative markers of life stages and development, see Berry, *Price for Their Pound of Flesh*.

11 This "genteel" form of slavery, perpetuated by liberal-minded whites, was signified visually by the silken choker that adorns Wheatley's neck in her famous portrait at the beginning of *Poems on Various Subjects, Religious and Moral*.

12 Indeed, in many of her elegies, Wheatley not only warns white readers about the coming of death but even she rushes them off to it. She often strategically displaces the site of mourning in her elegies from the site of the child or family member who has passed onto a reminder of the mortality of the one who commissioned the poem. For more on the politics of mourning in Wheatley and in African American elegy more broadly, see Cavitch, *American Elegy*, 180–232.

13 Brooks, "Our Phillis, Ourselves." On the libidinal dimensions of Wheatley's instruction see Rusert, "'The World Is a Severe Schoolmaster.'"

14 Brooks, "Our Phillis, Ourselves."

15 *Oxford English Dictionary*, "sable" (n. & v.), 2a., 3.a, accessed December 28, 2025, https://www.oed.com/dictionary/sable_n2?tab=meaning_and_use#24583149.

16 W. J. Wilson, "Afric-American Picture Gallery," 218.

17 Spires notes, "Unlike Wilson's city sketches for *Frederick Douglass's Paper*, where 'Ethiop's' ideas seem directly connected to Wilson, Ethiop in the *Anglo-African* functions increasingly as a dynamic character distinct from the author." Spires, *Practice of Citizenship*, 180.

18 Du Bois, "Phillis Wheatley and African American Culture."

19 Clytus, "Visualizing in Black Print."

20 Power-Greene, *Against Wind and Tide*.

21 See Rael on debates over racial nomenclatures in Black antebellum intellectual circles and political organizing. He says the term *Afric-American* has an anticolonizationist origin, noting its usage in Black anticolonization meetings in the early 1830s. Rael, *Black Identity and Black Protest*, 82–117.

22 W. R. Roberts, "Phillis Wheatley's Sarah Moorhead."

23 On the politics of war and slave rebellion in the eighteenth-century revolutionary Atlantic, see V. Brown, *Tacky's Revolt*.

24 Kelley, *Freedom Dreams.*

25 Warren, *New England Bound.*

26 Much recent scholarship and creative work has become interested in better understanding Wheatley's relationship to other Black people in her community and life, including intimacies made of her own volition. For example, Honorée Fannone Jeffers's *Age of Phillis* is at once a poetic and scholarly intervention that asks us to take seriously and reflect on a significant relationship in Wheatley's life that has been all but obscured by scholars: her marriage to a free Black man named John Peters after her manumission.

27 Jupiter Hammon, "An Address to Miss Phillis Wheatl[e]y, Ethiopian Poetess, in Boston, who came from Africa at eight years of age, and soon became acquainted with the gospel of Jesus Christ" (Hartford, 1778); Hammon's broadside poem is collected in Wheatley, *Complete Writings*, 204–8, and subsequent citations are drawn from that edition.

28 Bynum, "Phillis Wheatley on Friendship." See also Bynum's more recent book, *Reading Pleasures.*

29 Patterson, *Slavery and Social Death.*

30 Bynum, "Phillis Wheatley on Friendship," 43.

31 Slauter, "Looking for Scipio Moorhead."

32 In addition to drawing from her own surreal experience of traversing space and time through the Middle Passage, John Shields says Wheatley's poetics of mental flight were inspired by the Greek philosopher Longinus, "who introduces to literary aesthetics the possibility of cosmic flight of imagination and unmistakably identifies the imagination as the agent of this movement of mind." See Shields, *Phillis Wheatley and the Romantics*, 4. Wheatley's poetics of flight also resonates with diasporic tales of flying Africans; on the dynamic tradition of imaginings of return flights back to the continent, see Commander, *Afro-Atlantic Flight.*

33 Shields, *Phillis Wheatley and the Romantics*, 4.

34 Jay, *Downcast Eyes.*

35 Barnhill, *Gems of Art on Paper.*

36 Campt, *Black Gaze*, 103.

37 Campt, *Black Gaze*, 104.

38 See Eckstrom, "Untimely Verse," on this point and how Black writers themselves theorized the politics of circulation, ephemerality, and durability in antebellum print cultures.

39 W. J. Wilson, "Afric-American Picture Gallery," 216.

40 On the philosophical and existential significance of "physical and mental roaming for black freedom," see Cervenak, *Wandering.*

41 W. J. Wilson, "Afric-American Picture Gallery," 216; these lines were popularized by Sir Walter Scott.

42 W. J. Wilson, "Afric-American Picture Gallery," 216.

43 Gwendolyn DuBois Shaw has argued that the attribution of Wheatley's portrait to Moorhead lies more in cultural fantasy than in historical evidence. See Shaw, *Portraits of a People*, 26–43.

44 Reproductions of Wheatley's image in 1855 include Hale, *Woman's Record*, 553; Jones, *Illustrated American Biography*, 147; and Duyckinck and Duyckinck, *Cyclopaedia of American Literature*, 367.

45 W. J. Wilson, "Afric-American Picture Gallery," 218.

46 W. J. Wilson, "Afric-American Picture Gallery," 218.

47 W. J. Wilson, "Afric-American Picture Gallery," 218.

48 V. Jackson, "Apostrophe, Animation, and Racism." See also V. Jackson, *Before Modernism*. "[A] sold thing, a bought chattel" is Wilson's language. See W. J. Wilson, "Afric-American Picture Gallery," 218.

49 W. J. Wilson, "Afric-American Picture Gallery," 218.

50 Wheatley, *Complete Writings*, 144.

51 Wheatley, *Complete Writings*, 139.

52 W. J. Wilson, "Afric-American Picture Gallery," 218.

53 On the turn to force in Black abolitionist thought and practice, see K. C. Jackson, *Force and Freedom*.

54 Newman, *Black Founders*. See also Newman, *Freedom's Prophet*.

55 Newman, *Black Founders*, 1.

56 Newman, *Black Founders*, 1.

57 Adams, "Argument for the Defense."

58 Nell, *Colored Patriots*, 9.

59 *Martyrdom of the Colored American Crispus Attucks*.

60 W. J. Wilson, "Afric-American Picture Gallery," 54.

61 On the rich citational history in visual renderings of Attucks, see Kachum, *First Martyr of Liberty*.

62 W. J. Wilson, "Afric-American Picture Gallery," 54.

Chapter 4. Ethiop in the Black Forest: Cruising, Fantasy, Ambivalence

Some material in chapter 4 appeared in my contributions to a chapter coauthored with John Ernest, Rian Bowie, and Leif Eckstrom in the collection *Against a Sharp White Background: Infrastructures of African American Print*

Collection, edited by Jonathan Senchyne and Brigitte Fielder (University of Wisconsin Press, 2019).

1 Barrett, *Blackness and Value.*

2 Cervenak, *Wandering*, 17; McKittrick, *Demonic Grounds.*

3 In this way, the Picture Gallery represents a departure from the tradition of realism that has shaped African American literature from its beginnings. On African American writers' complex relationship to realism, see Jarrett, *Deans and Truants.*

4 Bonifacio, "Pastoral Escapes from the City." Interestingly, the travel narrative of Terance Ludlam appears in *Frederick Douglass' Paper* immediately after a Whittier poem titled "The Kansas Emigrants."

5 Williams, *Country and the City.*

6 On the sexual economies of enslavement, which both shadowed and shaped the market for free Black labor, see Owens, *In the Presence of Force*; and Jacobs, *Incidents.*

7 Roane, *Dark Agoras*, 22. Roane's idea of the plot draws from Wynter's theorization of that concept in "Novel and History."

8 Roane, *Dark Agoras*, 23. Roane is especially interested in plotting as a form of home-making for African Americans during the Great Migration; my understanding of the landscape of Black community-making in antebellum New York, where people came to the city from rural outposts and escaped from the plantation South, suggests that the plot pertained in this earlier context as well.

9 Roane, *Dark Agoras*, 9–10.

10 W. J. Wilson, "Afric-American Picture Gallery," 101.

11 W. J. Wilson, "Afric-American Picture Gallery," 103.

12 W. J. Wilson, "Afric-American Picture Gallery," 173, 174, 177.

13 W. J. Wilson, "Afric-American Picture Gallery," 101.

14 W. J. Wilson, "Afric-American Picture Gallery," 103.

15 I. Wilson, *Specters of Democracy*, 148.

16 Bloch, *Principle of Hope.*

17 I. Wilson, *Specters of Democracy*, 156.

18 W. J. Wilson, "Afric-American Picture Gallery," 54.

19 On the influence of Wheatley's image on British and Anglo-African portraiture, see Shaw, *Portraits of a People*, 26–43. Many thanks to Allison Lange and Connie King for their assistance locating nineteenth-century images of Wheatley at the Library Company of Philadelphia.

20 Both the 1834 frontispiece and the frontispiece that appeared in the third edition of Wheatley's memoir in 1838 were engraved at Pendleton's

Lithography in Boston, where Robert Benjamin Lewis's lithograph was also produced in the early 1830s. See Wheatley, *Memoir and Poems of Phillis Wheatley* (1834) and *Memoir and Poems of Phillis Wheatley* (1838). On Robert Benjamin Lewis's portrait, see Rusert, "Types of Mankind."

21 On the complicated role that sculpture played in transatlantic abolition, see Caitlin Meehye Beach's *Sculpture at the Ends of Slavery*. Beach says that abolitionist sculpture was a "highly visible" (4) but also "deeply unstable" (4) means of interrogating slavery, whose production and circulation were made possible "through the very regimes of wealth and bodily value that enslavement afforded" (20). On the racial and gender politics of neoclassical sculpture in the period, see Nelson, *The Color of Stone*.

22 Neil Roberts, for example, has made a compelling case for the political and conceptual possibilities of the term *maroonage*, perhaps even above that of *fugitivity*, from the perspective of Africana and Caribbean philosophy. See N. Roberts, *Freedom as Maroonage*.

23 Roane, *Dark Agoras*.

24 *Oxford English Dictionary*, "cruise" (v.), 1d., accessed December 27, 2025, https://www.oed.com/dictionary/cruise_v?tab=meaning_and_use. The OED says that the meaning of cruise as "To walk or drive about (the streets) in search of a casual sexual (*esp.* homosexual) partner" originates around the turn of the twentieth century.

25 Guerin, "Underground and at Sea."

26 Yacovone, "William J. Wilson," 400.

27 *Frederick Douglass' Paper*, May 13, 1852.

28 Douglass, *Narrative of the Life*, 101.

29 Douglass, *My Bondage and My Freedom*.

30 Thank you to Jordy Rosenberg for discussing the flying cloud during many walks in the woods.

31 Dorr, *Colored Man Round the World*, xi.

32 Quoted in Dorr, *Colored Man Round the World*, xxx.

33 Dorr, *Colored Man Round the World*, 87.

34 Wheatley, "On Imagination," in *Complete Writings*.

35 W. J. Wilson, "Afric-American Picture Gallery," 173.

36 *People's Advocate*, November 30, 1878.

37 Quashie, *Sovereignty of Quiet*.

38 Wellman, *Brooklyn's Promised Land*, 1.

39 Wellman, *Brooklyn's Promised Land*, 1.

40 Wellman, *Brooklyn's Promised Land*, 98.

41 On the cultivation of protected spaces by free Black women in the antebellum period, see Dunbar, *Fragile Freedom*; and Cobb, *Picture Freedom*.

42 Olvasky, *Most Absolute Abolition*.

43 W. J. Wilson, "Afric-American Picture Gallery," 321.

44 W. J. Wilson, "Afric-American Picture Gallery," 324.

45 W. J. Wilson, "Afric-American Picture Gallery," 54.

46 W. J. Wilson, "Afric-American Picture Gallery," 54.

47 W. J. Wilson, "Afric-American Picture Gallery," 54–55.

48 In the 1850s, free Black communities were also established in Canada, including the Ontario community where Mary Shadd Cary lived and published Canada's first antislavery newspaper, the *Provincial Freeman*.

49 W. J. Wilson, "Afric-American Picture Gallery," 55.

50 On the brutal anatomizing regimes of enslavement, and systems of valuation based on gender, age, and physical ability, see Berry, *Price for Their Pound of Flesh*; see also Baptist, *Half Has Never Been Told*.

51 W. J. Wilson, "Afric-American Picture Gallery," 54–55.

52 W. J. Wilson, "Afric-American Picture Gallery," 321.

53 On the turn to the use of force by Black abolitionists in the 1850s, see K. C. Jackson, *Force and Freedom*.

54 K. C. Jackson, *Force and Freedom*, 321.

55 *Frederick Douglass' Paper*, December 25, 1851.

56 Power-Greene, *Against Wind and Tide*.

57 Power-Greene, "Untitled."

58 Minutes of Colored Men's State Convention of New York, Troy, September 4, 1855, coloredconventions.org.

59 W. J. Wilson, "Afric-American Picture Gallery," 54.

60 W. J. Wilson, "Afric-American Picture Gallery," 54.

61 William J. Wilson to Henry Stiles, March 31, 1863, Henry Stiles Papers, Center for Brooklyn History, Brooklyn Public Library.

Conclusion

1 Butchart, "'We Best Can Instruct.'"

2 McHenry, *To Make Negro Literature*, 32.

3 For more on this periodical, along with other newspapers printed for use in the freedmen's schools, see Young, "Roads to Travel."

4 Yacovone, "William J. Wilson," 400.

5 *Brooklyn Daily Eagle*, July 8, 1863.

6 On the Draft Riots, see Harris, *In the Shadow of Slavery*, 280–88.

7 Harris, *In the Shadow of Slavery*, 285.

8 R. J. Weir, "Where All Eyes Are Turned: Letters from Washington in the *Anglo-African*, 1863–1864," *Civil War Washington*, accessed December 29, 2025, https://civilwardc.org/texts/letters/about.html.

9 National Lincoln Monument Association, *Constitution of the Educational Monument Association.*

10 "Notes from the Capital," *New National Era*, April 23, 1874.

11 *New National Era*, June 25, 1874.

12 *New National Era*, April 30, 1874.

13 *New National Era*, April 16, 1874.

14 For more on this emancipatory tradition of living free at the turn of the twentieth century, see Hartman, *Wayward Lives.*

15 *New National Era*, May 28, 1874.

16 *New National Era*, May 14, 1874.

17 For a firsthand account of Black women's cultures of fashion and high society in Reconstruction-era DC, see Elizabeth Keckley's 1868 narrative, *Behind the Scenes.*

18 *New National Era*, April 23, 1874.

19 Du Bois, *Black Reconstruction in America*, 599.

20 *New National Era*, December 14, 1874.

21 *New National Era*, December 14, 1873.

22 "Colored Refugees in Our Camps," *The Liberator*, April 10, 1863.

23 On the Civil War and its aftermath as a public health crisis, especially for African Americans, see Downs, *Sick from Freedom*. "The afterlife of slavery" is Saidiya Hartman's term. See Hartman, *Lose Your Mother.*

24 *New National Era*, July 16, 1874.

25 *People's Advocate*, November 30, 1878.

26 *People's Advocate*, November 30, 1878.

27 For more on the politics of African American burial practices, and the history of racism and segregation as they intersect with Black cemeteries, see Holloway, *Passed On.*

28 Kanakamedala, *Brooklynites*, 206.

29 Kanakamedala, *Brooklynites*, 206.

30 Somerville, *Queering the Color Line*, 3.

31 Channing Gerard Joseph notes that Swann served time for his criminalized activities and also demanded a pardon from President Cleveland for holding his drag balls; Joseph calls this a "historic act: It made Swann the earliest recorded American to take specific legal and political steps to defend the queer community's right to gather without the threat of criminalization, suppression, or police violence." See Joseph, "First Drag Queen."

32 Griffiths, "Bricolage Propriety," 2–3.

33 Scott, *Extravagant Abjection*, 6.

34 Abdur-Rahman, *Against the Closet*.

35 Glissant, *Poetics of Relation*; Clark-Hine, "Rape and the Inner Lives of Black Women."

Bibliography

Abdur-Rahman, Aliyyah I. *Against the Closet: Black Political Longing and the Erotics of Race*. Duke University Press, 2012.

Adams, John. "Argument for the Defense, 3–4 December, 1770." *Founders Online*, National Archives. https://founders.archives.gov/documents/Adams/05-03-02-0001-0004-0016#LJA03d031n1.

Bagneris, Mia. "Illuminating the Shadows of 'Liberty': George Washington and Blackness in American Art." *American Art* 35, no. 3 (2021): 2–14.

Bagneris, Mia. "The Radical Floriography of Sarah Mapps Douglass." *Smarthistory*, November 21, 2022. https://smarthistory.org/radical-floriography-sarah-mapps-douglass/.

Bailey, Moya. *Mysogynoir Transformed: Black Women's Digital Resistance*. MIT Press, 2020.

Baptist, Ed. *The Half Has Never Been Told*. Basic Books, 2014.

Barbash, Ilisa, Molly Rogers, and Deborah Willis, eds. *To Make Their Own Way in the World: The Enduring Legacy of the Zealy Daguerreotypes*. Aperture, 2020.

Barnhill, Georgia. *Gems of Art on Paper: Illustrated American Fiction and Poetry, 1785–1885*. University of Massachusetts Press, 2021.

Barrett, Lindon. *Blackness and Value: Seeing Double*. Cambridge University Press, 1999.

Barthes, Roland. *Camera Lucida: Reflections on Photography*. Hill & Wang, 1982.

Battle-Baptiste, Whitney, and Britt Rusert, eds. *W. E. B. Du Bois's Data Portraits: Visualizing Black America*. Princeton Architectural Press, 2018.

Beach, Caitlin Meehye. *Sculpture at the Ends of Slavery*. University of California Press, 2022.

Benjamin, Walter. "The Work of Art in the Age of Mechanical Reproduction." In *Illuminations: Essays and Reflections*, edited by Hannah Arendt. Schocken Books, 2007.

Bennett, Tony. *The Birth of the Museum*. Routledge, 2005.

Berry, Daina Ramey. *The Price for Their Pound of Flesh: The Value of the Enslaved, from Womb to Grave, in the Building of a Nation*. Beacon Press, 2017.

Blackwood, Sarah. *The Portrait's Subject: Inventing Inner Life in the Nineteenth-Century United States*. University of North Carolina Press, 2019.

Bloch, Ernst. *The Principle of Hope*. MIT Press, 1995.

Bonifacio, Ayendi. "Pastoral Escapes from the City: Alice Cary's Resistance to Patriarchal Romanticism in the *New York Ledger*." *J19: The Journal of Nineteenth-Century Americanists* 10, no. 1 (2022): 201–8.

Bowie, Rian, John Ernest, Leif Eckstrom, and Britt Rusert. "Visionary History: Recovering William J. Wilson's 'Afric-American Picture Gallery.'" In *Against a Sharp White Background: Infrastructures of African American Print*, edited by Brigitte Fielder and Jonathan Senchyne. University of Wisconsin Press, 2019.

Brand, Dionne. *A Map to the Door of No Return: Notes to Belonging*. Vintage Canada, 2001.

Brooks, Joanna. "Our Phillis, Ourselves." *American Literature* 82, no. 1 (2010): 1–28.

Brown, Kimberly Juanita. *Mortevivum: Photography and the Politics of the Visual*. MIT Press, 2024.

Brown, Kimberly Juanita. *The Repeating Body: Slavery's Visual Resonance in the Contemporary*. Duke University Press, 2015.

Brown, Vincent. *Tacky's Revolt: The Story of an Atlantic Slave War*. Harvard University Press, 2022.

Brown, William Wells. *The Black Man: His Antecedents, His Genius, and His Achievements*. Thomas Hamilton, 1863.

Buchtel, John, and Makeda Best, eds. *Framing Freedom: The Harriet Hayden Albums*. Boston Athenaeum, 2023.

Buck-Morss, Susan. *The Dialectics of Seeing: Walter Benjamin and the Arcades Project*. MIT Press, 1989.

Butchart, Ronald E. "'We Best Can Instruct Our Own People': New York African Americans in the Freedmen's Schools, 1861–75." *Afro-Americans in New York Life and History* 12, no. 1 (1988): 27–49.

Bynum, Tara. "Phillis Wheatley on Friendship." *Legacy* 31, no. 1 (2014): 42–51.

Bynum, Tara. *Reading Pleasures: Everyday Black Living in Early America*. University of Illinois Press, 2023.

Campt, Tina. *A Black Gaze: Artists Changing How We See*. MIT Press, 2021.

Casarino, Cesare, and Andrea Righi, eds. *Another Mother: Diotima and the Symbolic Order of Italian Feminism*. University of Minnesota Press, 2018.

Cavitch, Max. *American Elegy: The Poetry of Mourning from the Puritans to Whitman.* University of Minnesota Press, 2007.

Cervenak, Sarah Jane. *Wandering: Philosophical Performances of Racial and Sexual Freedom.* Duke University Press, 2014.

Clark-Hine, Darlene. "Rape and the Inner Lives of Black Women in the Middle West: Preliminary Thoughts on the Culture of Dissemblance." *Signs* 14, no. 4 (1989): 912–20.

Clytus, Radiclani. "'Keep It Before the People': The Pictorialization of American Abolitionism." In *Early African American Print Culture,* edited by Lara Langer Cohen and Jordan Alexander Stein. University of Pennsylvania Press, 2012.

Clytus, Radiclani. "Visualizing in Black Print: The Brooklyn Correspondence of William J. Wilson aka 'Ethiop.'" *J19: The Journal of Nineteenth-Century Americanists* 6, no. 1 (2018): 29–66.

Cobb, Jasmine Nichole. *Picture Freedom: Remaking Black Visuality in the Early Nineteenth Century.* NYU Press, 2015.

Cohen, Lara Langer, and Jordan Alexander Stein, eds. *Early African American Print Culture.* University of Pennsylvania Press, 2012.

Commander, Michelle. *Afro-Atlantic Flight: Speculative Returns and the Black Fantastic.* Duke University Press, 2017.

Davis, Theo. "Harriet Jacobs's 'Excrescences': Aesthetics and Politics in *Incidents in the Life of a Slave Girl.*" *Theory and Event* 13, no. 4 (2010). https://muse-jhu-edu.silk.library.umass.edu/article/407143.

Deleuze, Gilles, and Félix Guattari. *A Thousand Plateaus: Capitalism and Schizophrenia.* Translated by Brian Massumi. University of Minnesota Press, 1987.

Dorr, David. *A Colored Man Round the World.* Edited by Malini Johar Schueller. University of Michigan Press, 1999.

Douglass, Frederick. *Claims of the Negro, Ethnologically Considered.* Rochester, NY: Lee, Mann & Co., 1854.

Douglass, Frederick. *My Bondage and My Freedom.* New York and Auburn: Miller, Orton, and Mulligan, 1855. https://docsouth.unc.edu/neh/douglass55/douglass55.html.

Douglass, Frederick. *Narrative of the Life of Frederick Douglass, an American Slave.* Boston: Anti-Slavery Society, 1845. https://docsouth.unc.edu/neh/douglass/douglass.html.

Downs, Jim. *Sick from Freedom: African-American Illness and Suffering During the Civil War and Reconstruction.* Oxford University Press, 2015.

Duane, Anna Mae. *Educated for Freedom: The Incredible Story of Two Fugitive Schoolboys Who Grew Up to Change a Nation.* NYU Press, 2020.

Du Bois, W. E. B. *Black Reconstruction in America.* Free Press, 1992.

Du Bois, W. E. B. "Phillis Wheatley and African American Culture." In *The Oxford W. E. B. Du Bois Reader,* edited by Eric J. Sundquist. Oxford University

Press, 1996. Originally published as "The Vision of Phillis the Blessed (An Allegory of Negro American Literature in the Eighteenth and Nineteenth Centuries)." *Fisk News* 14 (May 1941).

Dunbar, Erica Armstrong. *A Fragile Freedom: African American Women and Emancipation in the Antebellum City*. Yale University Press, 2011.

Duyckinck, Evert A., and George L. Duyckinck, eds. *Cyclopaedia of American Literature*. Vol. 2. Charles Scribner, 1855.

Eckstrom, Leif. "Untimely Verse: Distressed Publishing and Exemplary Circulation in Antebellum America." PhD diss., Tufts University, 2018.

Eckstrom, Leif, and Britt Rusert. Introduction to "Afric-American Picture Gallery." *Just Teach One: Early African American Print* 2 (2015). https://jtoaa.americanantiquarian.org/welcome-to-just-teach-one-african-american/afric-american-picture-gallery/.

Eiland, Howard, and Michael W. Jennings. *Walter Benjamin: A Critical Life*. Belknap Press of Harvard University Press, 2016.

Emerson, Ralph Waldo. *The Essential Writings of Ralph Waldo Emerson*. Modern Library, 2000.

English, Darby. *How to See a Work of Art in Total Darkness*. MIT Press, 2007.

Ernest, John. *Chaotic Justice: Rethinking African American Literary History*. University of North Carolina Press, 2009.

Ernest, John. *Liberation Historiography: African American Writers and the Challenge of History, 1794–1861*. University of North Carolina Press, 2004.

Fabian, Ann. *The Skull Collectors: Race, Science, and America's Unburied Dead*. University of Chicago Press, 2010.

Fielder, Brigitte, and Jonathan Senchyne, eds. *Against a Sharp White Background: Infrastructures of African American Print*. University of Wisconsin Press, 2019.

Finley, Cheryl. *Committed to Memory: The Art of the Slave Ship Icon*. Princeton University Press, 2018.

Fleetwood, Nicole. *Troubling Vision: Performance, Visuality, and Blackness*. University of Chicago Press, 2015.

Ford, James Edward, III. "Notes on Black Ekphrasis." *Early American Literature* 58, no. 3 (2023): 591–618.

Foreman, P. Gabrielle. *Activist Sentiments: Reading Black Women in the Nineteenth Century*. University of Illinois Press, 2009.

Foucault, Michel. "Of Other Spaces." *Diacritics* 16, no. 1 (1986): 22–27.

Fox-Amato, Matthew. *Exposing Slavery: Photography, Human Bondage, and the Birth of Modern Visual Politics in America*. Oxford University Press, 2019.

Gardner, Eric. *Black Print Unbound: The Christian Recorder, African American Literature, and Periodical Culture*. Oxford University Press, 2015.

Glissant, Édouard. *Poetics of Relation*. Translated by Betsy Wing. University of Michigan Press, 1997.

Gonzalez, Aston. *Visualizing Equality: African American Rights and Visual Culture in the Nineteenth Century*. University of North Carolina Press, 2020.

Gould, Stephen Jay. *The Mismeasure of Man*. Rev. ed. W. W. Norton, 1996.

Griffiths, Timothy. "Bricolage Propriety: The Queer Practice of Black Uplift, 1890–1905." PhD diss., CUNY Graduate Center, 2017.

Guerin, Ayasha. "Underground and at Sea: Oysters and Black Marine Entanglements in New York's Zone-A." *Shima* 13, no. 2 (2019): 30–55.

Hager, Christopher. *Word by Word: Emancipation and the Act of Writing*. Harvard University Press, 2015.

Hale, Sarah. *Woman's Record; or, Sketches of All Distinguished Women, from the Creation to A.D. 1854*. New York: Harper & Brothers, 1855.

Harris, Leslie. *In the Shadow of Slavery: African Americans in New York City*. University of Chicago Press, 2003.

Hartman, Saidiya. *Lose Your Mother: A Journey Along the Atlantic Slave Trade*. Farrar, Straus and Giroux, 2008.

Hartman, Saidiya. *Scenes of Subjection: Terror, Slavery, and Self-Making in Nineteenth-Century America*. Oxford University Press, 1998.

Hartman, Saidiya. *Wayward Lives, Beautiful Experiments: Intimate Histories of Riotous Black Girls, Troublesome Women, and Queer Radicals*. W. W. Norton, 2020.

Helton, Laura, Justin Leroy, Max A. Mishler, Samantha Seeley, and Shauna Sweeney. "The Question of Recovery: Slavery, Freedom, and the Archive." Special issue, *Social Text* 33, no. 4 (2015).

Henkin, David. *City Reading: Written Words and Public Spaces in Antebellum New York*. Columbia University Press, 1998.

Hickman, Jared. "Douglass Unbound." *Nineteenth-Century Literature* 68, no. 3 (2013): 323–62.

Hinks, Peter. *To Awaken My Afflicted Brethren: David Walker and the Problem of Antebellum Slave Resistance*. Penn State University Press, 1996.

Holloway, Karla. *Passed On: African American Mourning Stories*. Duke University Press, 2002.

Holly, Theodore. "Thoughts on Hayti." In *Anglo-African Magazine*, vol. 1, edited by Thomas Hamilton. Arno Press and the *New York Times*, 1968.

hooks, bell. *Black Looks: Race and Representation*. 2nd ed. Routledge, 2015.

Irving, Washington. "Guests from Gibbet-Island: A Legend of Communipaw." *Knickerbocker; or, New-York Monthly Magazine of Literature, Art, Politics and Society* 14, no. 4 (1839): 342–50.

Jackson, Kellie Carter. *Force and Freedom: Black Abolitionists and the Politics of Violence*. University of Pennsylvania Press, 2019.

Jackson, Virginia. "Apostrophe, Animation, and Racism." *Critical Inquiry* 48, no. 4 (2022): 652–75.

Jackson, Virginia. *Before Modernism: Inventing American Lyric*. Princeton University Press, 2023.

Jacobs, Harriet. *Incidents in the Life of a Slave Girl*. Boston: Published for the author, 1861.

Jarrett, Gene Andrew. *Deans and Truants: Race and Realism in African American Literature*. University of Pennsylvania Press, 2006.

Jay, Martin. *Downcast Eyes: The Denigration of Vision in Twentieth-Century French Thought*. University of California Press, 1993.

Jay, Martin, and Sumathi Ramaswamy, eds. *Empires of Vision: A Reader*. Duke University Press, 2014.

Jeffers, Honorée Fanonne. *The Age of Phillis*. Wesleyan University Press, 2020.

Jones, A. D. *The Illustrated American Biography*. Vol. 3. New York: J. Milton Emerson & Co., 1855.

Joseph, Channing Gerard. "The First Drag Queen Was a Former Slave." *The Nation*, January 31, 2020.

Junker, Carsten. "Containing Bodies—Enscandalizing Enslavement and Movement at the Juncture of Slave-Ship Images and Texts." In *Migrating the Black Body: The African Diaspora and Visual Culture*, edited by Leigh Raiford and Heike Raphael-Hernandez. University of Washington Press, 2017.

Kachum, Mitchell. *First Martyr of Liberty: Crispus Attucks in American Memory*. Oxford University Press, 2017.

Kanakamedala, Prithi. *Brooklynites: The Remarkable Story of the Free Black Communities That Shaped a Borough*. NYU Press, 2024.

Keckley, Elizabeth. *Behind the Scenes: or, Thirty Years a Slave, and Four Years in the White House*. New York: G. W. Carleton & Co., 1868. https://docsouth.unc.edu/neh/keckley/menu.html.

Kelley, Robin D. G. *Freedom Dreams: The Black Radical Imagination*. Penguin, 2002.

Kelly, Michael. "Frederick Douglass's Prospective Aesthetic Theory." *Critical Philosophies of Race* 9, no. 2 (2021): 240–69.

Leigh, Simone. *Loophole of Retreat*. Exhibition, Venice Biennale, 2022.

Lewis, Sarah. *The Unseen Truth: When Race Changed Sight in America*. Harvard University Press, 2024.

Lorang, Elizabeth, and R. J. Weir. "'Will Not These Days Be by Thy Poets Sung': Poems of the *Anglo-African* and *National Anti-Slavery Standard*, 1863–1864." *Scholarly Editing* 34 (2013). https://www.scholarlyediting.org/2013/editions/intro.cwnewspaperpoetry.html.

Lorde, Audre. "Uses of the Erotic: The Erotic as Power." In *Sister Outsider: Essays and Speeches by Audre Lorde*. Crossing Press, 1984.

Lugo-Ortiz, Agnes, and Angela Rosenthal, eds. *Slave Portraiture in the Atlantic World*. Cambridge University Press, 2013.

Martyrdom of the Colored American Crispus Attucks, March 5th, 1770. Boston, 1863.

McHenry, Elizabeth. *To Make Negro Literature: Writing, Literary Practice, and African American Authorship*. Duke University Press, 2021.

McKittrick, Katherine. *Demonic Grounds: Black Women and the Cartographies of Struggle*. University of Minnesota Press, 2006.

McRee, Claire. "Mathew Brady and the Daguerreotype Portrait." *Visualizing 19th-Century New York*, Bard Graduate Center. https://visualizingnyc.org/.

Meer, Sarah. *Uncle Tom Mania: Slavery, Minstrelsy, and Transatlantic Culture in the 1850s*. University of Georgia Press, 2005.

Miller, Monica. *Slaves to Fashion: Black Dandyism and the Styling of Black Diasporic Identity*. Duke University Press, 2009.

Mirzoeff, Nicholas. *An Introduction to Visual Culture*. 2nd ed. Routledge, 2023.

Mirzoeff, Nicholas. *The Right to Look: A Counterhistory of Visuality*. Duke University Press, 2011.

Mitchell, W. J. T. *Picture Theory: Essays on Verbal and Visual Representation*. University of Chicago Press, 1994.

Moody, Joycelyn, and Howard Rambsy II, eds. "African American Print Cultures." Special issue, *MELUS: Multi-Ethnic Literature of the United States* 40, no. 3 (2015).

Moten, Fred. "Black Op." *PMLA* 123, no. 5 (2008): 1743–47.

Muñoz, José Esteban. *Cruising Utopia: The Then and There of Queer Futurity*. NYU Press, 2009.

National Lincoln Monument Association. *Constitution of the Educational Monument Association to the Memory of Abraham Lincoln: Organized May 16, 1865*. Washington, DC: McGill & Witherow, 1865.

Nell, William C. "Colored American Patriots." In *Anglo-African Magazine*, vol. 1, edited by Thomas Hamilton. Arno Press and the *New York Times*, 1968.

Nell, William C. *The Colored Patriots of the American Revolution*. Boston: Robert F. Wallcutt, 1855.

Nelson, Charmaine. *The Color of Stone: Sculpting the Black Female Subject in Nineteenth-Century America*. University of Minnesota Press, 2007.

Newman, Richard. *Black Founders: The Free Black Community in the Early Republic*. Library Company of Philadelphia, 2008.

Newman, Richard. *Freedom's Prophet: Bishop Richard Allen, the AME Church, and the Black Founding Fathers*. NYU Press, 2009.

Olvasky, Jesse. *The Most Absolute Abolition: Runaways, Vigilance Committees, and the Rise of Revolutionary Abolitionism, 1835–1861*. Louisiana State University Press, 2022.

Owens, Emily. *In the Presence of Force: Sexual Violence and Black Women's Survival in Antebellum New Orleans*. University of North Carolina Press, 2023.

Patterson, Orlando. *Slavery and Social Death: A Comparative Study*. Harvard University Press, 2018.

Peterson, Carla. *Black Gotham: A Family History of African Americans in Nineteenth-Century New York City*. Yale University Press, 2012.

Peterson, Carla. "Capitalism, Black (Under)Development, and the Production of the African-American Novel in the 1850s." *American Literary History* 4, no. 4 (1992): 559–83.

Phelan, Peggy. *Unmarked: The Politics of Performance*. Routledge, 1993.

Plasa, Carl. "Ekphrastic Poetry and the Middle Passage: Recent Encounters in the Black Atlantic." *Connotations* 24, no. 2 (2014/2015): 290–324.

Powell, Richard. *Cutting a Figure: Fashioning Black Portraiture*. University of Chicago Press, 2008.

Powell, Richard. "Sartor Africanus." In *Dandies: Fashion and Finesse in Art and Culture*, edited by Sudan Fillin-Yeh. NYU Press, 2001.

Power-Greene, Ousmane. *Against Wind and Tide: The African American Struggle Against the Colonization Movement*. NYU Press, 2014.

Power-Greene, Ousmane. "Untitled." Presentation to the American Antiquarian Society's American Studies Seminar, November 17, 2022.

Quashie, Kevin. *Black Women, Identity, and Cultural Theory: (Un)Becoming the Subject*. Rutgers University Press, 2003.

Quashie, Kevin. *The Sovereignty of Quiet: Beyond Resistance in Black Culture*. Rutgers University Press, 2012.

Rael, Patrick. *Black Identity and Black Protest in the Antebellum North*. University of North Carolina Press, 2002.

Raiford, Leigh, and Heike Raphael-Hernandez, eds. *Migrating the Black Body: Visual Culture and the African Diaspora*. University of Washington Press, 2017.

Rediker, Marcus. *The Slave Ship*. Viking, 2007.

Renner, Dennis K. "Leaves of Grass, 1881–82 edition." In *The Walt Whitman Archive*, general editors Matt Cohen, Ed Folsom, and Kenneth M. Price. Accessed May 18, 2026. http://www.whitmanarchive.org.

Roane, J. T. *Dark Agoras: Insurgent Black Social Life and the Politics of Place*. NYU Press, 2023.

Roberts, Neil. *Freedom as Maroonage*. University of Chicago Press, 2015.

Roberts, Wendy Raphael. "Phillis Wheatley's Sarah Moorhead: An Initial Inquiry." *Papers of the Bibliographical Society of America* 107 (2013): 345–54.

Rusert, Britt. *Fugitive Science: Empiricism and Freedom in Early African American Culture*. NYU Press, 2017.

Rusert, Britt. "Types of Mankind: Visualizing Kinship in Afro-Native America." *Common-place* 13, no. 1 (2012). http://www.common-place.org/vol-13/no-01/tales/.

Rusert, Britt. "'The World Is a Severe Schoolmaster': Phillis Wheatley's Poetry of Domination and Submission." *Early American Literature* 57, no. 3 (2022): 779–96.

Sanborn, Geoffrey. *Plagiarama! William Wells Brown and the Aesthetic of Attractions*. Columbia University Press, 2016.

Scott, Darieck. *Extravagant Abjection: Blackness, Power, and Sexuality in the African American Literary Imagination*. NYU Press, 2010.

Sekora, John. "Black Message/White Envelope: Genre, Authenticity, and Authority in the Antebellum Slave Narrative." *Callaloo* 32 (Summer 1987): 482–515.

Sharpe, Christina. *In the Wake: On Blackness and Being*. Duke University Press, 2016.

Shaw, Gwendolyn DuBois. *Portraits of a People: Picturing African Americans in the Nineteenth Century*. University of Washington Press, 2006.

Shields, John. *Phillis Wheatley and the Romantics*. University of Tennessee Press, 2010.

Slauter, Eric. "Looking for Scipio Moorhead: An 'African Painter' in Revolutionary North America." In *Slave Portraiture in the Atlantic World*, edited by Agnes Lugo-Ortiz and Angela Rosenthal. Cambridge University Press, 2013.

Smallwood, Stephanie E. *Saltwater Slavery: A Middle Passage from Africa to American Diaspora*. Harvard University Press, 2008.

Smethurst, James. *The African American Roots of Modernism: From Reconstruction to the Harlem Renaissance*. University of North Carolina Press, 2011.

Smith, Caleb. *Thoreau's Axe: Distraction and Discipline in American Culture*. Princeton University Press, 2023.

Smith, Valerie. *Self-Discovery and Authority in Afro-American Narrative*. Harvard University Press, 1987.

Somerville, Siobhan. *Queering the Color Line: Race and the Invention of Homosexuality in American Culture*. Duke University Press, 2000.

Spires, Derrick. "Seriality and Future Histories of Blackness." Paper presented at Early Black Utopias Symposium, Johns Hopkins University, March 29, 2019.

Spires, Derrick. *The Practice of Citizenship: Black Politics and Print Culture in the Early United States*. University of Pennsylvania Press, 2019.

Stauffer, John, ed. *The Works of James McCune Smith: Black Intellectual and Abolitionist*. Oxford University Press, 2006.

Stauffer, John, Zoe Trodd, and Celeste-Marie Bernier. *Picturing Frederick Douglass: An Illustrated Biography of the Nineteenth Century's Most Photographed American*. Liveright, 2015.

Taylor, Diana. *The Archive and the Repertoire: Performing Cultural Memory in the Americas*. Duke University Press, 2003.

Taylor, Elizabeth Dowling. *The Original Black Elite: Daniel Murray and the Story of a Forgotten Era*. Amistad, 2017.

Thompson-Spires, Nafissa. *The Heads of the Colored People*. Simon and Schuster, 2018.

Trachtenberg, Alan. *Reading American Photographs: Images as History, Mathew Brady to Walker Evans*. Hill and Wang, 1989.

Wallace, Maurice, and Shawn Michelle Smith, eds. *Pictures and Progress: Early Photography and the Making of African-American Identity*. Duke University Press, 2012.

Warren, Wendy. *New England Bound: Slavery and Colonization in Early America*. Liveright, 2016.

Watson, Sabrina. "Free Blacks in Accomack County During the Antebellum Period." *Black Perspectives*, March 27, 2024. https://www.aaihs.org/free-blacks-in-accomack-county-during-the-antebellum-period/.

Wellman, Judith. *Brooklyn's Promised Land: The Free Black Community of Weeksville, New York*. NYU Press, 2014.

Wells, Jonathan Daniels. *The Kidnapping Club: Wall Street, Slavery, and Resistance on the Eve of the Civil War*. Bold Type Books, 2020.

Wheatley, Phillis. *Complete Writings*. Edited by Vincent Carretta. Penguin Books, 2001.

Wheatley, Phillis. *Memoir and Poems of Phillis Wheatley: A Native African and a Slave*. With memoir by Margaretta Matilda Odell. Boston: Geo. W. Light, 1834.

Wheatley, Phillis. *Memoir and Poems of Phillis Wheatley: A Native African and a Slave*. With memoir by Margaretta Matilda Odell. 3rd ed. Boston: Isaac Knapp, 1838.

Wheatley, Phillis. *Poems on Various Subjects, Religious and Moral*. London: A. Bell, 1773.

Whitman, Walt. *Leaves of Grass*. Brooklyn: Rome Brothers, 1855.

Wilder, Craig Steven. *A Covenant with Color: Race and Social Power in Brooklyn*. Columbia University Press, 2000.

Williams, Raymond. *The Country and the City*. Oxford University Press, 1975.

Willis, Deborah. *The Black Civil War Soldier: A Visual History of Conflict and Citizenship*. NYU Press, 2021.

Willis, Deborah. *Reflections in Black: A History of Black Photographers, 1840 to the Present*. W. W. Norton, 2000.

Wilson, Harriet. "Preface." In *Our Nig: or, Sketches from the Life of a Free Black*. Boston: Geo. C. Rand & Avery, 1859.

Wilson, Ivy. "'Are You Man Enough?': Imagining Ethiopia and Transnational Black Masculinity." *Callaloo* 33, no. 1 (2010): 265–77.

Wilson, Ivy. *Specters of Democracy: Blackness and the Aesthetics of Politics in the Antebellum U.S.* Oxford University Press, 2011.

Wilson, William J. (Ethiop). "Afric-American Picture Gallery." In *Anglo-African Magazine*, vol. 1, edited by Thomas Hamilton. Arno Press and the *New York Times*, 1968.

Wilson, William J. "A Leaf from My Scrap Book." In *Autographs for Freedom*, vol. 2. Auburn, NY: Alden, Beardsley & Co., 1854.

Wilson, William J. "Terance Ludlam." *Frederick Douglass' Paper*, August 11–18, 1854.

Winch, Julie. *A Gentleman of Color: The Life of James Forten*. Oxford University Press, 2003.

Winch, Julie. *Philadelphia's Black Elite: Activism, Accommodation, and the Struggle for Autonomy, 1787–1848*. Temple University Press, 1988.

Wood, Marcus. *Blind Memory: Visual Representations of Slavery in England and America*. Routledge, 2000.

Wynter, Sylvia. "Novel and History, Plot and Plantation." *Savacou* (1971): 95–102.

Yacovone, Donald. "William J. Wilson." In *African American National Biography*, 2nd ed., edited by Henry Louis Gates Jr. and Evelyn Brooks Higginbotham. Oxford University Press, 2013.

Yao, Xine. *Disaffected: The Cultural Politics of Unfeeling in Nineteenth-Century America*. Duke University Press, 2021.

Young, Patricia. "Roads to Travel: A Historical Look at *The Freedman's Torchlight*—An African American Contribution to 19th-Century Instructional Technologies." *Journal of Black Studies* 31, no. 5 (2001): 671–98.

Index